ATLA Monograph Series
edited by Dr. Kenneth E. Rowe

1. Ronald L. Grimes. *The Divine Imagination: William Blake's Major Prophetic Visions.* 1972.
2. George D. Kelsey. *Social Ethics Among Southern Baptists, 1917–1969.* 1973.
3. Hilda Adam Kring. *The Harmonists: A Folk-Cultural Approach.* 1973.
4. J. Steven O'Malley. *Pilgrimage of Faith: The Legacy of the Otterbeins.* 1973.
5. Charles Edwin Jones. *Perfectionist Persuasion: The Holiness Movement and American Methodism. 1867–1936.* 1974.
6. Donald E. Byrne, Jr. *No Foot of Land: Folklore of American Methodist Itinerants.* 1975.
7. Milton C. Sernett. *Black Religion and American Evangelicalism: White Protestants, Plantation Missions, and the Flowering of Negro Christianity, 1787–1865.* 1975.
8. Eva Fleischner. *Judaism in German Christian Theology Since 1945: Christianity and Israel Considered in Terms of Mission.* 1975.
9. Walter James Lowe. *Mystery & The Unconscious: A Study in the Thought of Paul Ricoeur.* 1977.
10. Norris Magnuson. *Salvation in the Slums: Evangelical Social Work, 1865–1920.* 1977.
11. William Sherman Minor. *Creativity in Henry Nelson Wieman.* 1977.
12. Thomas Virgil Peterson. *Ham and Japheth: The Mythic World of Whites in the Antebellum South.* 1978.
13. Randall K. Burkett. *Garveyism as a Religious Movement: The Institutionalization of a Black Civil Religion.* 1978.
14. Roger G. Betsworth. *The Radical Movement of the 1960's.* 1980.
15. Alice Cowan Cochran. *Miners, Merchants, and Missionaries: The Roles of Missionaries and Pioneer Churches in the Colorado Gold Rush and Its Aftermath, 1858–1870.* 1980.
16. Irene Lawrence. *Linguistics and Theology: The Significance of Noam Chomsky for Theological Construction.* 1980.
17. Richard E. Williams. *Called and Chosen: The Story of Mother Rebecca Jackson and the Philadelphia Shakers.* 1981.

18. Arthur C. Repp, Sr. *Luther's Catechism Comes to America: Theological Effects on the Issues of the Small Catechism Prepared In or For America Prior to 1850.* 1982.
19. Lewis V. Baldwin. *"Invisible" Strands in African Methodism.* 1983.
20. David W. Gill. *The Word of God in the Ethics of Jacques Ellul.* 1984.
21. Robert Booth Fowler. *Religion and Politics in America.* 1985.
22. Page Putnam Miller. *A Claim to New Roles.* 1985.
23. C. Howard Smith. *Scandinavian Hymnody from the Reformation to the Present.* 1987.
24. Bernard T. Adeney. *Just War, Political Realism, and Faith.* 1988.
25. Paul Wesley Chilcote. *John Wesley and the Women Preachers of Early Methodism.* 1991.
26. Samuel J. Rogal. *A General Introduction of Hymnody and Congregational Song.* 1991.
27. Howard A. Barnes. *Horace Bushnell and the Virtuous Republic.* 1991.
28. Sondra A. O'Neale. *Jupiter Hammon and the Biblical Beginnings of African-American Literature.* 1993.
29. Kathleen P. Deignan. *Christ Spirit: The Eschatology of Shaker Christianity.* 1992.
30. D. Elwood Dunn. *A History of the Episcopal Church in Liberia, 1821–1980.* 1992.
31. Terrance L. Tiessen. *Irenaeus on the Salvation of the Unevangelized.* 1993.
32. James E. McGoldrick. *Baptist Successionism: A Crucial Question in Baptist History.* 1994.
33. Murray A. Rubinstein. *The Origins of the Anglo-American Missionary Enterprise in China, 1807–1840.* 1995.
34. Thomas M. Tanner. *What Ministers Know: A Qualitative Study of Pastors as Information Professionals.* 1994.
35. Jack A. Johnson-Hill. *I-Sight: The World of Rastafari: An Interpretive Sociological Account of Rastafarian Ethics.* 1995.
36. Richard James Severson. *Time, Death, and Eternity: Reflecting on Augustine's "Confessions" in Light of Heidegger's "Being and Time."* 1995.
37. Robert F. Scholz. *Press toward the Mark: History of the United Lutheran Synod of New York and New England, 1830–1930.* 1995.
38. Sam Hamstra, Jr. and Arie J. Griffioen. *Reformed Confessionalism in Nineteenth-Century America: Essays on the Thought of John Williamson Nevin.* 1995.

39. Robert A. Hecht. *An Unordinary Man: A Life of Father John La-Farge, S.J.* 1996.
40. Moses Moore. *Orishatukeh Faduma: Liberal Theology and Evangelical Pan-Africanism, 1857–1946.* 1996.
41. William Lawrence. *Sundays in New York: Pulpit Theology at the Crest of the Protestant Mainstream.* 1996.

Father John LaFarge in his office at *America*, about 1960.

An Unordinary Man
A Life of Father
John LaFarge, S.J.

by
Robert A. Hecht

ATLA Monograph Series, No. 39

The Scarecrow Press, Inc.
Lanham, Md., & London

SCARECROW PRESS, INC.

Published in the United States of America
by Scarecrow Press, Inc.
4720 Boston Way
Lanham, Maryland 20706

4 Pleydell Gardens, Folkestone
Kent CT20 2DN, England

British Cataloguing-in-Publication Information Available

Library of Congress Cataloging-in-Publication Data

Hecht, Robert A.
An unordinary man: a life of Father John LaFarge, S.J./by Robert A. Hecht
p.   cm.—(ATLA monograph series; no. 39)
Includes bibliographical references.
1. LaFarge, John, 1880–1963. 2. Jesuits—United States—Biography.
3. Civil rights workers—United States—Biography. I. Title II. Series.
BX4705.L237H43   1996   282'.092—dc20   95-38738   [B] CIP
ISBN 0-8108-3094-9 (cloth : alk. paper)

♾ ™ The paper used in this publication meets the minimum requirements of
American National Standard for Information Sciences—Permanence of
Paper for Printed Library Materials, ANSI Z39.48—1984.
Manufactured in the United States of America.

For Helen, my wife

Contents

Preface

Father John LaFarge, S.J., was born in 1880 in Newport, Rhode Island and died in New York City in 1963. One of the most prominent American Roman Catholic clergymen of his time, he achieved recognition as a major civil rights activist in the years before and after World War II, and as an editor of *America,* the Jesuit weekly journal of opinion and current events, until his death. His own writings are voluminous, including eleven books and more than one thousand signed articles.

LaFarge was the youngest of the seven surviving children of John LaFarge, the well-known nineteenth-century American artist. His mother descended from Benjamin Franklin and Oliver Hazard Perry, hero of the Battle of Lake Erie during the War of 1812. Other important names abound in the LaFarge family, including his brother, C. Grant LaFarge, one of the architects of Saint John the Divine Cathedral in New York City, and author-nephews Christopher and Oliver LaFarge, the latter a Pulitzer Prize winning novelist.

In researching this biography, I went through a large collection of Father LaFarge's private papers, mostly family letters, at the New York Historical Society, photocopying more than four hundred of them. They gave me an intimate picture of his personal life. Most of these letters are well written and eminently quotable. There is also a large collection of his papers at Georgetown University in Washington, D.C. These deal mainly with his professional life.

I was able to interview (in person and on the telephone) many of his relatives, as well as several clergymen who worked with him at *America.*

Then there are Father LaFarge's published works, his autobiography and his books and articles dealing with racial problems in the United States. For fifteen years he worked in Jesuit rural parishes in southern Maryland, where for the first time he experienced racial prejudice against blacks. In 1934 he founded the Catholic Interracial Council of New York, currently headquartered at 16 West Thirty-sixth Street in New York City. In 1938 Pope Pius XI asked him to write an encyclical on racism. Pius died before it was issued, however, and his successor decided against its publication.

In a very real sense LaFarge was a white man ahead of his time, one who showed a deep concern for blacks as early as the second decade of the twentieth century. This part of his life should interest anyone studying the civil rights movement of more recent years.

In writing about blacks, LaFarge, as was customary then, used the words *Negro* and *colored*. Where I quote directly from his letters or published works, I use those words as he used them. In my own text, however, I use the word black.

Robert A. Hecht
College Point, New York

Chapter 1

Newport

Father John LaFarge, S.J., descended from several illustrious American families. On his mother's side were Oliver Hazard Perry, hero of the Battle of Lake Erie in 1813, and his nephew, Matthew Galbraith Perry, who opened up Japan to the world with his "great black ships" in 1853. La-Farge's grandmother, Fanny Sergeant Perry, was a great-granddaughter of Benjamin Franklin and the daughter of Thomas Sergeant, chief justice of the Pennsylvania Supreme Court. Fanny, according to what La-Farge's mother told him, "had a fanatical hatred for everything Catholic. She firmly believed that the Church was the Scarlet Woman," and that just before the last judgment the sun would turn blood red. One of his mother's earliest memories was seeing the sun setting over Newport, Rhode Island, and believing that the end of the world was near.[1]

Margaret Perry, LaFarge's mother, spent her youth and most of the rest of her life in Newport. A very pretty, intelligent woman, she had a number of ardent suitors. Among them, and the eventual winner of her hand, was John LaFarge, the outstanding nineteenth- and early twentieth-century artist. Born in New York City in 1835, he was the oldest of the nine children of Jean-Frédéric de la Farge and Louisa Josephine Binsse de Saint-Victor, the daughter of French émigrés to America. Born near Angoulème, France in 1786, Jean-Frédéric served in Napoleon's navy in the West Indies and was captured by some of Toussaint L'Ouverture's Haitian soldiers during the 1803 uprising against France on that island, where for three years he served as a slave to a Haitian leader. He managed to escape in 1806 on a ship that first took him to Philadelphia. Soon thereafter he came to New York, where he became successfully involved in commerce. Among other activities he shipped goods to and from New York and Le Havre, France. He also became involved in real estate in New York City and northern New York State, founding the village of LaFargeville near Watertown, where he built a large house. He later

1

bought an estate in Glen Cove, Long Island, where he died in 1858, leaving a sizable inheritance to his family.

Jean-Frédéric's artist son (Father John's father) made a considerable impression on his intellectual and artistic contemporaries. Although a Roman Catholic, he moved freely in the Protestant-dominated upper class of late nineteenth-century America, numbering among his closest friends William and Henry James and Henry Adams. Briefly studying art in Paris, he returned to the United States in 1857, about six months before his father's death. The death of his father (who had anglicized his name to John by this time), who had wanted his son to study law, was a crucial point in the artist's life. He was now free to choose his own profession and had, at least for a time, enough money to support himself while preparing for it. He thought of returning to France to continue his art studies there, but decided instead to go to Newport in 1859 to work under the painter William Morris Hunt. Hunt had two other budding artists in his studio, the future pragmatist philosopher William James and his writer brother, Henry. It was probably through one of the James brothers that he met Margaret Perry. Henry James remained attached to the LaFarge family, and especially Margaret, during the remainder of his life. He mentioned her several times in his autobiography, and wrote to her from England during his long self-imposed exile there.

It was a momentous introduction for them both. LaFarge soon fell in love with Margaret. When she went to Louisiana during the winter of 1859–60 to stay with a friend at her family's plantation he pursued her, first with long letters, then in person. He determined to have her for his wife, but knew he had to move quickly to beat the competition. William James was already mischievously spreading a rumor that she had been proposed to by a man named Johnson, but had refused his suit.[2]

This had not been Margaret's first visit to Louisiana. In 1923, two years before her death, she reminisced with her son Oliver about the first time she had been there. Oliver made notes of the conversation. Margaret and her mother made the long journey together. While she dated this trip to the period 1856–57, she was mistaken. Her first visit to Louisiana actually occurred two years later, 1858–59.

Margaret had been ill, and her mother felt that getting out of cold Newport for the winter and spending it instead in the South would hasten her daughter's recovery.

> I had been very ill with what we should now call typhoid, and my mother was persuaded that the change would be good for me. Mrs.

Porter was a great friend of my mother and had often asked her to
spend the winter with her. The Porters lived in the Stone house on
Greenough Place. We went by New York and Albany, Rochester,
Syracuse, and Cincinnati, I think, stopping each night, and traveling by railway each day till we struck the Ohio River and took a
boat to Louisville and from there by steamer to New Orleans on the
Mississippi. We were three weeks on the way altogether. The boats
were comfortable, and the Porter's plantation was some miles from
New Orleans.

The Porters owned a huge plantation at Bayou Teche, not far from
New Orleans. In the 1850s wealthy southerners built expensive homes
in Newport, so their families could escape the intense summer heat of the
Deep South. Mrs. Mary Porter and Margaret's mother became close
friends in Newport. The Porters owned many slaves, which does not
seem to have disturbed Margaret. She was told that there were five hundred slaves on the plantation, the great bulk of them field hands. Margaret "came in contact with only about 20 on the immediate grounds, and
in the house, they were trained as servants and excellent."

The following winter Margaret returned to Bayou Teche for a second
stay. This time, however, it was not her health that brought her there, but
rather the amorous intentions of John LaFarge. As she told her son Oliver
in 1923, "I think my mother took me away to try to break off the matter
for she was not favorable to my marriage with Mr. LaFarge—mainly on
the ground of his being Catholic."[3]

Already in love with Margaret, John immediately started his epistolary campaign to win her hand. While properly called "love letters," his
long missives to Margaret were carefully composed so as not to sound
too amatory in case they fell into the wrong hands, especially those of
her mother. In his autobiography, *The Manner Is Ordinary,* LaFarge
quoted from several of his father's letters to Margaret. Some of the passages are ardent, though not sensual. More often they referred to books
or authors he thought she should read. One paragraph reflects the generally accepted husband-wife relationship of the time. The woman was expected to become the adored possession of the man, and to remain his
possession regardless of his behavior.

I have spoken of you to my mother, who is ready to love you, nay
who loves you already . . . not, dear, (as I wished to tell you), that
I am in a hurry to marry—(to marry you is another thing, for I thus
own you) even with you my dear, dear Margaret, it is to me a sad

step. I feel how serious it is, trust me, and its pleasures cannot conceal from me its dread chances. But with you, dearest dear, a life, I believe, will pass happily: recollect that you are to love me *forever*—and *that*—even if my love for you were to die, which indeed I cannot believe it will. Does that appear too hard to you?[4]

Another letter dated March 1859, but almost certainly misdated, since LaFarge did not meet Margaret Perry until several months later (it must have been written in March 1860), is filled with poetic anticipation at the prospect of soon seeing her in person at the Porters' plantation in Bayou Teche. (This is a hitherto unknown letter from the artist to his future wife. It was found by the author in the original in the private collection of Margaret LaFarge Hamill, the daughter of Oliver LaFarge, Father John's brother.)

> I look forward to making my trip (to Louisiana) as being my ideal of my desire of spring. It seems to me often at night as I sink to sleep that I wander about with you in a country all green and soft and full of flowers. As I used to as a boy when spring came. Of the green transparent water in which it seemed to me that I spent days and weeks floating from place to place—islands fringed with grass rising and falling in the smell of the sea-clear grained rocks warm in the sun and reflected far below me—piles of white clouds rosy in the morning light.[5]

Although John might not have thought so, he probably had no serious competition for Margaret's love. His biggest obstacle was her mother—not rival swains. Reminiscing in 1923 with her son, she remembered being urgently pursued by a southern gentleman during her second stay at the Porters. She had met him on a visit to New Orleans, where she had gone for a round of parties.

> I remember one young man, whose name I do not recall, who was very violently in love with me, and used to write me impassioned notes and used to serenade me—I think one night he played all night—but I went to sleep and forgot all about him! On our return to the Plantation he wrote me two letters which were violently amorous and which Annie made fun of. I never cared in the least for the youth, showed the letters to my Mother, and I forget what happened, but I think the man was killed in the war.[6]

John took no chance of losing her. He made the long journey to Bayou Teche in April 1860. Somehow he persuaded Margaret's mother to ac-

·cept him as a son-in-law. He proposed marriage and Margaret accepted. They were married in Newport on October 15, 1860. Three weeks later in New York City, Margaret, to her mother's horror, was converted to Roman Catholicism.

LaFarge explained the delay in his mother's conversion until after the wedding by noting that she did not want to seem to be changing her faith just to marry her Catholic husband. Even before the marriage, however, she was convinced of the truth of the Catholic religion. "As she explained to me," he wrote, "her faith came naturally. It was the unfolding of a spiritual blossom that had already begun to grow."[7]

Margaret's conversion greatly distressed her mother, a practicing Episcopalian. It was one thing for her daughter to marry a Catholic, but to become one herself was nearly unbearable. Margaret wrote of her situation to Father Isaac Hecker, founder of the Paulist Fathers and a good friend of the LaFarge family. Hecker was indirectly responsible for one of LaFarge's largest commissions, the decoration of the Paulist Church in New York. Hecker died in 1888, but his family was a major financial supporter of that huge edifice.

Hecker was himself a convert to Catholicism. His Paulist Fathers' special, self-assigned mission was to convert non-Catholics to the true faith. It was not surprising, therefore, that Hecker had instructed Margaret in her new faith before her conversion. In her unhappiness about her mother, she turned to the priest for advice and consolation.

> Although I have not met with any practical difficulties in the way of my faith about which I especially need your advice, I still feel that I can write to you as my Father to ask of you if you can to send me either advice or encouragement, and at least to remember me very often in your prayers.
>
> My greatest trouble has been, as I expected, from my Mother who received the news with the greatest grief, and has tried every argument to dissuade me from continuing faithful. Your words to me on the danger of delay, and your promise to pray for us, came to my mind in a great many moments of weakness. My dear husband too has faithfully fulfilled all his duty towards me. I need not tell you Sir, how he has encouraged and helped me—it has taught me, at least, what a Sacred thing Marriage can be.[8]

She wrote Father Hecker again the following April, after the birth of their first child, Christopher Grant. By this time she seems to have convinced her mother that she was a Catholic to stay. She was certainly on good terms with her younger brother, Thomas, who later became a significant older male relative in Father John's life. Her letter to Father Hecker was ostensibly to thank him for sending her some Palm Sunday palms, but was more likely a good opportunity to let him know how she was getting along as a Catholic.

> We have been very remiss not to acknowledge the receipt of the palm which came safely—I can only write my thanks for it, but I hope John will see you himself, as he has again gone to New York and I always advise him to see you before he returns—I have had to strip off some of the palm to distribute among some of my Catholic friends, who prove very true friends although nearly all are Irish—Miss Vernon and I are becoming very good Catholics; it is not as hard as expected, and we help each other along. . . .Our little boy is a very good Catholic already, he goes every Sunday to Church in his nurse's arms, and on Good Friday was taken by her to the railing and had the Cross laid on his lips, besides going twice around the stations. He is a fine healthy child and the pet of the Irish population.[9]

In his autobiography, LaFarge wrote of the difficulties faced by his convert mother in the early years of her marriage. At the time of her conversion, Roman Catholics in Newport were a distinct minority, a situation that would change as more Catholic immigrants came into the city after the Civil War. During her youth Margaret had "vividly impressed on her imagination" the specter of Newport Irish Catholics being "stoned by rowdies." After her conversion, "to attend the Catholic service she had to pass by Trinity Church on Spring Street, pass by the graveyard where her ancestors from the founding of the colony were buried, pass by the pews where they and all their friends and relatives had worshipped, and make her way to a back street to which she came as a complete social stranger."[10]

The first home of John and Margaret LaFarge was a large house on Key Street in downtown Newport, not far from William Morris Hunt's studio. LaFarge had already become less than enthusiastic about Hunt's teaching and artistry, but had remained in Newport to court Margaret. They paid nine thousand dollars for the house, a considerable sum for that time. Children followed rapidly, and in quantity. Margaret went through ten pregnancies, but only seven of her children lived to maturity.

Though they started life with a fine house and a small, inherited fortune, the LaFarges ran though their money rapidly. The young artist, while totally absorbed in his work, painted much but sold little. The time would come, after he had established his reputation as a leading American artist, when he was paid generously for his work. Even then, however, money would pass through his hands like water through a sieve. By 1864, according to Henry James, he and his family actually had to flee Newport at night to escape their creditors, "leaving prodigious debts behind them, and one silver spoon in the side-board drawer; the servants wages unpaid, the house dismantled of its prodigious ornaments."[11]

They moved temporarily to Roxbury, Massachusetts, possibly to remove themselves from Rhode Island, where their creditors presumably were located. Years later Margaret remembered that they "had rather an attractive house but I do not remember the location except that it was on Cedar Street and had considerable grounds about it. I think about 20 acres."[12]

Their exile lasted only a few months, however, for LaFarge recovered financially somewhat by selling the Newport house for twice what he had paid. Over the next seven years he and his family rented various houses in Newport, and occasionally stayed with Margaret's mother in her home on Catherine Street, or at the LaFarge family estate at Glen Cove, Long Island, where his mother lived.

From about 1860 on, John also maintained a studio in New York at 51 West Tenth Street, traveling back and forth between New York and Newport by steamer. Over the years he filled this studio with thousands of drawings and other works. A year before his death he wrote to an editor friend, "I don't know if I have ever told you that my studies go by the thousands. I have numbered and stamped 8,000 for glass, and a little more, say for general subjects, and there must be 50,000 or 60,000 more."[13]

In 1873 they bought the house on Sunnyside Place in Newport, not far from St. Mary's Church. LaFarge's brother Oliver, who was four at the time, remembered moving into that house. "To me," he wrote, "was given the duty of carrying a clock." He described the house as "quite an old house, two stories high with ample friendly roof, facing a quiet, sleepy land." At the time they took over there were no other houses close by. Oliver reminisced about the house's surroundings many years later.

> About us was a child's paradise, for back of the house over a stone
> wall, sufficiently tempting for climbing and walking on, was a large

orchard and adjoining it a little grove of oak saplings, and farther
away in the meadow, there seemed to be a perennial growth of
splendid daisies, long grass and large buttercups. On one side of us
stretched away a gentle sloping field, containing traces of old paths
and dotted here and there with a few apple trees and little clumps
of evergreens.[14]

Father John LaFarge was born in that house in 1880. Seventy-four
years later he described the house, and his attachment to it, in a letter to
an acquaintance. "Sunnyside Place in Newport is right off the Old Beach
Road to the east of the Old Stone Mill. My sister—twelve years older
then myself—still resides in the old house where she has lived since she
was a child of four. When I return there I sleep in the room where I was
born, which few people do these days."[15]

After the death of his sister Margaret in 1956, the house was sold, although it is still occupied at the present time. Writing in 1958, LaFarge
poignantly described his last visit to the house the year before, shortly
before its sale.

Last year, toward the end of summer, I made a final visit to the old
house in Newport that had been familiar to me since childhood. The
last—and the most devoted—occupant had passed on and been laid
to rest. It was the final phase before the moment when the house's
furnishings, books, pictures, "estate" of every kind would be duly
and lovingly parcelled out and distributed among the heirs and
friends. There was a chill enough in the damp sea air to warrant
filching some old newspapers and a few sticks out of the traditional
wood closet and lighting up the old fireplace in the library, arrang-
ing kindling and pine splits in proper order, drawing a match-stick
from the cloisonne-silver box on the gray stone mantelpiece, starting a bit of a blaze, and settling in the presumably eighth uphol-
stered version of the easy chair for a few moments solitude before
the fire.[16]

The fire was not a big one, and soon burned itself down to a few glowing embers. As he walked through the rooms each item recalled some
connection with his past. "The bookshelves recalled the school and college days, and the visits to the library. The prayer book, the parish church
and all its associations. The china bowl in the hallway where formal
summer-colony visitors left their calling cards. . ."[17] The house had been
in the LaFarge family for some eighty-five years. When he left after an
hour or so of musing about the past, it was the end of any formal ties with

Newport. It is doubtful that he ever entered the house on Sunnyside Place again.

Only Father LaFarge and his sister Frances were born in that house. All the others entered the world before the family moved in. The oldest, Christopher Grant, better known simply as Grant, was born in 1861. He became an architect, and together with his partner, George Lewis Heins, husband of his father's sister Aimée, was the original designer of St. John the Divine Cathedral in New York in Morningside Heights of Manhattan. One of Grant's sons, Oliver, achieved fame as author of the novel *Laughing Boy,* for which he received the Pulitzer Prize in literature in 1929. Emily, the second born, came along in 1863, followed by Bancel (1865), Margaret (1867), Oliver (1869), Frances (1874), and lastly John. Except for Emily, who died in 1919 from an accident at the age of fifty-six, they all lived into their seventies and eighties.

Among Oliver's reminiscences was the LaFarge's parish church, St. Mary's, now a national landmark. (John F. Kennedy and Jacqueline Bouvier were married in that church in 1953.) He remembers himself, his brother Bancel, and his sister Margaret leaning out of an open window on the second floor of the house watching Father Grace, the pastor of St. Mary's, walking by. "With a devilish spontaneity, known only to children," he wrote, "we thought this so funny, that we yelled in unison from the window, as Father Grace kept step: "Father Grace, with the dirty face. Father Grace, with the dirty face!"

The priest ignored the brazen LaFarge children, but they were stricken with guilt, compounded by the "severe punishment from my much humiliated mother, whose devotion to and reverence for the Church was known throughout the parish."[18]

As for Father Grace, he does not seem the type to be nettled by the insults of a few unruly children. Oliver went on to describe him as a powerful pastor, who would sometimes exhort his parishioners to greater efforts in the collection basket by openly commenting during mass on their generosity—or lack thereof. After the annual collection to pay off the church debt he would read the names of everyone who contributed.

> Bridget Sullivan—25 cents. That's good for Bridget. She's a hard working woman. God Bless her.

> Thomas Dolan—25 cents. Now that's disgraceful. Thomas gets good wages and knows better than that. Saturday night away from the saloon would enable him to give more for God's Glory.[19]

Many years into his priesthood LaFarge delivered an Easter sermon at
St. Mary's. He also recalled Father Grace. "Few of us," he said, "could
understand Father Grace's sermons, but all of us respected his zeal and
air of authority with which he spoke."[20]

The principal authority figure in LaFarge's life was of course his own
father, although as a youth he had little contact with him. The son would
come to appreciate the father's high standing in the artistic and intellectual worlds only when he grew to manhood. The elder LaFarge was wed-
ded to his work, especially in his later years, and all but abandoned his
family for long stretches at a time. LaFarge began the first chapter of *The
Manner Is Ordinary* with this lament.

> In 1891, when I was a boy of eleven, Father returned from his trip
> to the South Seas with Henry Adams. I went down to Long Wharf
> to meet him and we drove to our house in Sunnyside Place, the old
> Grant cottage, in a Long Wharf cab. I was charmed to see that Fa-
> ther was a real person, who wore an impressive black beard. I was
> glad to know that I really had a father, in fact, since my picture of
> him before that time had been quite indefinite.[21]

Only for brief periods did the father and his youngest son spend serious time with one another. It is proper to say that the young LaFarge was
wary of his father, who had a well-known temper and could be distant
and aloof from his wife and children. So distant, in fact, that Margaret
once confessed to her son that by the time Emily, her second child, was
born she no longer had a real marriage. She came to this realization while
staying with her mother-in-law at the LaFarge estate in Glen Cove, Long
Island. "I knew then," she said years later, "that your father no longer
had the same affection for me. I knew there was no sense in weeping. He
was going to lead his own life, and I said to myself, this will be my life
henceforth; I must face it and do the best I can."[22]

Her husband's "own life" apparently included a long-term romance
with Mary Whitney, one of his studio assistants who had artistic and poetic abilities. James Yarnell, a recent biographer of the artist, identifies
her as a member of a "socially prominent family from Broome County,
New York, near Binghamton." She seems to have joined his studio staff
sometime in 1882, but little is known about her personal appearance or
background.[23]

In *The Manner Is Ordinary* LaFarge commented obliquely about his
father having many admirers, including "women of intellect and high social standing," but only hinted at the possibility of any extramarital af-

fairs. "Possibly there was something graver in the case," he wrote, "but reports of such did not reach us."[24]

The fact is, however, that when LaFarge wrote his autobiography, he had in his possession some dozen or so letters from his father to Mary Whitney that can only be described as love letters. How he came to possess these letters is not clear. He did not mention them in his book. But after completing the manuscript he proceeded to deposit these letters in the LaFarge family collection at the New York Historical Society in New York City, thus assuring that some future researcher, less emotionally involved with the family, would discover and use them.

The romance between the artist and Mary started sometime in the spring of 1882, shortly after she came to work as one of his assistants. Its beginning was innocent enough—an exchange of bouquets between them. As he wrote to her at Easter of that year, "Many thanks and it was nice of you to remember me—so I send you some [flowers] from another bunch with good wishes."[25]

The relationship, however, soon deepened into love, which lasted until the artist's death in 1910. It continued even after Mary married a man named Lawrence sometime before 1890. How physically sexual their love became is not known. There are no references to love "scenes" in the letters—only passages that reveal LaFarge's yearnings for her. On Thursday night, September 8, 1882 he wrote her:

> I have reread your letters this moment to be able to ask you this *something* about it—can I really save you from the feeling of depression you suffered from last winter? You say so, dear, and it makes me ask you for you will probably not tell me on paper.

> Can my love for you tide over such moments? My dear Mary, the more you will let me know of your mind and of your wishes and feelings the more certainly can I be with you in mind, and wishes, and feelings. Otherwise, love has such a selfish side, is so jealous and so absorbing that it will wound and make sore especially any heart trusting only to it. Lucky it is that the cause of the wound can also be a cure—[26]

The letters from the artist to Mary continued until less than a year before his death. The last one on file was written from the Albemarle Hotel on New Year's Day, 1910. It is short and poignant. "I thought a letter from you would come and it does give me courage." In a postscript he wrote, "I am here, I hope not long. I have been very ill as you may know and was taken here."[27]

That Margaret knew about Mary Whitney and her place in her husband's life is reasonably certain. To keep the family together, however, she chose not to act on her knowledge. A divorce, especially for a Catholic woman with seven children, was all but unthinkable. Many years later her daughter Margaret, responding to a request from her own nephew Henry for any letters from or to the artist that might be used in a collection of his correspondence, wrote that her mother had destroyed much of it. "The difficulty about publishing any of his letters," she wrote on March 12, 1947, "is that which still exists and which she dreaded as I do too, that references to her married life with him, which was very grim, would creep in despite all care to keep them out. She hid as much as she could from the public and suffered much in doing so. . . . It is not pleasant to write you all this, for I don't want your generation to have to listen to old family tragedies which had best be forgotten."[28]

In his father's defense, LaFarge insisted in his autobiography that despite the artist's neglect of his family, "We were still his, as he was always ours."[29]

While the senior LaFarge was temperamental and forbidding, he could also at times be warm and caring about his family, at least about his children. His son Oliver, the one who carried the clock into the new house on Sunnyside Place, described one such time.

> Nothing bored him as much as being surprised, and once when I returned from the west after an absence of four years, burst in on him at his studio in Tenth Street, in New York, he was quite indignant and refused even to be polite. I left at once to receive later in the evening a most docile note asking me to be sure to dine with him that night at the Century Club. He was interested in our most trivial happenings and when on this same trip I gave him an account of Henry James in the west and his short stay in Seattle, telling him how Mr. James sat on top of an old board fence with me, overlooking beautiful Lake Washington and talked of the comforts of London clubs and the difficulties of finding proper valeting in the west, it tickled him immensely.[30]

Young John was normally cautious and diffident with his father, but he certainly loved and admired him, despite his treatment of the family, and especially his mother. Somehow with the passage of time, the artist became a family icon, and his work, the house where he was born, even his former studio, holy places to stand before and wonder about. In 1935, one hundred years after his father's birth, LaFarge wrote about him in *America,* the Jesuit magazine published in New York, which LaFarge helped to edit.

> Once on a stormy afternoon I undertook to explore what was left of No. 30 Beach Street, in New York City, where my father was born a hundred years ago this writing, March 31, 1835. Dodging among trucks emerging from loading platforms, stepping over rain puddles, I found nothing at the end of the quest that was even a remote reminder that once a dwelling house had been there, or even a number thirty: it was merely a conjectural spot in the grim area of an immense brick warehouse. As I made my way to normal streets and sidewalks, I wondered to myself if it would be likely that John La-Farge's memory would in a few years be reduced to naught but a few museum titles or catalogue references in the public libraries.[31]

He need not have worried. John LaFarge's reputation as an outstanding American artist is firmly established. Two of his early paintings hang in the American Wing of the Metropolitan Museum of Art in New York City, and exhibitions of his work are held regularly around the country. While he was an excellent water colorist, his greatest fame stems from his church murals and stained glass windows. Among his most artistically successful commissions were the murals for Trinity Church in Boston, murals and windows of the Church of the Ascension in New York City, and the windows of Trinity Church in Buffalo, New York.

Royal Cortissoz, his friend and confidant for over twenty years, published a biography of LaFarge in 1911, one year after the artist's death. It is a "friendly" biography, basically uncritical of the man and his work. Still it is a good starting point for anyone interested in the life and times of John LaFarge. Much of the book is really autobiographical, since a good part of the text is drawn verbatim from LaFarge's letters to Cortissoz. A recurring subject was his health. During much of his adult life he suffered from real or imaginary illnesses—some thought him a hypochondriac. Real or not, however, they were a continuous worry to his family. He wrote Cortissoz about his health in the fall of 1908.

> As I am led into talking about myself, I wish to note a matter which is interesting to me, and which is also interesting in a general manner, and this is that I have been off and on an ill man since the years 1866 and 1867. I was paralyzed by what was later supposed to be

lead poisoning, which affects some of us painters very much, and which can be continued in the practice of the art of what is called "stained glass," where lead is much used and fills the air, and the hands, etc., of the people engaged.[32]

Two of his closest friends, Henry Adams (with whom he toured Japan and the South Seas) and Henry James attested to the influence he had on their own appreciation of art and the intellect. In his autobiography James wrote of LaFarge as if he were some sort of cultural magician, who made arcane things clear and the exotic both less and more so.

John LaFarge became at once, in breaking on our view, quite the most interesting person we knew, and for a time remained so; he became a great many other things beside — a character, above all, if there ever was one; but he opened up to us, though perhaps to me in particular, who could absorb all that was given me on those suggestive lines, prospects, and possibilities and made the future flush and swarm.[33]

As for Adams, he also admitted to LaFarge's genius and influence on himself. Cortissoz emphasized LaFarge's unique place in nineteenth-century art as "an inventor in his glass . . . He knew where that was concerned he had no predecessors in America, that none of his numerous followers had ever quite rivaled him or was likely to do so."[34] Adams went even further in his tribute to LaFarge's skill in stained glass. In *The Education of Henry Adams,* his autobiography written in the third person, he rhapsodized about his friend.

This vehemence, which Whistler never betrayed in his painting, LaFarge seemed to lavish on his glass. With the relative value of LaFarge's glass in the history of glass decoration, Adams was too ignorant to meddle, and as a rule artists were if possible more ignorant than he; but whatever it was, it led him back to the twelfth century and to Chartres where LaFarge not only felt at home, but felt a sort of ownership. No other American had a right there, unless he too were a member of the Church and worked in glass. Adams himself was another interloper, but long habit led LaFarge to resign himself to Adams as one who meant well, though deplorably Bostonian; while Adams, though nearly sixty years old before he knew anything either of glass or of Chartres, asked no better than to learn, and only LaFarge could help him, for he knew

enough at least to see that LaFarge alone could use glass like a thir-
teenth-century artist.[35]

Since his father was well into his fifties by the time he really started
to know him, the young John LaFarge had never seen him in his youthful and more vigorous years. The father often perplexed the son, at times
shunning him, at other times warm and even chummy. Although intellectually gifted himself, young John was not a creative genius. He understood music well, but only to play and not compose. He does not seem
to have had much appreciation of the pictorial arts either. He confessed
this years later in a letter to one of his nieces. "Since any knowledge of
art that I have is largely acquired by a sort of osmosis from the family,"
he wrote, "I could not make one of those wise pronouncements that one
would like to utter when Ben showed me your recent class-room work
on Thursday evening."[36] He once asked his father if there were any point
in his studying art. His reply settled the matter. "No," he told his son,
"you have absolutely no talent for drawing or painting. Just forget all
about it."[37] His father wrapped himself in those arts. A restless, searching man, he had to see things with his own eyes, hence his several trips
to Europe, Japan and the South Seas.

The young LaFarge was a rover also, but not for the same reasons. He
was more concerned about people as human beings, rather than subjects
to display on a one dimensional surface. And he was far more religious
than his father. While the artist retained his Catholic faith to the end, it
was much lower on his scale of priorities. The son admitted that he
"never could quite make out my father's religious practice. He believed
in going to church, he knew he ought to go to church. He would go to
church if he could get organized and straightened out and somehow arrive there, and *then* his attendance was thoroughly simple, childlike, and
reverent."[38]

While living apart from each other so much of the time—Margaret in
Newport, he either abroad or working in his New York studio—the artist
did return home often enough to sire ten children, only seven of whom
lived to maturity. The death of his third child, Raymond, in infancy particularly distressed him, and for the next two years he spent at least the
summers with his family in Newport. In 1865 Father John's favorite
brother was born. Christened John Louis Bancel (Bancel after one of the
French relatives), he was soon simply called Bancel. When LaFarge was
born, therefore, the name John was considered available, and that was
how he was baptized.

It is not unusual for a Catholic priest to be emotionally attached to his mother. For a celibate man she is often the closest female figure in his life. LaFarge was no exception. Until her death in 1925, he made her his principal confidant, and poured out to her the details of his life, his religious feelings and beliefs, his successes and failures. His long letters to her, which she kept, are a major source of information about his early life. Several years before his own death in 1963, he deposited these letters, along with others, in the LaFarge family collection at the New York Historical Society in New York City.

Father John LaFarge was born in his mother's bed in her home in Newport on February 13, 1880. Margaret was forty years old. Although he does not state it explicitly, LaFarge implied that this was a most unwanted pregnancy. At the time, he wrote, "her health was failing, she was in considerable straits financially, and our home life was a very complicated affair indeed."[39]

In her distress, his "sadly troubled mother decided to ask the advice of her confessor . . ." She told her son "many years later that she asked her confessor whether it would be wise, good, or prudent to have another child with the probability of its death or of adding to her burden." The priest, a young French-Canadian Jesuit stationed at St. Francis Xavier on Sixteenth Street in New York, "simply told her, go ahead and try it again and trust in God."[40]

Margaret concealed her pregnancy from her husband—not too difficult since he was preoccupied with his work in New York. Not until the baby's birth did she tell him he once again had a newborn mouth to feed. In truth, however, the child was so weak and puny that he was not expected to live. LaFarge wrote of this in his autobiography.

> I was brought into daylight by a colored midwife in the southwest second-story room of the old house on Sunnyside Place. . . . According to legend, people would stop my mother as she wheeled me in a perambulator and express a word of sympathy when they saw her feeble baby, pale and apparently half-lifeless. It was assumed I would not live so there was not much bother about formalities at my baptism. As a matter of fact I was baptized not in the church itself, but in the convent rectory. . . . The priest significantly forgot to register my baptism in the register, something I discovered at the time of my ordination.[41]

The Newport that LaFarge grew up in was, at least a good portion of it, a rich man's playground in the latter half of the nineteenth century.

From about the 1840s to the start of the Civil War it was increasingly filled with wealthy southern families who merged and mingled with the Newport Yankees, and with the social and intellectual elite from Boston, Providence, New York and Philadelphia. The tycoons of the Gilded Age built their "cottages" along a three-and-one-half-mile stretch of waterfront called Bellevue Avenue, or the Cliff Walk. James Huneker, a travel writer, described Bellevue Avenue in a 1915 book. "The Cliff Walk is three miles and a half of the pure picturesque. From Easton's Beach to Land's End there is a series of surprises; not alone in the villas, but in the coy turns of the walk, the unexpected change of marine physiognomy, and then the sheer romance of the entire coast."[42]

The most lavish and best known of the Bellevue Avenue mansions was The Breakers, built for Cornelius Vanderbilt by the architect Richard Morris Hunt, brother of the painter William Morris Hunt, between 1892 and 1895. It was facetiously described by Huneker as looking "like a mediaeval fortress, full of torture chambers."[43] During the summers the Astors, Belmonts, Vanderbilts, and dozens of equal or lesser members of the American plutocracy vied for social dominance, spending the kind of money for "conspicuous consumption" mocked by Thorsen Veblen in his *The Theory of the Leisure Class* published in 1899, and satirized by Edith Wharton in her novels and short stories.

Newport also attracted artists and intellectuals such as William and Henry James, the naval historian Alfred Thayer Mahan, and some of the nation's best architects (Newport was where the money was), who came to design and build the pleasure domes of their wealthy patrons. Some of LaFarge's earliest paintings were of scenes in and around Newport. His son John, however, was not impressed by the opulent splendor of his hometown. He was more interested in the sea, at least during his youthful years. He wrote of his feelings about Newport in *The Manner Is Ordinary.*

> Greater and lesser lights on Bellevue Avenue and the Ocean Drive were more the social concern of my older brothers and sisters. My own summer friends were for the most part from a different group. I preferred the nautical-minded folk who occupied the old houses on Washington Street and "The Point," as it was called, fronting on the outer harbor north of Long Wharf and to the east end of the Naval War College, which was the chief exploit of canny, old white-bearded cousin George Mason. From Philadelphia every summer came the Quaker families, the Hallowells and the Smiths: white-haired, ruddy, robust Hester Morton Smith, her sister Anna,

her brother Bill, close friend of my brother Bancel. Bill was
drowned on a Sunday morning trying to save a crippled friend
when their boat had capsized off Brenton's Reef in a sudden squall.
The event was particularly poignant because Bancel was to be one
of the party, but at the last moment he figured in his sober way that
he did not want to miss Mass. I haunted the marine workshops of
Bill Smith's younger brother, Ed. The Smiths, strict disciplinari-
ans, were my nautical advisers. They helped me rig up my first
craft, a Swampscott dory. I was long pursued by their reproaches
when I returned to the wharf late one August evening, after allowing myself to be caught in a tide rip off Rose Island.[44]

Julia Ward Howe, the suffragist and author, was living in Newport at the
time of LaFarge's birth, and was well acquainted with the LaFarge family.
"An object of my occasional pilgrimage out on the island," LaFarge wrote,
"was the awesome Julia Ward Howe, who wrote 'The Battle Hymn of the
Republic.' "[45] She described some happenings in Newport which, had he
been old enough, would most certainly have intrigued him. At the end of
March 1882, for example, when LaFarge was just past his second birthday, she wrote in her diary, "Today the Zuni chiefs and Mr. Cushing, their
interpreter and adopted son, came to luncheon at 1:45. There were twelve
Indian chiefs in full Indian dress. Reception afterwards."

The Zunis had come from Arizona on their annual pilgrimage to the
sea. Usually, they went to the Pacific, much closer to their homeland, but
this year they decided on Newport and the Atlantic. At sunrise they
waded into the ocean to offer prayers to the Great Spirit, and to fill
their tightly woven grass baskets with salt water for use in their ceremonies. Hundreds of early-rising Newport residents gathered to watch
them.[46]

From the end of the Civil War there was a permanent American naval
presence in Newport. In 1883 Commodore Stephan B. Luce established
the Naval Training Station on Coaster's Island. Luce persuaded Captain
Mahan to join his Naval War College in 1884. Mahan's most important
work, *The Influence of Sea Power on History,* evolved from his research
and teaching at the college. The book was published when LaFarge was
ten years old.

With Narragansett Bay at its doorstep, Newport offered a myriad of
salt water activities, including the holding of many America's Cup races.
LaFarge learned to swim and sail his boat in that bay, although he first
had to overcome a fear of deep water. One of his closest childhood
friends was Neil Fairchild, whose family had their own wharf. "Off that

wharf," he wrote, "I first learned to swim by the simple process of falling overboard when nobody was around and deciding the best thing to do was to strike out. It was from their slowly moving cat-boat that I overcame my timidity and plunged into the brilliant, clear, green salt depths five or six miles offshore on lazy summer afternoons."[47]

Despite his sickliness as a baby, and his mother's fear that he would not survive, LaFarge became a handsome, alert child. A photograph taken of him when he was three (wearing a frilly white dress) shows him with long curly hair hanging down his neck, and a very serious expression on his face. Another, taken at eight, shows him in a sailor suit with a big-brimmed straw hat on his head. At eleven he is still in a sailor suit (a different one) smiling impishly at the camera with a dog on his lap.

He and his mother took long walks together along the beaches and cliffs surrounding Newport. It was on one of these walks along Easton's Beach that she told him of her problems with his father. "You ought to know," she said, "that your father does not look properly after us. He means well, but nevertheless I am at times forgotten and there are times when I must turn to Almighty God for help."[48]

Until his father died in 1910, when LaFarge was thirty, the two managed to love each other, although most of the love came from the son's side. In 1940, thirty years after his father's death, LaFarge wrote to Harold Voorhis of the Hall of Fame of New York University, asking why John LaFarge had not been one of the artists "nominated for the Hall of Fame on the ballot of the Ninth Quinquennial Election." He disclaimed any "personal interest in the matter," explaining that he had written only because it seemed "strange to Mr. Royal Cortissoz, his biographer, and many others who have traditionally considered him one of the two or three outstanding artistic figures in this country. . . ."[49]

The explanation came back a few days later that he had not been nominated because no one from the public had submitted his name. "The next election," he was told, "will be held in 1945, at which time I hope someone will have the foresight to present the name of John LaFarge."[50] (The author checked with the Hall of Fame recently and was informed that the artist John LaFarge had never been inducted. No explanation could be found.)

When he was seventeen LaFarge left Newport for Harvard. While he would return for occasional visits in the years ahead, he never again really lived there. Until his death in 1963 at the age of eighty-three, he moved from place to place following the orders of his Jesuit superiors, only rarely returning to the city of his birth. Still, Newport was where he grew up, and his memories of his youth there were strong. One incident near the end of his life points up his and his family's attachment to the town.

His mother, his brother Bancel, and several close relatives are all buried in St. Columba Cemetery in Newport. For years the LaFarge plot was surrounded by a low stone wall, marking it off from other family plots. But in the early summer of 1961, in accordance with new cemetery regulations, the wall was removed. When he learned of this, LaFarge wrote to the Bishop of Providence requesting that the wall, or some other demarcation, be restored. "The carefully planned unity of that little plot has always been, since its inception, a precious bond with the Church for my family; and it has always been for me an infinite consolation that so many of them have died and been interred in the Holy Catholic faith. With the removal of the low wall, however, that unity is necessarily destroyed, and the plot as a plot no longer is noticeable."[51] Despite his pleas, however, the wall has never been replaced.

Before leaving for Harvard in 1897 LaFarge received all his formal education in Newport. Oddly enough, especially for a man who would consistently urge all Catholics to send their children to parochial schools, he received no regular Catholic school training himself until entering Innsbruck University in Austria in 1901.

Chapter 2

The Secular Education of John LaFarge

An advocate of Catholic education for Catholics, LaFarge had a largely secular education. His mother sent him to public grammar and high schools in Newport, while his father, along with other friends and relatives, persuaded him to attend Harvard, although his first choice had been Georgetown. When he was twenty-one he finally entered a Catholic institution, Innsbruck University in Austria, where he began studying for the priesthood. During those twenty-one years, however, he spread his fertile mind far beyond the classroom, earnestly seeking knowledge, both secular and religious, wherever it could be found. In a very real sense, despite his formal education, he was primarily a self-taught man.

His intellectual precocity revealed itself early. By the age of five he was reading the *St. Nicholas* magazine. In his autobiography he confessed that it bothered him to be considered a prodigy, but he was happy that the Newport boys and girls his own age did not taunt him about the "prodigy business," but simply took him for granted.[1]

A number of his letters on file in the library of the New York Historical Society suggest both the depth and breadth of his intellectual interests, mainly in literature, theology, music and languages. Some years later, when he left the Jesuit missions in Maryland to join the staff of *America* magazine in New York, he started digging deeply into history as well. His ability to learn foreign languages, especially the Germanic ones, was phenomenal. When he had to memorize "Longfellow's pathetic poem, *The Skeleton in Armor*," he was impressed by the possibility that Norsemen might have settled in southern New England before the English colonists arrived in the early seventeenth century.[2] At age ten he began to look through books in the family library about the Norsemen, written in Danish, Swedish and Icelandic, collected by his father during a European tour before his marriage. "I saw no reason," he wrote, "why I shouldn't learn to read these books. Mrs. George Bliss, the wife of the librarian of Redwood Library in Newport, knew Danish and was so taken with my interest that she undertook to teach me."[3]

At the same time he also began studying French with a Belgian lady, both in the school he attended and at her home. Shortly before his fifteenth birthday he wrote his mother that he had "given up reading Danish with Mrs. Bliss and have started reading German with her instead, since I have practically learnt Danish . . ."[4]

LaFarge's formal education began at age five in a private day school run by Mrs. Walter N. Hill, a non-Catholic, whose two sons were near his age, and who became his earliest best friends. Two years later Margaret, probably because she could no longer afford the tuition in private school, sent him to the Coddington Public School on Mill Street, then on to Rogers High School. In his sophomore year he suffered an attack of appendicitis, missing the entire second half of that school year, "much of the time merely resting in bed, too weak even to do much reading." He "developed an intense antipathy toward various kinds of food and lost weight and was generally miserable." At the end of the term Margaret decided to take him to New York, where they could be near his father, and where he could recover.[5] They spent nearly two years in New York. The first year they rented a house from Richard Watson, publisher of *Scribner's* magazine, at 55 Clinton Place. The following year they moved to a red brick house at 22 East Tenth Street, just a short distance from his father's studio at 51 West Tenth Street.

LaFarge's mother could have afforded to send him to their parish Catholic school, since it charged no tuition. Margaret, however, apparently never seriously considered doing this, which is not surprising. While a devout Catholic herself, she also came from the upper social stratum. Although within easy walking distance from St. Mary's Church and School, the pastor would have been shocked if LaFarge had been sent there, since the parochial schools in Newport were intended for the education of the local poor Catholics, and especially for the children of recent Irish immigrants. One woman whose family knew the LaFarges well, and who came from that same social level, stressed how embarrassing it would have been all around if LaFarge went to St. Mary's. This woman, who went to private school herself, but whose parents generously supported the parish, remembers her own embarrassment when she went to make her first confession in the church in preparation for her first communion. She had already been privately prepared at home by a nun, and she would later be taught, again at home, by a priest for her confirmation. There was a long line of children from the parish school waiting their turn outside the confessional. As soon as the priest saw her, however, he quickly took her hand and led her to the front of the line. After all she was gentry and did not have to wait her turn along with the ordinary children. She remembers being personally mortified, but the other children seemed not to mind at all. All the priests at St. Mary's, she recalls, were of Irish descent.[6]

LaFarge's brother Oliver, in his reminiscences, also remembered the lower class Irish of St. Mary's, albeit with some fondness.

> Father Philip Grace was the pastor of St. Mary's Church and no easy job it was, for in the parish were many turbulent people. Real Irish, not second generation Irish-Americans, but the real thing with sod upon many of them. Good, pious, faithful, sober, drinking, bad, ready for 'ructions and full of humor. All mixed together.[7]

Ordinarily, as a child of an important Newport family, LaFarge would have gone to private school, or even had tutors. Since his parents could not afford this he went to public school. LaFarge recalled, however, that the two public schools he attended were of a high academic quality. "The teachers," he wrote, "were strict, of the good old New England variety, showing full consideration for my religious beliefs."[8]

One of LaFarge's grandnieces who knew him well, speculated that his decision to go to Harvard, another non-Catholic institution, stemmed in part from family prejudices against the offspring of Irish and other immigrants, who were heavily represented among the student bodies of the Catholic colleges and universities.[9] LaFarge himself might have been free of these prejudices, but he was influenced by his family and his family's friends, including Theodore Roosevelt, to pick Harvard for his higher education rather than Georgetown, his initial choice.

Curiously, considering his superior intelligence, LaFarge did not do well academically in grammar school. The earliest extant letter from him to his mother in the New York Historical Society collection is dated June 8, 1893, when he was thirteen. He wrote that his rank in class was low, "being 59 when there are 80 people in the class, but it might have been worse."[10] Since he was sickly during this time he probably missed a lot of school suffering from periodic bouts of stomach and other disorders, which were, perhaps, a not-yet-diagnosed case of appendicitis. While he spent Christmas holidays with his sister Emily in Philadelphia at the end of 1894 he wrote his mother, "I write to tell you that Emily says I had better stay till Friday." He had been "rather sick," and "was in bed part of yesterday and all this morning. I felt quite weak, but all the pain and sickish feeling from which I have been suffering is gone, and now I feel better than I have since Christmas."

There were some further advantages in staying over the extra days in Philadelphia—music and language. "If I stay I can hear another concert on Thursday at the Academy of Fine Arts. It will be all Beethoven." Also, he could get out "to see Father Heuser, a friend of Emily's, who was here to dinner the other night. He teaches at Oldbrook Seminary and knows nearly every language you can think of, such as Irish, Chinese, Sanskrit, etc. He is very learned, very holy, and very good natured and pleasant." He invited LaFarge to visit him and go through his library.[11]

LaFarge returned to his Newport high school in early January, apparently recovered from his illness. By the end of the month he had taken examinations in all his subjects and could proudly report on his grades to Margaret, who was visiting somewhere away from Newport at the time.

> Last week we had the examinations. Each counts 25% in the term averages. In English Walter and I did better than any of the class. I got nearly 100. In German it is a long story, and I have much to tell you when you get home. In Latin I got A. Highest except Ed Sherman's. We were the only ones whose term mark was raised by the examinations. In Greek B+. In geometry C . . .[12]

The "long story" about the German could not wait until Margaret's return, so he wrote her another letter a week later explaining what had happened. Besides being unintentionally amusing, the letter reveals the driving intensity to succeed in the things that mattered most to him, in this case his school work.

> I said that the German was a long story. I have done well in German during the term work, and I know about as much German as any boy in the class, and yet I got only B in the test. It seems to me that it is hardly my fault. Mrs. Smith, in the first place, got me nearly frantic by mixing the classes all up, and then going around the room yelling the questions at the top of her voice. I had not brought my Grimm with me, though that perhaps was my own fault. I had to keep borrowing from someone else, and also do my translation in a terrible hurry. Secondly, she corrected the most insignificant and natural mistakes, as writing "stay" for "remain. . . ." I have learnt hardly any German since I have been with her, compared with what I could have learned with another teacher. It makes me perfectly frantic to see the snail's pace at which she makes me creep along. With her I shall never have much, if any, chance to talk German.

In this same letter he thanked his mother for sending him a volume of Schiller, "for his German is not very bad."[13]

He also read widely on his own, both in English and in the several languages he was learning or had already learned. He read both secular and religious works. Nor did he neglect his music. In Newport he took piano lessons from a Miss Annie Kelly. "I was so eager to begin," he wrote, "that I struggled to attend my first lesson through drifts of snow on the day of the worst blizzard that, to my knowledge, Newport had ever known."[14]

He did much of his reading at the Redwood Library in Newport. At the rear of the building was a large porch that was nearly always deserted, and which he used as a "magical hiding place . . . and spent long summer afternoons there sitting on the floor of the porch poring over sea stories and biographies."[15] It was here, at age thirteen, that he first read Boswell's *Life of Johnson,* and was so desolate when he finished the two "fat volumes" that he read them through twice more. He also read Kipling's *Soldiers Three,* Cardinal Newman's *The Idea of a University,* Cardinal Manning's *The Eternal Priesthood,* and the Bible "conscientiously three times from cover to cover, reading much that I could not understand. The heroes and heroines in the Old and New Testament formed an inspiring picture in my mind and when I was troubled I took refuge in the book of Wisdom or the Psalms."[16] At home in the long evenings, his mother read aloud most of Dickens, Trollope and Jane Austen.[17]

By his early teens, therefore, the young John LaFarge had found the intellectual and cultural interests that would accompany him through the rest of his long life—literature, theology, music and languages. While having less time to cultivate these early interests during his priesthood, and at the same time adding new interests along the way, he never abandoned any of them.

LaFarge would finish his senior year at the Newport high school, and would go on from there to Harvard. Of the two years he spent with his mother and father in New York, there is no record of his receiving any formal education. It is almost certain that he did not. But he did take advantage of his sabbatical to enrich his cultural life, attending Philharmonic concerts at Carnegie Hall and joining a group of "elderly Gaelic-speaking Irishmen who met every week or so over beer and cheese somewhere around Second Avenue and Thirty-fourth Street and cultivated the mysteries of the Gaelic language." His father was "infinitely amused" when the Irishmen elected him secretary of the group.[18]

Just about the time he was learning Gaelic, his father received a letter from Henry Adams asking if he would play host to a young Polynesian boy who was touring the United States. The artist sent back an amusing but revealing reply.

> The boy seems younger than mine, and if he turned up this way I don't exactly know what they would do to amuse him, unless by the usual course of taking him to the theatre or shows; I suppose he has that in San Francisco. If you determine to do anything about it, I am at your service as far as I can use the younger machinery. Unfortunately my youngest boy might be a college professor, and I don't know how amusing he would be to the young savage. He would certainly be interested in the savage and get out of him the declinations of the irregular pronouns in Polynesian, as lately he has assuaged his rage on the Gaelic and is now the secretary of the Gaelic Society of New York.[19]

There is no evidence that the Polynesian "savage" showed up in New York. The letter to Adams, however, gives a glimpse into the artist's feelings about his son. He recognized young John's abilities, but at the same time was somewhat derisive about him, calling him a potential "college professor." Had he thought John might someday become a Jesuit priest, he would have been even more distressed, as did happen when he received that piece of news some years later.

While his mind was a grab bag of interests, LaFarge's most important and last contacts during his teens were with theologians, since by that time he was determined to become a priest. He wrote of this in *The Manner Is Ordinary*. "As my twelfth year approached I experienced the growth of an all dominant purpose of my life. That was to become a Catholic priest."[20]

Two of these theologians were Father John Prendergast, S.J., who was the first Jesuit he had ever talked to, and Rev. Dr. Herman Heuser, the professor of scripture he had first met at his sister Emily's house in Philadelphia during Christmas week of 1894. At that time Heuser, who must have recognized LaFarge's inordinate craving for knowledge, warned him not merely to cultivate his intellect while neglecting his heart, advice that impressed him "profoundly."[21]

In the spring of 1897 he had to select a college. Having missed so much formal education during his nearly two years in New York, it was at first doubtful that he could get into either of the colleges he was applying for—first Columbia, then Harvard. "The Georgetown plan had been dropped," he wrote. "Columbia was almost my choice, but fair Harvard prevailed."[22]

"Fair Harvard" turned out not to be so fair to LaFarge, as he revealed in his autobiography, and in letters and articles written by him during his undergraduate years and long afterward. He had already taken preliminary entrance exams for Columbia in the spring of 1897 when he suddenly decided on Harvard. Through W. Kirkland Brice, a Newport friend of the family, he was allowed to take the Harvard exams in September, just before the start of the fall semester. The dean of Harvard, LeBaron R. Briggs, was so impressed with his showing that he wrote Brice: "I scarcely dreamed of his passing enough examinations to warrant our admitting him as a regular student. Certainly he more than justifies your account of him; and if you can send us some other fellows who will come up on the second day of the examinations and get in . . . we shall gladly consider them. I regard this kindness on your side rather than on mine."[23]

Dean Briggs would write another, not so favorable letter about LaFarge in May 1899, when he was nearing the end of his sophomore year. LaFarge had broken a college rule by leaving the campus one day before spring recess officially started. "We have to look strictly at records of attendance when recesses approach," he wrote his father, "if we are to keep the students within bounds."[24] There is no evidence that LaFarge's father chastised him for this transgression.

The youthful Briggs's appointment as dean in 1891 by President Charles Eliot came as a surprise to the rest of the faculty. Observing that students flocked to Briggs's office for counsel, he decided to make the assistant professor of English the dean of the college. "In Briggs," wrote Hugh Hawkins in his biography on Eliot, "the students found a friend, to him they told the truth, and even those penalized admitted his fairness."[25]

The Harvard of LaFarge's day was intensely class- "divided between society men (members of selective clubs) and nonsociety men. Among the latter there was a great deal of personal isolation."[26] This was especially true of sons of new immigrants, and even more true of Jewish students, for whom there was an admissions quota. These students were too diverse among themselves to be able to band together for solace and company. LaFarge was not a society man, but neither was he isolated. He made friends easily, both on and off campus, and was content to hone his intellect—for which he would receive recognition while still a Harvard undergraduate.

His biggest difficulty at Harvard was not social but economic. Insufficient funds were a recurring problem for him. He went to Harvard, but he went there on a tight budget. His brother Bancel sometimes came to his rescue. In early spring of his freshman year he wrote Margaret, "Yesterday I got $75 from Bancel, to my great relief; for I was reduced to 25 cents."[27] At one point, terribly strapped for funds, he was forced to sell his dory to his brother Grant. "I have just received a cheque of $30 from Grant," he wrote his mother, "he thinks that the dory is worth that to him. I think it very likely is."[28] One senses a bit of sarcasm here—that Grant, taking advantage of his need, paid less for the boat than it was worth.

LaFarge did not find Harvard congenial to Roman Catholics. He regarded some of his professors as distinctly anti-Catholic, although he conceded that he did not suffer from any overt or formal discrimination.[29] For a while he attended the Wednesday night poetry readings of the philosopher and poet George Santayana. After a few sessions, however, he perceived that Santayana was not only hostile to the Catholic faith but to Christianity in general. He felt that Santayana singled him out with his "penetrating glance" and insinuating manner. He angered the young freshman, who told him "rather bluntly" that he resented the "tone of his inquiry." LaFarge left the meeting and never returned.[30]

He never forgave Santayana. Learning of the philosopher's death in Italy in 1952, at age eighty-eight, he wrote, "I have personal knowledge of the influence he then wielded in weakening the religious faith of young men and drawing Catholics and believing Protestants away from their religion."[31]

One question often asked of LaFarge in later life was how, as a member of the Jesuits, a teaching order, he felt about studying at a secular university. He did not equivocate in his answer. "I believed," he wrote in response, "and still do, that a Catholic youth is apt to suffer a definite loss in not attending a Catholic college."[32] In a 1945 letter to a fellow priest in London, he gave a more expanded answer to the same question.

> I believe that I myself have an extraordinary impartial view of the whole question, since I am a product of a secular school, Harvard University, yet have taught in our Jesuit institutions and have seen the thing very intimately from both sides and continue to have close contact with both types of instruction. I find that the products of the Catholic colleges here, while they lack some of the boldness and initiative of those that have been in secular schools and have had to battle to some extent against a surrounding atmosphere, are in the long run more inclined to wear well. They have some principles clearly fixed and, in constructive work of organized Catholic Action, you can rely on them to a much greater extent than you can

the others. A man who is a Catholic school product yet has some
breadth of view and some worldly wisdom is a strong power in public life.[33]

To compensate for the lack of religious teaching at Harvard, except
for the divinity school, LaFarge tried to revive the moribund Harvard
Catholic Club, which had first been formed by Irish Catholics in 1893.
He arranged for various priests to give talks to the Catholic students under the club's auspices. The lectures, he wrote, were a "feeble substitute
for the religious atmosphere of a Catholic college," but rewarded those
who attended, or so he believed.[34] By LaFarge's time at Harvard, compulsory attendance at morning chapel was no longer required, although
it had been not too many years before he arrived. To a Catholic of La-
Farge's devoutness this would have been intolerable.

To further stimulate Catholic students to practice their faith, he persuaded the administration to grant the Catholic club two hundred dollars
to furnish its room with a library. In his sophomore year he took on the
job of chairman of the library committee. In the Georgetown collection
there is an undated copy of a memorandum from him soliciting donations for the library. "The books desired," he wrote, "are standard apologetic works: standard works dealing with dogma, morals, philosophy, or
history; biographies of saints and eminent men, or any of the best books
from the great body of Catholic writings."[35] After working hard to amass
the collection, he "noticed that nobody ever read them. It was discouraging."[36] After he left Harvard, however, the club, named the St. Paul's
Catholic Club, came back to life, aided by the acquisition of the Newman House as a gathering place.

Writing more than two decades after leaving Harvard, he seems to
have had a change of mind on creating enclaves of Catholics studying in
secular colleges and universities. This would only set Catholics apart
from non-Catholics, bringing upon them even more prejudice. He would
rather see money spent to make it possible for more Catholics to be educated at Catholic institutions.[37]

While focusing his formal studies at Harvard on Greek and Latin, he
did not abandon his music. He took two elective courses in harmony and
counterpoint with the "desultory professor J.K. Payne and the scholarly
Walter Spalding."[38] He even tried his hand at composing music, and
played one of his piano preludes for Emma Forbes Cary, a family friend
in Boston and a brilliant pianist herself. According to LaFarge she lis-
tened placidly and at the end remarked graciously, "It is very impres-

sive." He knew then that his talent for music was in performing and interpreting, not writing original scores.[39]

Some of his letters to Margaret during the Harvard years point up his great pleasure in playing and listening to good music. In his sophomore year, for example, he wrote to her of a very enjoyable evening spent at the home of the Napoleonic Era historian John Ropes. Included in the company were a man named Palmir Welsh, another called Russell, and Martin Joyce, "a very agreeable freshman . . . I played for them after dinner. Russell played too, and Mr. Ropes was so warmed up that he treated us all to a Sousa concert. It was interesting, though long and deafening and was enlivened by a bat that had some way got into the theatre, and circled around to the great amusement of the audience."[40] It appears that LaFarge was no great admirer of John Philip Sousa.

He shared his love of music with Margaret, who was his first piano teacher, but not with his father. Once he asked the artist what was his favorite kind of music. "John," he replied, "the music that makes the least sound."[41] He once tried to bribe his mother into a longer visit with him in Cambridge with promises of concerts and other musical entertainments. In a letter of November 27, 1899, when he was a junior, he wrote, "We could have a good deal of music, as we can go on Sundays to hear Mr. Spalding play the big organ, or you could go to the symphony in town: and we can hear Mrs. Yellison sing by the hour at Miss Cary's, as Miss Cary being unable to read amuses herself by getting Mrs. Yellison to sing Bach and Handel. . . ."[42]

In addition to music and religious studies done largely on his own, he continued his strong interests in literature and languages. Since he expected to be a priest, and might someday teach scripture, he reasoned that he should be able to read the texts in their original languages. So for his last three years at Harvard he "studied the Semitic languages, Hebrew, Syriac, and Aramaic . . ."[43]

He took freshman English under Charles "Copey" Copeland, one of the truly great and inspiring teachers of that generation. Harvard's President Eliot hired Copeland as an instructor in 1892, but refused to promote him to assistant professor since he had insufficient publications.[44] Copeland, however, outlasted Eliot, and in 1925, three years before his retirement, he was appointed Boylston Professor of Rhetoric and Oratory at Harvard. Copeland took a "dim view" of one of LaFarge's essays "on the psychology of emptiness of thought since the paper was empty of thought." But he encouraged LaFarge to write, with the result that he was elected to the editorial board of the Harvard monthly.[45]

In his junior year he made the O.K. Literary Society and the Shakespeare Club, which elated him. He wrote to Margaret immediately about his twin triumphs.

> I have had good fortune. I have been elected to two of the most wished for clubs: The O.K., the literary society, and the Shakespeare Club. The O.K. is composed of sixteen men, all of one class, eight of whom are chosen by the outgoing senior class, which eight choose eight more. Just remarkably I have been chosen as one of the first eight without having been in one of the lower societies. . . .
>
> The Shakespeare Club is a small informal club of about the same number of men of generally similar character. It is what the name implies, for reading Shakespeare in a sociable way, with beer and crackers.
>
> In this way I shall make the acquaintance with a good many of the best men in my class. Bancel is much pleased.[46]

The tone of this letter implies that LaFarge was becoming something of an intellectual snob. Perhaps he was, briefly, but if so it did not last long. It was not part of his makeup. These two literary honors — coming on the heels of one another — must have been heady stuff for the young man who had for so long lived in the shadow of his father, and he would have been more than human had he not crowed about them to Margaret. What would characterize LaFarge's personality throughout his life, however, was caution and self-restraint about his accomplishments.

At no time, either in his autobiography or his known correspondence, did he mention any physical attraction to the opposite sex. If he had such feelings he kept them to himself. He very much enjoyed the company and conversation of women, but his early decision to enter the priesthood probably discouraged him from any thoughts of romance.

One family that he visited regularly in Boston during his Harvard years was that of Edward Hooper and his five daughters, one of whom, Mabel, married his brother Bancel. Of the Hooper girls he wrote, "The five slender blonde girls, with their subdued voices and measured language, would be seated in low chairs in their mansion parlor on Mount Vernon Street. You also sank into one of these chintz-covered chairs, and the conversation was just stimulating enough, avoiding violent controversy." He added, however, just in case the reader got the wrong idea, that he "never felt as if the girls were anything but my older sisters."

LaFarge felt so comfortable at the Hoopers because his father was an intimate friend of Edward Hooper, father of the "five slender blonde girls." Hooper had been treasurer of Harvard for over twenty years. He was wealthy, distinguished, and an important art collector. According to Henry LaFarge, nephew of Father John, who attended Harvard twenty years after his uncle, many of his acquisitions were made on the advice and encouragement of John LaFarge senior, "including works by Delacroix, Courbet, Constable, Whistler, Winslow Homer, and a marvelous collection of William Blake's prophetic books."[47]

Henry believed that LaFarge benefitted socially and intellectually from the Hooper connection, "because it was the touchstone of the wider community." Had LaFarge been interested in social advancement he could have capitalized on this connection. To a degree he did, but not in a social climbing sense. Henry, nevertheless, thought that his uncle got more out of Harvard and his four years in Boston than he was willing to admit. He reflected on this in a 1982 letter.

> Edward Hooper, as already indicated, belonged to an enlightened group of Bostonians which included personages like Henry Lee Higginson—founder of the Boston Symphony—the naturalist Alexander Agassiz, son of Louis Agassiz, the architect H. H. Richardson, the historians George Bancroft and Henry Adams, the Orientalists Feneloss and William Sturges Bigelow. It was a transitional period for Harvard, which although lacking the religious foundations of the great centers of learning in Europe—Oxford, Paris, etc.—was beginning to rival them in fields of secular culture, in law, medicine, scientific research. Judging by LaFarge's recollections, I always had the impression that despite the spiritual shortcomings, he valued his associations there and made the most of what there was to offer.[48]

To a point, LaFarge would have agreed with his nephew. As far as courses, amusements, and intellectual contacts were concerned, Harvard lived up to its reputation. He could not have asked for a more congenial atmosphere for pursuing knowledge. Still, at graduation, he knew that something had eluded him during his Harvard years. What it was he did not realize until he came to teach at a Jesuit institution years later. What Harvard did not give him was a sense of his humanity, despite the great knowledge and wisdom that poured from the mouths of its faculty.

> For marvelous as all those other achievements are, if we look through the history of our civilization, we find that the most durable

prestige usually is attached to the school which, while it gives to positive science and erudition the priceless need that is due them, nevertheless glories, as its crowning achievement, in the interpretation of man to man.[49]

LaFarge's mainly secular education came to an abrupt end on graduation day from Harvard in 1901. He would return for class reunions and other functions in the years ahead. To his considerable surprise he was invited to give the annual Dudleian Lecture on Religion at Harvard in 1947, the first Catholic priest to be so honored. "It never occurred to me," he wrote in his acceptance letter, "that this request would come my way."[50]

Of his graduating class he wrote:

By general agreement of its members, the class of 1901 was a vast improvement over the expiring nineteenth century's last gasp in the class of 1900. We also felt we were setting a standard which the class of '02 might admire but never obtain. The genius of the class was the poet Robert Frost, and some lesser celebrities clustered around his melodious name. In general, however, the class of '01 prided itself through the years on being the class of the *homme moyen,* standing on its widely distributed merits, not on the borrowed radiance of a few celebrities.[51]

In the fall of 1901 John LaFarge began his theological studies at the University of Innsbruck in Austria, and for the first time in his life going to school in a Roman Catholic institution.

Chapter 3

Innsbruck

Innsbruck University in the Austrian Tyrol, which LaFarge entered as a theology student in the fall of 1901, had been established by edict of the Austrian Emperor Ferdinand I in 1562. The town of Innsbruck, which rises some nineteen hundred feet above sea level on the south bank of the Inn River, sits at the foothills of an Alpine range, and is a mecca for tourists, skiers and mountain climbers. Briefly annexed to Germany from 1938 to 1945, it has been part of Austria for many centuries.

Officially titled the Royal Imperial Leopold Francis University in Innsbruck, it is much better known simply as Innsbruck. From its beginning, except for the period 1773–1857, the Jesuit Order dominated the school of theology. Since the latter year, and until LaFarge's ordination in 1905, only two non-Jesuits had taught theology there. The university church, also controlled by the Jesuits, was built during the years 1620 to 1640. LaFarge would be ordained and say his first mass in that church. It is not surprising, therefore, that he became a Jesuit himself. It was not a foregone conclusion, but the myriad of Jesuit influences at Innsbruck certainly pointed him in that direction.

With two of his Harvard classmates, Henry Varnum Poor of New York and Benjamin Blake of Boston, LaFarge sailed for Europe on the German liner S.S. *Grosser Kurfürst* in July 1901. He had never been to Europe, so before heading for Innsbruck he decided to make an abbreviated Grand Tour of the continent. The three young men landed at Bremerhaven in northern Germany in early August. The city came as a "complete disappointment" to LaFarge. On August 5 he wrote his mother "Bremerhaven is ugly, and the country around here is dull, like New Jersey, though occasionally you see quaint cottages." He found the people "horribly dressed, at least the ordinary people. Clothes five sizes too large, and horrible hats."[1]

This reaction to a less fortunate group of people would have been uncharacteristic of LaFarge only a few years later. At this juncture in his life (as a recent graduate of Harvard) he was not wealthy, but still a pampered American aristocrat. He had not yet been exposed to the lower levels of life, and was sometimes annoyed at poverty, which in this case he interpreted as bad taste in clothing.

His impressions of Bremen, his next stop some miles from Bremerhaven on the banks of the Weser River, were only marginally better. "Last night," he wrote Margaret, "we went to the one beer garden in Bremen, which was only half filled, and of course second rate . . . but nevertheless amusing. There was a little stage where people sang outlandish songs in Tyrolese costume, and really sang pretty well. But everything here has a shabby second rate air, which I suppose is partly because it is foreign and partly because this is a socially unimportant place."[2]

Within days, however, his initial disappointment with Europe, including Germany, began to fade. His "spirits lifted" as he started covering more ground.[3] His next letter to Margaret came from Amsterdam. By this time he was even happy with the German and Dutch trains. "We came down from Bremen to Amsterdam yesterday afternoon," he wrote, "leaving at 4:31 and arriving at 9:40. It is delightful traveling in parlor cars, and a second class German or Dutch train is as comfortable as a parlor car in America."[4]

Amsterdam offered an "endless variety" of things to do and places to see. No two houses were alike. "I had forgotten all about the canals," he enthused, "and I cannot get used to seeing them everywhere, numberless canals with their green trees and walks beside them." The people were "quite different from the Bremen Germans . . . They are a uniquely nice looking lot as a general rule," one type looking "strangely Anglo-Saxon."[5]

He found the Rijksmuzeum in Amsterdam magnificent. His European tour, before he settled in for serious study at Innsbruck, was going increasingly well. "I feel as if I have been in Europe for months," he wrote. "One gets used to the strangeness so quickly, but the interest does not therefore diminish. *Everything* is interesting now, and of course the more so it is German or Dutch. The language here fascinates me, but I cannot understand it, but very little. It is not half as distinct as German. . . ."[6]

Rotterdam, where he arrived on Saturday, August 10, gave him not just a cultural, but a spiritual experience as well. When he saw Rembrandt's *Presentation of Our Lord,* he "felt as if time had vanished."[7] Later, he came across a "charming little Gothic Church . . . white washed, like all the northern churches, and with a splendid Gothic carved wood altar and pulpit." But he missed not having his mother with him to share these foreign delights. "And yet I cannot fully enjoy it without you," he wrote her. "I have to have you to show things to. We must have things together. Otherwise what I see is but something that flits before my eyes and stores itself in my brain, without taking any place in my heart."[8]

On that Saturday evening in Rotterdam he felt the need for confession. He found a "shabby little Jesuit church, and confessed to a delightful old gentleman in French, which was very rattling, as it perturbed my mind . . ." As penance the priest gave him an unfamiliar prayer, so he "had to borrow a Dutch prayer book from a lady who knew no other tongue." He guessed he "did all right."[9]

The next morning, Sunday, he attended the eight o'clock mass at the same church, still hoping to catch the nine o'clock boat to Delft with his two companions, and then go on to The Hague. The church was right around the corner from the dock, but the priest gave a half-hour sermon. Despite leaving immediately after the sermon he missed the boat and had to take a train by himself, since his friends had gone ahead without him. He reached The Hague at 10:30 and searched until he found another Catholic church where he could finish his mass. He described his frustration at what happened next to Margaret.

> Then I tried to find the picture gallery. I asked several citizens, and I don't know how many gendarmes. I asked them in English and German and French and Dutch. It was awful. They were all very polite, but I had great difficulty in speaking anything but Dutch. One very kind gentleman volunteered German, but got hopelessly mixed on the genders, just like myself. However, after going round and round and round I found it. It does give you a queer feeling, though, to walk along a street full of people not one of whom you can talk to. Even gendarmes are pretty scarce. I wish guides were. I wonder if anyone is ever arrested.[10]

His next stop was Munich, where he said good-bye to his fellow travelers. A few days later, going by stagecoach, he finally came to Innsbruck. His first visit there, however, was a brief one, intended mainly to register as a student and get the feel of the town and university. Then it was on to the Schloss Palau at Brixen on the outskirts of Innsbruck, where he stayed a few days at the summer home of the Baron and Baroness Schönberg-Roth-Schönberg. It was the first of many visits to their palace during his Innsbruck years. The baron, a convert to Catholicism from the Church of England, held the post of papal chamberlain and spent his winters with the baroness in Rome. His wife was an American, born Elizabeth Ward, daughter of Thomas Ward of Boston, and aunt of George Cabot Ward, one of LaFarge's Harvard classmates.

After spending a few pleasant days at Brixen, he returned to Innsbruck to settle down to his first year of studies. Although a theology student, he did not have to live, at least for the time being, in the Canisianum, the Jesuit-run residence. He chose instead to live in the town, walking each day to his classes in the university. He described his quarters in *The Manner Is Ordinary*.

> My room on the second floor at No. 3 Adamgasse was separated from the street by a cold, green, rushing mountain stream that ran right though the town. There was a coffee or chicory factory in the building, and the water wheel which operated the machinery turned day and night.[11]

It was not long before he became "appallingly homesick" in that room. To ease the pain of his loneliness he rented a grand piano—a Bluthner—for a modest sum. It was less, in fact, than he had paid for an upright at Harvard. Somehow he got the large instrument into his small apartment, to the "amazement" of his landlady.[12]

Classes began in October. For LaFarge these classes included lectures in philosophy under the renowned Father Joseph Lercher and scripture with Leopold Fonck. He found the faculty calm and dignified, in sharp contrast to the uproarious student body, a melange of competing religions (including atheists) and nationalities. The fiery nationalisms that tore much of Europe apart in 1914 were much in evidence at Innsbruck in 1901, as LaFarge sometimes found to his despair and frustration. The German-speaking students, the majority in the university, objected to lectures given in Italian by the Austrian-Italian professors in the school of law. In their turn the Italian students demanded their own university in either Trent or Trieste, two Italian cities in Austria. The student demonstrations became so disruptive that the administration closed the entire university for the semester.

LaFarge noted with some satisfaction that the German Catholics took no part in the protests. They instead petitioned against the closing, reminding the university officials that together with the German students in the school of theology, they numbered six hundred. Writing with hindsight more than half a century later, LaFarge saw forecasts of the future in this particular student unrest. "The student affair was my first sampling of the German-Italian dissensions that continued to plague the Austrian Reich during the successive years: the fruit of a hopeless conflict between pagan German nationalism and an extreme, often highly anti-clerical Italian nationalism; a foretaste of Hitler and Mussolini."[13]

Despite the closing of the university for the fall semester, LaFarge's first year there was a busy one as he adjusted to his new surroundings and made new friends. Not surprisingly, he sought the company of fellow Americans, a sizable group that dubbed itself the "American Exiles." He also joined the Blessed Virgin's Sodality, whose members included students from the law, medicine, and philosophy departments, as well as theology majors. LaFarge played the harmonium for the hymn-singing in the Prince's Chapel of the Jesuit University Church at the sodality's weekly meetings. When he visited Innsbruck in the spring of 1951 he went to see the old chapel where he had said his First Mass in 1905. "It had been badly bombed out during the war," he wrote, "but to my delight I found it completely restored, the same old chapel with a window looking into the sanctuary of the church, and even a harmonium like the one I had played fifty years ago."[14]

Three months of living alone in his room in town left him even more depressed and lonely. To relieve the boredom he took long walks "in the dusk through the nooks and byways of half-medieval Innsbruck, wearing an old raincoat." One night a young boy, observing his furtive figure, called out to him, *'Bettelstudent!'* "a hobo student."

Fortunately, his ability to charm women, both young and not so young, came to his rescue. He remembered an introduction some friends at home had given him to an English lady who lived in Innsbruck, Miss Mary Howitt, daughter of the poets William and Mary Howitt, best known for the ditty, "Will you walk into my parlor, said the Spider to the Fly?" She invited him to her villa in a better part of town, where she lived with a companion, the Baroness Frankenstein.

> She offered me a good cup of hot British tea, with British muffins to boot, talked of common friends, and made me feel as if I had escaped from the grim Alpine surroundings. It was absurdly trifling, yet it broke the spell, and I began to feel more like a normal human being. I have often thought of that experience in dealing with young people who come from abroad to this country.[15]

During Christmas vacation that first year he visited Munich again, staying in a plain small hotel called the "Three Ravens." While there he went to the museums and the Court Theater, and attended his first midnight mass.[16]

When he returned from Munich he decided he had experienced enough solitude and was ready to move into the Jesuit seminary, the Theologisches Convict, better known as the Canisianum, a "plain, fairly modern four-story building." The accommodations were truly Spartan.

> Outside of the bedrooms there was no heat whatsoever in any part of the buildings. Corridors, dining hall, capacious lecture rooms where the professor climbed up in a lofty pulpit and the listeners sat on the hardest of wooden benches, were completely devoid of heat. In the chapel the holy water froze solid in the bronze founts, and an acolyte serving Mass had to beware lest he freeze his fingers on the heavy eighteenth-century silver cruet trays. In the evening we lined up in the courtyard to fill our jugs for drinking and washing. During the first two years there was no plumbing and nature's needs were cared for in fairly medieval fashion.[17]

Despite the discomforts, which he called the "primitive features of the life," he began to thrive and enjoyed during his Innsbruck years "a health he had never known before."[18]

One year after leaving Newport, bound for a new life, his mother and sister Margaret visited him. Together they toured the Tyrol, stayed for a while with the Schönbergs at Brixen, and traveled through parts of Bavaria. The following Easter they returned, this time meeting in Rome, where LaFarge "had the privilege of seeing Pope Leo XIII in a general audience in his very last months."[19] While he had to return to Innsbruck after the brief vacation (classes would not let out for the summer until July 31), his mother and sister continued the tour.

Once again, in the summer of 1903, the two Margarets sailed to Europe to be with him, their third Atlantic crossing in three years. LaFarge met them in Paris, and together they toured the cathedrals in northern France and the Loire Valley. They also visited LaFarge relatives in Brittany, near the town of Morlaix. One of them, Auguste la Barre de Nanteuil, was first cousin to his father through the Binsse side of the family.

While at Morlaix LaFarge experienced at firsthand the conflict then raging between the French government and the Catholic Church. He described Auguste as a "faithful Ultramontane: a Catholic first, and with all his patriotic fervor a Frenchman afterward." LaFarge, of course, sided with his family and his Church, accusing the government of being "fanatically anti-clerical." During his brief stay at Morlaix he "witnessed the cruelty and undemocratic action of Emile Combes, recently elected Prime Minister, in demanding the expulsion of the religious congregations."

In his youth Combes had studied for the priesthood, and even taught for a while in Catholic schools. Later he turned against the Church, insisting that it, and the military, exercised too much power in French politics. He was an ardent believer in the innocence of Alfred Dreyfus, the Jewish French officer convicted of high treason in a case fraught with overtones of anti-Semitism and conspiracy. He rigorously enforced recent laws forbidding religious congregations to teach, and in 1904 broke diplomatic relations with the Vatican. In describing Auguste as a faithful Ultramontanist first and a loyal Frenchman next, LaFarge was really confirming the charge that his cousin, and others, were giving their loyalty to a power outside France, namely the Church of Rome.

Still the government's demands were harsh and sudden. The Sisters of the Holy Ghost of Brittany, who had a house in Morlaix, were ordered dissolved immediately. The government gave them the choice of returning to the world, or exile. With LaFarge helping to see them off they boarded a train that would lead them to asylum and a new life in England. The affair left him with strongly bitter feeling against the French government.[20]

Following the visit to the Brittany relatives the LaFarges sailed to Southampton in England, then rode by train to Rye in Sussex to spend a couple weeks with Henry James, their longtime Newport friend. The enigmatic Henry was then in the midst of his self-imposed exile at Lamb House, his "stately, square brick residence." The LaFarges took rooms at a picturesque nearby inn, where "the food was not quite equal to the artistic surroundings." They dined occasionally, however, at Lamb House, where the cuisine was a treat after the indifferent fare at the inn. James and the LaFarges took long walks through the English countryside, of especial delight to Margaret, who had never been to England before. "She felt," she told her son, "as if she had stepped into one of the novels of Jane Austen or Anthony Trollope, most of which she already knew by heart."[21]

Years later Margaret let drop to her son "that she was the only woman with whom Henry James was ever deeply in love." LaFarge was skeptical of her claim, although he conceded that certain cautious comments from his mother over the years did lend some credence to her story.[22]

A letter written to Margaret by James in June 1904, while not exactly amatory, does suggest his strong feelings for her.

> My dear Margie: . . . The months revolving in their terrifying way
> brought round again the aspects (*some* of them, that is, not, thank
> heaven, *all!*) that prevailed in this little place simultaneously with
> your and Margaret's presence here so that, the past seeming to join
> hands with the actual, it is as if there had verily been no interval at
> all, and I had only to walk around to the musty Mermaid to find
> you.[23]

LaFarge left the two Margarets in England in early October 1903
when he returned to Innsbruck for the fall semester. He described his
journey back in a long letter from Innsbruck dated October 4, 1903.

> The journey, except for the crossing of the channel was by no means
> fatiguing or unpleasant. In crossing I remained on deck, having no
> idea there would be a sea on. I hired a rubber coat from a sailor, and
> placed myself in a steamer chair. There was soon, however, a dread-
> ful sea—almost everyone had gone below, but I felt too sick to
> move. Of course I was wet, and my valise was drenched,—all the
> labels being washed off, but except for the wrecking of my collar
> no damage done. It was a horrible experience—the cold darkness,
> sickness, showering torrents of saltwater, etc.[24]

The rest of the trip, by train from Boulogne to Bale to Zurich and
thence to Innsbruck, was in happy contrast to the channel crossing—lots
of sunshine and cold, brisk air. It was "delightful to be back," he wrote
his mother. At that moment the world, for the young seminarian, was a
fine place to be.[25]

The weather would soon turn frigid, however, as he settled down for
his third year of studies at Innsbruck. In one of Henry James's letters to
Margaret in early January 1904, the author referred to LaFarge's Ty-
rolean life. "I hope," he wrote, "you get uplifting news from John—
whom I can't think of, however, in his fine wintry Dolomite scenery,
without the impulse immediately to stir the fire."[26]

LaFarge himself alluded to Innsbruck's cold weather in a letter to his
mother in mid-November. "The only thing I am much in need of is shoes,
for my feet are still uncomfortable. I want a pair of stout warm shoes
(boots) with strong sides and wide enough and high enough at the toes."[27]

A few weeks later he wrote expressing relief that mother and sister had
arrived safely back at Newport after a good Atlantic crossing. He asked
that she send him some books and other things from home, including his
copy of *The Confessions of Saint Augustine,* which he remembered was
either a little green or a little blue book, "a Danish volume called *Tarvis*

with a red back, and a thick black book, cloth covered, the title of which I have forgotten treating the history of the 19th century in the different countries of Europe." He suggested that if anyone wanted to give him a Christmas present, "the most acceptable would be a year's subscription to the *Harvard Graduate Magazine.* As for more practical items he asked her to send him "another washbag which you might make and send by mail." Also a "decent photograph of yourself which Margaret ought to try again to take. The only other things are the shoes, but those I trust will be no difficulty."

His most important news was that he would receive minor orders at the end of December, following a retreat. This meant that ordination to the priesthood could take place sometime in 1905 or, at the latest, 1906. He also wrote of his coming vow of celibacy, which he would take when he became a sub-deacon the following summer. The vow did not present any problem for him. "So it is before the sub-deaconate," he wrote, "that the real decision for or against one's vocation comes—which for me is as certain as it could well be." He ended this upbeat letter with the news that while "today is all deep snow, a regular wintry day," that his health was "first rate, and all is well."[28]

Until ordination in July 1905 LaFarge continued to absorb theology from the highly competent Jesuits who taught at Innsbruck. Except for Church history the classes were conducted in Latin. He enjoyed the easy personal access to his professors, so unlike the Harvard faculty, where the professors tended to be aloof outside the classroom. His only disappointment was lack of opportunity to learn much scholastic philosophy. What was taught in that area, he thought, was taught in "uninspiring fashion." This problem hit him hard, he wrote in his autobiography, "precisely because I had learned no scholastic philosophy at Harvard and had thereby missed the key to the more speculative part of doctrinal teaching."[29] His failure to obtain a good grounding in scholasticism would bother him for the rest of his life. In his mind he never really made up this deficiency in his education.

His exposure at Innsbruck to the national and religious differences that plagued Germany and Austria-Hungary, from which countries most of the students there were drawn, both intrigued and disturbed him. Austria-Hungary, he discovered, contained at least twelve different nationalities, some mutually antagonistic to one another and to Hapsburg Vienna. As for the Germans, he was "surprised to find how strong was their consciousness of their particular land or section of the country, how little feeling there was for Germany as a whole. This was, of course, before World War I. If you asked a German his nationality he would say, I am a Bavarian, a Württemberger, a Pfalzer, or a Saxon, as the case might be. But if he said *'Ich bin ein Deutscher,'* you knew that he was Prussian."[30] LaFarge would have many opportunities in the 1930s and 1940s, after he joined the staff of *America,* to draw upon his personal knowledge of central Europe to understand and explain events there in his articles and editorials.

His third year at Innsbruck was a busy one, filled with making plans and traveling, both in Europe, and in the summer of 1904, a transatlantic crossing, this time to Newport, for his first visit home in three years. As of January of that year, however, his thoughts for the near future were more modest. On the twenty-first he wrote Margaret thanking her for sending the books and boots he had requested some weeks before. In referring to the summer ahead he thought he "should probably go to Austrian Poland if nothing else turned up and perfect my tongue in that charming language—I have already since summer progressed a good deal and am very glad to know it will be useful at home."

His spiritual condition had recently received a substantial boost from a retreat given by Father Hugo Hurter, a Jesuit at Innsbruck, who had given a similar one two years before. The priest made a "remarkable impression" on the young seminarian.

> P.H. is quite indescribable. He delighted me this time by his wonderfully cheerful and hopeful tone which he put into everything—reminding me a little of good Miss Cary—together with great seriousness. Even single words, as "Der Wille Gottes! Der Wille Gottes!" he would repeat with such a childlike confidence, such a fervent intonation they sufficed for all one could think. Some of course was a repetition of what we had heard before, but not all. I will copy out some points and send them to you eventually. I cannot tell you how much help I had from it, and how much clearer my way had become for me, especially in the precise things that troubled me.
>
> Of course the practical matters were often illustrated by his little jokes, which were indescribably enlightening and to the point. He spoke of our duty regarding confession, especially that we should approach it, not with fear and trembling, but cheerfully, with a certain impulse; just as before a visit he washes not unwillingly but gladly.

He ended this letter to Margaret with a warning that he would probably not have much news to write about until Easter, when he was think-

ing of going to Vienna. The final sentence, however, called her attention
sharply back to his impending vocation. "How I wish I could bring all
the world to make a retreat with P. Hurter."[31]

The winter and early spring that year passed uneventfully for him. His
letters home, though infrequent, were pleasant and chatty and, as usual,
full of questions about Margaret's well-being and what was happening in
the family. He was delighted that his brother Oliver had come east from
the West Coast, and that Margaret herself was planning a trip west in the
spring. Among his own projects were efforts to get some formal Catholic
presence at Harvard, but he received some discouraging reaction. "I have
talked recently," he wrote her at the end of February, "to the P. Rector of
the Jesuits about the conditions at Harvard; I must make inquiries about
the actual state of things at present. He was sympathetic and explained a
good many things—at first told me that from Rome alone could matters
be changed, and neither the Jesuits nor the Archbishop of Boston were to
be blamed—because they only follow the universal policy of the Church."

By the time he wrote this letter the Russo-Japanese War had broken
out in the Far East. Increasingly interested in foreign affairs, he felt frustrated at the paucity of information available to him on the course of the
conflict. "I subscribed to the *Telegraph* for a month," he wrote, "but it is
not good for the war: an enormous amount of news and letters and descriptions but all tremendously pro-Japanese and anti-Russian. I feel no
sympathy for one or the other. Russia is however at least Christian."[32]

During the Easter break he managed a trip to Italy, where he visited
Verona and Venice, among other Italian towns and cities in the north of
Italy. Judging from his enthusiasm, the trip was a success, including both
the sightseeing and the making of new acquaintances. He sent a letter off
to Margaret shortly after his return.

> Let me tell you the last news of Venice. I think it was Friday after-
> noon out to the old church of Torallo, formerly a Cathedral. I went
> in the steamer, on a glorious afternoon to Burano, where there are
> lace factories; thence I took a gondola to the Franciscan monastery
> of S. Francesco in Deserto, and thence round to the old cathedral of
> Torallo. The former (S. Fran.) is a marginal sort of spot, a little con-
> vent and garden, delightfully quaint and dreamlike, in the midst of
> vast sand-banks and lagoons. . . .

While in Venice he met two young Scots women, who tried to be
friendly, but whom LaFarge at first rebuffed, since he suspected them of
having romantic intentions. The women had no idea he was grooming

himself for the priesthood, since he usually kept that side of his life secret from strangers. But they did at last gain his friendship, as he wrote somewhat prissily to his mother, who must have been amused by his customary delicacy in dealing with members of the opposite sex.

> The Scotch ladies asked me a second time to go out in their gondola with them, and I did not quite see how to get out of it. However they seemed perfectly respectable and well-meaning, so I went, and it was quite agreeable. The gondola is very delightful for that sort of thing. . . . I asked the Scotch ladies a good deal about life in Venice, for in case you ever *should* care to stay there, such little facts would be useful . . .

On Sunday he heard mass at St. Mark's, where he found the music "solemn and beautiful, being the simple Gregorian melody after the papal prescription." The return to Innsbruck took him through Verona. The train trip was "beautiful — all brilliant sunshine, coloring with delicious luxuriance the tender green orchards and lawns, and the glorious blossoming trees and shrubs, through which occasional glistening rivers wound languidly. In the distance the hazy Padua hills. I had never realized that Italy could look so intensely verdant and flowery."

Among the letters waiting for him at Innsbruck were two from Margaret. One told of his father's recent illness. While not close to the artist, LaFarge worried about his father deeply. He let out some of his feelings about him to Margaret in the same letter that he described his trip to Italy. "It seems," he wrote on April 20, "as if he might be growing a little more frail, tho it is also likely that the events of the winter, especially the cold and the change of dwelling have upset him. As it is I should feel very badly if anything serious happens to him before I again return home, and I have come to the conclusion that if I do not hear news of his having a marked improvement, and if you don't intend coming over during the summer, the best thing I could do would be to come home for the summer."[33]

Although the senior LaFarge recovered somewhat that summer, young John decided to come to Newport anyway, where he could be near him both physically and emotionally, perhaps for the last time in their lives. It had been years since the two men had spent any extended time with each other, and at that point LaFarge was still a boy, and his father a distant and aloof parent. The coming summer would be especially propitious for them to get to know each other, since Margaret planned an extensive trip to the West Coast, and would be gone for most of the time that LaFarge would be in Newport. He wrote of his plans to her from Innsbruck on May 28.

I have finally, after much thought, decided to return to the U.S. for the summer. I received your letter the other day, of May 8, in which you tell me about the improvement in Father's condition. There seems to be no particular reason for any worry about him, and I am glad you're going on to Seattle. I thought however that it would anyhow be a good thing for me to be with Father this summer, as it is so long since I have seen him, and I do not know when I shall again be able to be with him for any length of time. For that reason I wrote to him, asking him to cable me "Come," if he really wanted me, and would be able to send me money right off. He answered, "Come, shall remit," so I have no doubt that he really wants me to be with him.

He expected to sail from Antwerp on the S.S. *Finland* of the Red Star line on July 9, which would bring him to New York on about the eighteenth. He would have to head back to Europe sometime around September 20, giving him altogether about two months in the United States. "How much I look forward to returning!" he wrote Margaret.[34]

His first reaction on landing in New York, however, was regret that he had come home when there was so much he could have seen and done had he remained on the continent. But by the time he reached Newport he felt differently. His father was at the house all by himself. "My mother and sister," he wrote, "were out on the West Coast and, for the first time in my life, I found myself alone with him, and he in a relaxed and genial mood."[35]

Long, and sometimes profound, were the many conversations that father and son enjoyed with each other that summer of 1904. It would be the last time the two men could get together and really see and hear each other out. It seemed to come as a surprise to each that they could get such pleasure from the other's company. The boy-son was now the man-son, both physically and mentally, unlike the seventeen-year-old that left for his freshman year at Harvard seven years before. They could now talk as equals. The artist wrote of this discovery to a friend. "John returned from Europe in due ecclesiastical form. I have him here now in Newport, where he has turned out to be quite charming and human, and will probably be improved by the acquaintance of the laity. He is really very charming, though I say so, and I shall miss him when he goes."[36]

The two talked of many things. The artist told his son of his trips to Japan and the South Seas many years before with Henry Adams, and the cultures and people they experienced in those places, and their reactions to them. They discussed the medieval schoolmen, a topic very close to

LaFarge's heart and mind. He found his father a natural scholastic as far as the search for truth was concerned. "What I had picked up at Innsbruck of the scholastic theory of knowledge seemed to fit in closely with Father's concept of the artistic perception of truth—that the mind correctly perceived truth, but perceived it according to the mind's own mode and intelligible activity." In other words, one's perception of truth was objective, since truth had only one form, but one's presentation of that truth was subjective. His father, he thought, "lucidly distinguished between the accuracy with which all artists, from the cave men to Rembrandt and Valasquez [sic], have always *felt* the visible world, and the inaccuracy with which they have represented it."[37]

While much of LaFarge's time that summer was spent with his father, he also kept busy visiting friends and relatives, many of them in and around Boston. And all the while he waited impatiently for his mother's return from the West Coast. He also discovered, while visiting various diocesan priests, including Father William Simmons of the Church of the Blessed Sacrament in Providence, a building designed by his architect-brother Grant, that he had formed a different view of his own future priestly life. "I felt that as a priest," he wrote, "I might better live under a rule bound more strictly to poverty and to obedience than was the case with the diocesan priests. It was only a vague feeling of disquiet, but it laid the foundation for thoughts that were to mature some months later."[38] That maturing process soon led him to the Jesuits.

He found it difficult in the early autumn of 1904, "to quit the fireside in Newport, with its conversations and comfort and peace, and start across the ocean to the distant crags and glaciers of the Alps." He took a slow steamer from New York to Genoa. Of the seventeen passengers on board, one was a relative by marriage to a cousin of his on the French side of his family. He then headed north toward Brixen, but ran out of money on the way. Confessing his poverty, he threw himself on the mercy of the proprietor of the Hotel Zum Elephanten in Brixen. He told LaFarge that all the rooms were taken "save the sacrosanct archducal suite." He led LaFarge to the suite, opened the doors, and told him to have a good night's rest. He "never felt more like an Emperor than after that endless journey," he wrote. He settled his account with the proprietor sometime later.

On reaching Innsbruck he was told that he could be ordained in July of the following year. He expected to receive the subdeaconate in February, followed by the full deaconate around Easter. There were still a few formalities to observe, such as getting permission from the bishop of Providence, his home diocese. Until these details were completed he asked Margaret to make no announcements of his coming ordination to anyone outside the immediate family. He was confident his father would design a suitable ordination announcement for him, and his anticipation of the event left him highly charged emotionally, as he revealed in a letter to Margaret on October 21, 1904.

> I feel that the few months remaining before the ordination—if it be in July, for you understand it is not yet absolutely settled—are a very solemn time of my life. It seems as if my whole life, with all its failure, all of its lukewarmness and neglect of grace, yet its ideals of the many great incalculable benefits of God, were rolled out like a scroll before my eyes, and over it were written: *unworthy servant! All, all is the gift of God.* It is the knowledge that all which I ever do is in obedience to God's calling which gives me peace and confidence.[39]

Even though the Jesuits were foremost in his mind at this point, he had not yet fully decided his future after ordination. This was apparent from his correspondence with Bishop Harkins of Providence who, in order to give him permission to be ordained in Innsbruck, had to be assured that LaFarge would have means of support after becoming a priest. As a diocesan or order priest he would be provided for, although as a member of the latter type of clergy he would take an oath of poverty. "At that time, however," he wrote, "the pledge, or mission oath as it was called, to the service of an American bishop contained also a pledge not to join a religious order. This pledge I could not utter in conscience." The bishop, therefore, had to permit his ordination on the "title of poverty," meaning that he assumed responsibility for supporting himself.[40]

During his annual retreat in January 1905, LaFarge all but committed himself to the Jesuits. The retreat profoundly affected his thinking about himself and his religion. After the fourth day, during which the participants meditated on the visit of the Christ Child to the Temple, he decided that his only option was to become a religious. "The idea of being a priest and not sharing the poverty of the great High Priest seemed to me intolerable. I could not reconcile myself to the idea of owning property, having anything of my own when He Himself was without a place to lay his head."[41] He discussed his feelings with the retreat master, who told him simply that he had a vocation to the Jesuits. For LaFarge that was it. He would be a Jesuit.[42]

It was not so easy, however, to break the news to his father, whom he suspected would not be happy to hear that his son was to become an order priest, and especially a Jesuit, although why he believed this is not clear. On March 22, 1905, he wrote Margaret from Innsbruck that she should be circumspect about whom she told, presumably to prevent word from getting back to his father. But he had dropped a few hints to him that soon he would no longer be financially responsible for his youngest offspring. "I have written nothing about it to Father, and I shall not for a while," he wrote his mother. "I told him, however, that he might expect me to be able some time during the year to make an arrangement which would relieve him of the further obligation to support me—but that it was only a perhaps. I did not explain, however, what the arrangement might be, and told him not to speak even to you about it,—in order that he might not be asking you what it was."[43]

In April, during Easter vacation, he journeyed to Rome in the company of Tom McLaughlin, a newly ordained priest, where he contacted the Jesuit General's office, which sent him on to the English assistancy, since a separate American office had not yet been established. "I paused a long time at the door," he wrote, "on which was the sign Assistentia Angliae. I even held my hand up in the air and reflected that all I needed to perform was to bring it down on the door and my fate would be sealed forever."[44] Whatever hesitation he felt was momentary. He knocked on the door and it was soon arranged that he would enter the Society of Jesus. He was first told that it would be best to delay ordination until he finished his Jesuit training. LaFarge agreed to wait, although he hoped it would come sooner. As he later wrote:

> Nevertheless I did hope that I could have the privilege of being ordained first, since my family was coming over, quite a bit of preparation had been made for my first Mass in July of that year and, moreover, I was concerned about my father. Father had been so much won over to my priestly vocation and showed himself so sympathetic on my recent visit and so interested in the prospect of my ordination, that I felt if it were postponed he would become discouraged and possibly alienated.[45]

Permission for an early ordination was soon obtained, and on July 26, 1905 John LaFarge was ordained a Catholic priest at the University Church of the Holy Trinity at Innsbruck. Three days later, with "trembling hands," he said his first mass in the Prince's Chapel in the tower of the same church.[46] Present were his mother, his sister Margaret, his cousin Henry Bancel Binsse, the Baron and Baroness Schönberg, and some friends. His mother described the event as part of a long letter to her daughter Frances. She and Margaret had arrived in Innsbruck on the afternoon of the twenty-eighth. They spent the night at a local inn, and at 8:30 in the morning gathered in the chapel for the mass. She wrote that John was very "composed and quiet and it was wonderfully peaceful and lonely. He was assisted in his Mass by Pater Meyer who is the Pater Rector. I called on him afterwards and am sure you would be pleased to have heard the things he said about John."[47]

LaFarge had a somewhat different recollection of the Pater Rector. "Father Rector Mayr, of his own accord, offered to be my assistant at the Mass. He was so old and feeble that I was in acute fear every moment lest he tumble over, and two or three times had to stretch my arm out to support him. However, all went happily and I was infinitely glad that after so many vicissitudes the great goal had at last been reached."[48]

His brother Bancel, although living in France at the time, did not attend. Neither did his father. Shortly before his son's ordination he wrote to a friend, "Of course my wife and Margaret are abroad with John at Innsbruck. I send you a clipping from the newspaper regarding him, which has been so serious to me."[49] While willing to write to a friend about his son, the artist was unwilling to write to his wife about anything. In the same letter to Frances, she wrote "I was truly thankful to hear that your father was in Newport. I hope he is well. When you write again do give me any news about him, for he never writes to me himself."[50]

Forty-three years later LaFarge reflected on his Innsbruck years.

> It is interesting to know that you visited Innsbruck. I was ordained in the old university church, most of which was destroyed by the bombardment. During the Second World War Innsbruck was hit by allied warplanes. This church is not the same as the monumenal hofkirche a little farther down the street. I said my first Mass in the wonderful little sodality chapel which was high up in the tower of the church, beautifully decorated. That chapel, however, was entirely destroyed. I felt so badly, because it had been one of my dreams to go back there again and renew old memories.[51]

This was the chapel he visited in 1951, finding to his delighted surprise that it had been completely restored.

LaFarge was surely disappointed that his brother Bancel did not attend his ordination and First Mass, especially since he was in France at the time. Bancel sent him a lengthy letter apologizing for his absence, but not clearly explaining why he had not come. In *The Manner Is Ordinary* he surmised that Mabel, his brother's wife, was ill at the time and he could neither bring her along nor leave her behind. In fact Mabel was having a severe and protracted nervous breakdown, at times requiring treatment in a sanitarium in Lausanne, Switzerland.

To help Bancel and Mabel out somewhat, LaFarge's sister Margaret went to Switzerland for a few months in the fall of 1906. When she arrived back in Newport, Margaret senior wrote Mabel about her safe return. It was a warm, kind letter, not solicitous, but emphatic.

> Margaret enjoyed being with Bancel. He is indeed all that you say of him as no one but yourself knows better than I. Very few men are as sweet and as strong as he. I am glad he has been painting so much for that is good for him and for his work, which of course everything that he paints helps and it must be an interest for you too.
>
> I worry dearest child that your thoughts trouble you. Your poor body is weak and that makes it hard for you. I have never had a real nervous breakdown but I have at times been so tired and so weak that I have had something of the same trouble. As you get stronger physically you will find it easier to steady your mind.[52]

According to Ben LaFarge, one of Bancel's grandsons, Bancel and his father had seriously quarreled over money matters. "What happened," Ben wrote the author, "was that Bancel, as manager of his father's studio, agreed to work without salary for a while when the artist was in financial straights [sic], and even loaned him money. When he failed to repay the loan, Bancel sued him (circa 1900), and as a result of the ensuing schism fled to France with his wife and two children."[53]

As mentioned earlier, Bancel was a second father to LaFarge. This quarrel between his two close relatives must have pained him deeply. Bancel himself was in a very troubled state at this time. The letter he sent LaFarge explaining his absence from Innsbruck, while warm and full of good wishes, was also gloomy and self-deprecating.

> You are my brother, so that the great step which you have taken means much to me, inasmuch as it sets an example and awakens in me a desire to perfect my own efforts in giving to my fellows the best that I am. It seems at first as if our lives were far apart but in reality they are not, because we are here chiefly to do the best we are able and help those who are about us. . . .
>
> Your life has so far been marked by great success while mine has been about a failure, but fortunately I am not discouraged and one

reason is because I have you as an example. It is a great comfort to
know that I have you to turn to for advice and help at times. . . .

Now, dear John, you have all my love and sympathy; I have nothing else to give you except my friendship which, of course, you
have always had. That I may seem distant and unsympathetic is
nothing more than a characteristic peculiarity of mine which will
always exist at times, whereas my interest in you is always increasing and I hope my admiration for you will continue as hereto-
fore. I expect to, anyhow.

It was hard for me to decide not to go to your first Mass and I can't
get over feeling my regret and absolute chagrin at not being there,
but I had so much to consider that I think in fact I know for my work
at least it has been much better that I stayed here and threw myself
into it rather than have another serious interruption.

Bancel noted somewhat ruefully near the end of the letter that "We hear
that Father has sold about $75,000 worth of paintings to the Whitneys,
so that I suppose he is a rich man now."[54]

The bitterness of this letter was not misplaced. Bancel's father had indeed wronged him. But the artist was an impossibly complicated man,
whose art overruled every part of his life. Family, filial obligations, and
financial problems took second place to his art. Near the end of his life
he realized, belatedly, how important Bancel was to him. According to
Margaret it came to him almost as a revelation.

Its denoument [sic] was like the end of a long and painful romance.
As to yourself you are now fully reinstated in his affection. He
seems most anxious to do everything he can to let you know it. In
fact he told some members of the family not long ago that he loves
you the most of all his children.[55]

At this point, while ill, the artist was still lucid. He probably meant
what he said. Unfortunately, he died before a reconciliation could be
made.

Bancel, Mabel and their four children did not return to America until
1915, the year after war broke out in Europe. For some fifteen years La-
Farge did not see the brother he so loved and admired. During those years
he had graduated from Harvard, gone to Innsbruck, became a Jesuit, and
was well into his career as a missionary priest in Maryland.

Chapter 4

The Manner Is Ordinary

LaFarge began the eighth chapter of *The Manner Is Ordinary* with a reflection on the Jesuit Order and its founder, St. Ignatius Loyola.

> Of life in the Society of Jesus its founder, St. Ignatius of Loyola, remarks (Rule 4): "For good reasons, having always in view God's greater service, the manner of living as to external things is ordinary, and has no regular penances or corporal austerities obligatory on all." This means that the novice coming from a seminary for priests, as I did, finds a regime which in general resembles that of his seminary. The Jesuit wears no prescribed or traditional habit. He does not recite the Divine Office in choir, and penitential practices are voluntary. This absence of certain typical monastic customs, however, is partly made up for by longer periods of prescribed mental prayer and examination of conscience and certain specific community devotions. The difference lies in the manner in which all life is carried out, as expressed in the Institutes (rules of the Order). The spirit is one of complete simplicity, and a poverty which makes up for the lack of austerity by its absolute dependence, even in the smallest details, upon explicit permissions and conformity to common life.[1]

For the rest of the summer of 1905 and through early autumn LaFarge, although now a priest, was not yet a Jesuit. That would soon change, but for the time being he was, in his own words, an "ecclesiastical freelance," attached to neither an order nor a diocese.[2] Until he entered the New York-Maryland Province of the Society of Jesus in Poughkeepsie, New York, in November, he was free to wander on his own, a situation of which he took full advantage.

Although he had been to London before, he decided to stop off there once more before returning to the United States. On the way he visited Lourdes in France, the shrine where in 1858 the miller's daughter

Bernadette experienced visitations from the Blessed Virgin Mary. Just a few years before LaFarge's visit, a large church had been built to accommodate the many pilgrims who came seeking cures for their illnesses from the waters of a spring flowing from a nearby rock. "It was an ineffable privilege," he wrote, "to offer Mass in the shrine, and I was deeply touched when a bishop undertook to serve a Mass for myself, a very young neophyte."[3]

The London visit lasted only a few days, which he spent as the guest of Father Hamilton MacDonald, chaplain of the Church of the Religious of the Sacred Heart in the Hammersmith section of the city. He also looked up some friends of the Schönbergs, including Lady Herbert of Lea, who introduced him to some of her own friends. Another transatlantic crossing to New York followed. He would not see Europe again until 1938, when Father Francis Talbot, editor-in-chief of *America* magazine, sent him there as a special correspondent to cover an international religious conference in Budapest, Hungary.

In New York he went directly to the Jesuit church of St. Francis Xavier on Sixteenth Street, where Father Thomas J. Gannon, the provincial, directed him to enter the Jesuit novitiate at St. Andrew-on-Hudson in Poughkeepsie on November 13, the eve of the feast of St. Stanislaus. Although almost missing the train at New York's Grand Central Station, he arrived in Poughkeepsie on time. He was admitted to the novitiate and shown to his room by the Jesuit who met him at the door. To his relief he discovered that he could sleep in his pajamas as he always did. Somehow he had thought all Jesuits wore long white nightgowns.

The next morning, after a good night's sleep, he found that the Jesuit who had greeted him at the door and shown him to his room the night before was the novice master, Father George A. Pettit, who suggested, among other things, that LaFarge write regularly to his parents while in the novitiate. LaFarge knew that this would relieve his father's mind, since the artist had feared his son would be held incommunicado for some years to come. The LaFarges had much to learn about Jesuit customs and practices.

LaFarge spent the next two years at St. Andrew-on-Hudson, further studying his faith while learning to live by the rule of St. Ignatius. A strong sense of God's presence continued to pervade his life. Shortly after arriving he wrote Margaret:

> We learn that even the little duties and occupations of the Novitiate all tend to the one great end. God's glory and the saving of souls.

It is to perform all these little duties with the due fullness of spirit
and care and intention that seems to be the chief difficulty of the
Novitiate: it is the consciousness that God looks alone on our good-
will, and is ever ready with all his transforming grace that makes
everything easy.[4]

While his Poughkeepsie years were mainly given over to preparation
for the religious life, they were sometimes punctuated by family problems. As was often the case during these years his father, working inces-
santly in his New York studio while his wife remained in Newport, cast
his long shadow over the lives of the people closest to him, and especially
over those of Margaret and John. On New Year's Day of 1906, for
example, he wrote LaFarge, without explanation, that he was very sick.
The letter caused his son "some anxiety, as it was more than usually odd,
and complained particularly seriously of being ill . . ." As it turned out,
the illness either passed over with no serious consequences, or his father
stopped mentioning it. But it does seem probable that the artist, now in
his seventies, was in failing health. Shortly after receiving the alarming
letter, LaFarge received a more cheerful one "saying all was well."[5]

LaFarge's correspondence with his father differed radically in tone and
content from that with his mother. With Margaret he was open, cheerful,
and gossipy, eager to report on the mundane events of his life. He often
gave her advice on what books to read, whom she should visit or write to
(sometimes, even what to say), and in general how to conduct her life.
With his father he was diffident, apologetic, and self-critical, as if he were
imposing on the great man merely by writing to him. "Just a few lines on
Christmas Day," he wrote at the end of 1906. "I don't want to burden you
with much writing, as I had written to you so shortly before."[6]

But while family problems did burden the young priest, they did not
overwhelm him. He was increasingly caught up in his vocation, more
than ever before in his life, especially on a pragmatic level. He was discovering new powers in himself, not only to experience God personally,
but to bring him to others as well. On his first St. Patrick's Day at St. Andrew's he said mass at the nearby Hudson River State Mental Hospital.
During the middle of his sermon "a patient stood up and yelled: 'Grand
work, old boy, let's have more of it!' I sensed then," he wrote, "my possibilities as a preacher."[7]

As was the case with order priests then and now, he was frequently
sent to local parishes to say mass on Sundays. He especially enjoyed going to Kingston, he wrote Margaret, "a small, old-fashioned town up the

river . . . to hear confessions, and celebrate two masses on Sunday . . .
There is always a great deal of happiness in participating in the more
priestly life, especially when one really feels the help or enlightenment
one can bring to souls, especially in the confessional."

In this same letter he also displayed that charming bent for humor that
characterized his life. He described to her some work being done on the
grounds of the seminary by the New York Central Railroad.

> Spring has come back. I hope to stay, and it is beginning to be very
> beautiful here. There is an immense amount of desultory digging
> and blasting going on, in hopes of eventually smoothing the rugged
> outlines of our grounds. The N.Y.C.R.R. giving us aid, I believe,
> here and there. My only regret is that they cannot blast out the frogs,
> whose continued symphonies, some six months in length, weary
> one's ears a little, especially when all is still within, — for the frogs
> have learned as yet no religious recollection. However, they may
> reckon their chanting as a sort of divine office, and keep it up be-
> yond the canonical hours, to make up for the Jesuits, who do no
> chanting at all.[8]

He would have happily stayed at St. Andrew-on-Hudson indefinitely,
but as a novice he had to expect sudden, sometimes radical, changes in
his life. This did not disturb him. "Wherever I am," he wrote Margaret,
"I know I shall be thoroughly happy, especially as one learns always
more and more to see God's holy and most loveable Will in every disposition and turn of circumstances."[9] Shortly after returning from a va-
cation-retreat at Fordham, during which the novitiates were treated to a
picnic at Glen Cove, Long Island, he received orders to head north for
the Jesuit college of Canisius in Buffalo, where he was to teach human-
ities that fall to male freshmen students. He had to pack quickly and leave
on a few days' notice.

He wrote his mother the news from Canisius on August 18. "The
above address will doubtless surprise you, as it still surprises me a little,
tho a pleasant surprise. Three days ago, just after our annual retreat,
which finished on the eve of the Assumption, I received word from Rev.
Fr. Provincial to go directly to Buffalo, to teach in Canisius College. In
the hurry of departure I had not time to write anyone, else I would have
spared you some of the surprise."

Teaching was a new experience for him, and he hoped he would be up
to it. "Were it anything but God's will that sent me here, I should feel extremely diffident," he wrote her. "As it is, I know that the task given me

is the very best thing for my own perfection and for the help of others, provided I am quite faithful to the charges committed to me."

He expected to be at Canisius for at least a year. He was to teach Greek, Latin and English, including many of the same authors he had studied in his last year at Innsbruck — as well as Virgil, Plato, Homer and Cicero. "The class, I believe, will be small: about 20 young men. . . . Doubtless I shall profit by change from the quiet, retired life I have had for so long a time."[10]

His stay at Canisius, however, lasted only one semester, admittedly to his relief. As usual, with everything else in his life, he had thrown himself hard into the assignment. On October 20 he sent Margaret his first letter to her in about two months, apologizing for its being overdue and so brief. His excuse was his work. "The chief time consumer is theme-correcting, a useful but laborious occupation. For every class I need preparation, even in familiar matters — for it is one thing to know a matter and make twenty-two young men learn it."[11]

He found the Canisius experience exacting and, at times, bewildering. There is reason to believe that he had trouble maintaining discipline in class. The Jesuits at the college were mostly Germans who still belonged to the Jesuit mission in Buffalo, a German province. That would soon change when the order dissolved that mission and placed its members under the two Jesuit provinces of Maryland-New York and Saint Louis. To his distress LaFarge found himself in the middle of a raging culture clash between the older traditional priests, who insisted on teaching and preaching in German, and the younger, more moderate priests, who were ready to accept changes. He felt relief when his superiors transferred him from Canisius to Loyola College in Baltimore for the spring semester, and then, from the fall of 1908 to the spring of 1910, to its seminary at Woodstock, Maryland, for studies in philosophy and theology.

As with Canisius, his stay at Loyola lasted only one semester. He was probably sent there in the first place, at least partly, because of frayed nerves and mental exhaustion. LaFarge seldom took on a role without throwing himself into it. The experience of teaching at Canisius, preparing the courses, and being thrown into the middle of a divided clergy left him weak and shaky.

The students at Loyola were apparently more respectful and self-controlled than the ones at Canisius. He wrote that he could hardly believe his ears when "at my first entry into the classroom, the boys one by one walked up to me and said, 'Good morning, Father.'"[12]

A few weeks after his arrival at Loyola he could write Margaret that his health was improving "under the favorable conditions of Baltimore." The work was lighter than at Canisius. He found life there very agreeable. "Baltimore is an attractive city, a sort of specialized Philadelphia."[13] In July, however, he was reassigned again, this time back to Woodstock for more education for himself.

He arrived at the same time as another young priest, Father Daniel Callahan, in the midst of a freakish midsummer snowstorm. He settled in quickly, despite the unusual weather, and wound up calling his two years at Woodstock a "golden opportunity" to acquire a grip on the fundamentals of scholasticism. His stay there, he wrote many years later, was "the time of the greatest natural intellectual satisfaction that I have ever experienced." He wallowed in Thomism for the first time, grasping some of its essence. "Certainly," he admitted, "the strict scholastic method can be exaggerated and it would be absurd to confine philosophical discussion to that single pattern. Nevertheless," he confided, "I have never shared the extreme distaste for it. One of the most stimulating experiences for the human mind is to combine both methods, that of rigid syllogistic demonstration along with a free commentary and informed exposition."[14]

During those two years at Woodstock his letters continued to reflect his joy at being there. "Though Father Callahan and I had heard that we should certainly come here sooner or later," he wrote his sister Margaret, "we did not expect to be here so soon, for various reasons had made it seem probable that we should be needed for another year's teaching."[15] His pleasure at being at Woodstock, however, was tempered by a heavy regimen of work or study, undoubtedly stemming in large measure from the pressures and demands he put upon himself. His immersion in scholasticism left him mentally exhausted. With his other duties there was little time to relax. Fortunately, his days were occasionally broken up with walks about the countryside.[16]

It was prayer, however, even more than study, that gave his life meaning. His very existence, he wrote his mother, was "so entirely built on supernatural principles and for supernatural ends, that if the support of prayer be removed, the whole structure falls to pieces." At that point prayer was especially important to him in regard to his father's health, which started to deteriorate seriously while he was at Woodstock. It was not so much that he feared his father's death, as that he feared he would not die in a state of grace. He and Margaret worried that this might happen if he did not come back to the Church. To bring him back, however, did not call for threats about his immortal soul, which they knew would be worse than useless, but tact and diplomacy. He alluded to this in a letter to Margaret written shortly after Christmas in 1908.

> I have heard no news recently from Father; and I am still waiting for more favorable circumstances. I agree with you and M. in thinking that not much can be done just at present, especially as I have not yet come upon a person who would seem to be quite suitable in case Father were willing to see any one. His disposition is so peculiar that it might take a real apprehension of danger to arouse him to a more sensible view of things. Certainly his letter to the *Tribune* betrays no very anxious state of mind. It is best, therefore,—I should judge,—to leave him in peace until an opportunity presents itself. Anyhow, we must keep on praying.[17]

Whether because of his loved ones' prayers, or a growing awareness of his mortality, the artist did start drawing closer to the Church and to the possibility of making a good confession. For several months he and John had been corresponding with each other with greater frequency than ever before. Their letters, however, were still painfully formal and brief, as if neither man wanted to intrude on the other's privacy. Although LaFarge did not know it at the time it happened, his father suddenly became quite ill in the summer of 1906. Only months later did the artist write to his son about it. "I had to prepare for death in a very short number of hours," he wrote. "It is a curious experience, and I think out of all proportion with our habits. Only it seems a little severe that one should have to go through that several times over."[18]

What kind of illness the senior LaFarge suffered from that summer of 1906 (which might have killed him) is not at all clear, but he obviously made a recovery since he lived another four years. While at Woodstock LaFarge wrote to his father with some frequency, but as usual his letters remained stilted and unemotional. Their epistolary exchanges on art, philosophy, life, and even death, were nearly always in the abstract. There were no overt expressions of love, though they certainly loved each other. Writing from Baltimore in June 1908, for example, LaFarge suggested, since he would be in New York for a day, that he and his father meet for dinner somewhere.

> I expect to be in New York the morning of next Sunday, the 28th of June, spending the day and night at St. Francis Xavier's, 30 West 16th St. The following day I leave for my vacation at Keyser Island, in Long Island Sound. I can see you of course *any* time in the

afternoon or evening: or you can put me off till Monday morning if you wish. I hope it won't trouble you to have me walk in so unceremoniously: yet I do wish to see you again. If you would leave word at the studio, I would call there after lunch on Sunday, and I know when and where to find you. If you prefer, send a note to await me at St. Francis Xavier's: it is all the same to me. Could we dine together? Will call at the studio if no note awaiting me.[19]

While his father's letters continued to deal mainly with intellectual interests, they also occasionally began to touch upon spiritual matters. LaFarge was encouraged by what he perceived as a growing closeness and intimacy between them. "I have had a great deal of correspondence recently with Father," he wrote Margaret at the end of September 1908, "and relative to Father. He himself has his little hobbies, as you know, and writes to me often on various points, which I encourage, as it evidently gives him pleasure. . . ."[20]

Somehow or other LaFarge persuaded his father that it might not be a bad idea to see a confessor. But it had to be the right confessor, somebody who could do the job properly without offending or embarrassing the artist-intellectual. It had to be a "good" confession, so the confessor could grant him full absolution for his sins, some of which, at least in his son's eyes, were serious. It was also important that the confession be made quickly.

In early June 1909 LaFarge sent his father the names of two priests he considered up to the task. They were Father Henry C. Semple of St. Ignatius Church on Park Avenue in New York, and Father Edmund B. Spillane, stationed in Washington Square. LaFarge called Semple a "peaceable, thoughtful man, and very considerate, and spiritual in the best sense." Of Spillane he could only write his father that what he knew of him was "most favorable."[21]

During the last year or so of his life the senior LaFarge did flirt with the thought of returning to the Church as a possible communicant, but in the end he apparently backed away, to his son's bitter disappointment. During those last months LaFarge vacillated between optimism and despair over his father's soul. In mid-February 1910 he believed the artist was about to make his peace with the Church. He joyfully wrote Margaret, "I was more than delighted to hear that Father gave you to understand that he has really approached the sacraments. This is the main, the essential difficulty: and since this has been conquered, the others will give way in their turn. Our Lady of Lourdes has not failed us."[22]

Just six weeks before his father's death, however, LaFarge once more wrote disappointingly of his resistance to the sacraments. By then his father was in the Butler Hospital in Providence, where he finally agreed to go for a complete rest and checkup. He was seeing a priest, but LaFarge wondered just how spiritually productive were these visits. "It is a great satisfaction to know Father is being visited," he wrote Margaret. "If he is *capable of profiting* by any visits I think he will appreciate them, if, e.g., Father Rooney sees him. But if he acts strangely I suppose he will hardly be able to derive from them much benefit."[23] Later he would refer to his father's "general senile breakup during the last weeks of his life."[24]

In later years LaFarge would assure the world that his father had died in a state of grace, reconciled with the faith of his childhood. In the May 27, 1911 issue of *America* he wrote a brief biography of his father's religious beliefs, asserting that he was always a good, practicing Catholic who received the sacraments regularly. But this is not born out by LaFarge's own correspondence during his father's last years. It strains credulity to accept LaFarge's claim that the artist's final words to the priest who attended him for the last time before his death were "Place your hand upon my head; I wish to have the blessing of the Holy Catholic Church rest upon my head before I die."[25]

By LaFarge's own account his father was out of his head for weeks before he died. He could hardly have uttered these words at the last moment. LaFarge was not with him when he died quietly, suddenly, and in his sleep at about six o'clock in the evening of November 24, 1910. "I was deeply distressed that I had not been able to be with Father at the end," he wrote in *The Manner Is Ordinary*. "However, I was comforted later on when I learned he was kindly cared for in his last days by the Catholic chaplain of the Hospital."[26] It would be pure guesswork to speculate why he could be so positive about his father's last words to a priest in 1911, and so vague in writing about the same episode in 1953.

LaFarge's father had been sent to Butler Hospital because Margaret could no longer care for him at home. At the end of September she wrote a letter of both despair and relief to Bancel, who was then living in Switzerland.

> The summer here as you must know has been a very trying one as
> for heat. The worst we have had since 1876 and all the rain seems
> to have been on the other side of the world, for we have had so lit-
> tle here. In other respects it has been a very, very hard one for us

all. The relief of feeling that your father is where he can no longer get himself in debt, and make everyone around him perfectly miserable is indeed very great as you may imagine. While it was a dreadfully painful thing to have to decide to commit him to the hospital, and I can never forget all that I suffered in doing so, however, he is without doubt in the right place and as far as we can see he is peaceful and contented and likes his surroundings. The doctors all say there is nothing to regret and we shall never make any change. The money question as you may know also has been a pretty desperate one. A mountain of debts and nothing to meet them or to pay the hospital bills. At one time the Sheriff sitting in the Studio just as we had hoped to arrange for money to pay up a little. However, between us all we managed to keep off the worst.[27]

LaFarge had hoped to be with his father at the end. He had written Margaret that the Reverend Father Provincial promised he could "return when news comes of the end *really* approaching; when it is really unmistakable."[28]

But his father died before he could reach his bedside. The rector of Woodstock had to awaken him in the middle of the night to tell him of his father's death so he could catch the early train from Baltimore to New York. The artist was buried after a solemn high mass at the Church of St. Francis Xavier in the LaFarge family vault in Brooklyn's Greenwood Cemetery, although he had wished to be buried in the more fashionable Woodlawn Cemetery outside of New York City. But Margaret, because of her desperate financial situation, refused to spend the extra thousand dollars or so that this would have cost.

Many years later LaFarge wrote of his father "He was convinced that the most genuine merit of all that he crowded into his busy seventy-five years was the inspiration for others to do the same, but do it far better, and with still loftier and purer intent."[29]

He wrote with less certainty about him, however, in a long, rambling letter to Margaret about a month before his father's death. Sensing that this death was near, he was apparently contemplating a eulogy when the time came, but was very unsure what to say. This rather odd and tentative paragraph was written on October 19, 1910.

Ever so many thanks for your delightful letter of October 16th, and for the letters that you sent me. I have not had time to look over them as yet, but I imagine that they will offer some of the testimony that I want as to Father's essentially Catholic principles. I have

written Uncle Tom Perry, asking him for some ideas, and am thinking of writing in a tentative way to Henry James and to Mr. Osborn
Taylor, though I don't know if either of these wd. help much. What
I am looking for are more or less fundamental impressions of Father as a man and as a thinker. Some of his remembered sayings and
characteristic criticisms of life and literature wd. be especially
helpful as bearing out general remarks that I might make. Henry
Adams wd. of course be better than almost anyone, and I might call
on Mr. Adams in case I go down to Washington sometime during
the winter. But I have never even seen Mr. Adams, and moreover
some difficulty seems to have arisen between him and Father in recent years. Have you any idea what the relations have been, or
whether the trouble is merely some oddity on Father's part which
Mr. Adams would easily pass over in meeting with any of the family? I hope not, because a few talks with Mr. Adams might help
more than anything else. Then there might be one or the other of
his old French friends. I had thought of cousin de Nanteuil, of
Mme. Blanc, of Bourget and Bruntiere. Some of their estimates,
though less intimate, might be very just. Anyhow let us think and
pray over the matter, and I shall be very glad to hear any sugges-
tions you may have.[30]

On this same day he wrote an equally tentative, somewhat morose letter to Uncle Tom Perry, who was about fifteen years old when his sister
Margaret married John LaFarge. Perry was very close to the artist and
Margaret. John painted his brother-in-law's portrait at least twice, once
in 1860 in Bayou Teche, Louisiana, and again in 1865 in Newport. La-
Farge wrote Perry asking for advice on a short biography that he was
preparing about his father, while assuring Perry that the artist was not in
imminent danger of dying. He was trying hard, he wrote, to understand
his father.

> I should be happy if I could find even a few features by a word of
> quotation or reminiscence, so that those who knew him could say,
> "Yes, this is John LaFarge." Yet I am at a far greater disadvantage
> than at first would seem. For in earlier years I saw really very little
> of Father, and did not always appreciate that little. In the last nine
> years, however, I have hardly seen him at all, save in his severe ill-
> ness last year. My hope therefore is to gather from the one or two
> who have known him over the span of his life, especially his ear-
> lier life, such as you and perhaps Mr. Henry James—no others oc-
> cur to me at present.[31]

In this last month of his father's life, LaFarge was clearly frustrated that he had not gotten closer to him. He did not blame himself for this. Nor did he blame his father. It was not in the nature of either man to discuss his deeper feelings. They remained closed books to each other to the very end.

John LaFarge's death brought to his widow Margaret her first sense of peace in many years, as she wrote to Bancel on December 5, 1910, "It is indeed a blessed relief to know that all is over and that the terrific perplexities have come to an end so peacefully. I suppose there never was a complicated nature in one person than your father or a more difficult one to manage."[32]

Soon after writing this harsh letter, however, her bitter feelings gave way to sympathy and understanding for her deceased husband. "I know," she wrote Bancel's wife Mabel, "and feel still more from all that you have said, that you understand just how sad and trying this last year has been for me and how great a consolation it was to me that I could have been near Mr. LaFarge in the end. My only feeling about him after the nature of his illness declared itself was one of the greatest pity and tenderness—all else had faded into the past and much of it has been accounted for."[33]

Although his father dominated his thoughts during the Woodstock years, and periodically for the rest of his long life, at the same time other worlds and other ideas were coming together to frame out LaFarge's future. In the year before his father's death he had his first experience with the Jesuit missions in southern Maryland where, although he could hardly have predicted it at the time, he would spend more than a decade of his life.

Among other groups, the region contained a large black population. Segregation of the races was still very much the law in this part of the country, and would not change for years to come. Being sent briefly to St. Mary's County in 1909, where the most defining years of his life would be spent, brought LaFarge, for the first time, into contact with blacks and the black situation in America. He had, of course, seen and talked to blacks before, but the blacks of Newport and other northeastern cities did not much intrude upon his lily-white world. They were, in Ralph Ellison's phrase, the "invisible men." There were few blacks in Newport while LaFarge was growing up there. In Maryland he found matters very different. For one thing there were many more of them; for another, he was thrown into instant and intimate contact with them. Nothing in his experience had prepared him for this contact. His first reactions to their condition were somewhat naive, reflecting his own ignorance. Gradually, however, he would gain much greater understanding of what it meant to be a black in America. And with that understanding would come a rising anger at their plight, and a growing determination to do something about it.

In the early summer of 1909 he arrived at St. Inigoe's Jesuit Mission in St. Mary's County in Maryland. He had never been that far south in the country before. "St. Inigoe's is a peculiar spot," he wrote his sister. "If you look up the map of Maryland you will find the St. Mary's River (really an arm of the sea) running into the Potomac at its mouth."

At this point it is doubtful that he thought he might spend a good portion of his early life as a Jesuit along the Maryland Shore. This visit, he was led to believe, was to be a brief mission assignment combined with a vacation. "There has always been a parish church here," he wrote his sister, "with a number of missions attached. Sunday last I said the ten o'clock Mass and preached in the church—the congregation being white in the body of the church, and colored in the gallery above. I believe practically all the negroes in this county (and Charles) are Catholics; and they seem to be decidedly superior to the ordinary run of darkies, and enjoy a high reputation for morality and piety."[34]

During his second, and final, year at Woodstock LaFarge experienced two crises. The first was his father's last illness and death. The second was his own health, damaged, he believed, by his passion for study and learning. This was not a recent phenomenon in his life. It had started in his early youth and caught up with him at Woodstock in the late fall of 1910.

What he was suffering from was probably nervous exhaustion, caused by a combination of worry over his father and overwork in the library. It brought him to a state of near collapse, which was fortunately recognized by the rector of the college. Shortly after his return from his father's funeral, the rector put it to him clearly and succinctly. "You have the choice, Father LaFarge, of being a live jackass or a dead lion. Personally, he said, I think it is better to be a live jackass."

> This meant, in less metaphorical language, that the time had come to give up the idea of pursuing a strictly intellectual speculative career. The Rector judged, as did Father Provincial, that I would recover my strength better if I were in some active work which would not be too much of a strain.[35]

He was sent again briefly, this time mainly for a rest, back to the Maryland Shore, to St. Thomas's Manor at St. Ignatius Church in Charles

County. Three weeks later he moved on to a parish in Philadelphia, and three weeks after that to New York, to become Father John W. Casey's assistant on Blackwell's Island, later renamed Welfare Island, in the East River. It is now known to New Yorkers as Roosevelt Island. In this capacity as assistant to Father Casey he "experienced eight of the most tremendous months" in his life. They opened up for him "a vast vision of the tragic as well as the human side of life. I had," he wrote in *The Manner Is Ordinary*, "a glimpse of this in Poughkeepsie State Hospital, but Blackwell's Island was the real thing."[36]

Today the island can be reached by bridge from the Queens Borough side of the river, and by cable car from Manhattan. Now there is a huge apartment complex there, and the rents are high. In LaFarge's time, however, it housed a state penitentiary and a New York hospital. (The author's grandmother died in that hospital in 1934.) Also then, in the center of the island, was a city shelter for some thirty-three hundred inmates, most of them Catholics, and a workhouse with a population of nine hundred men and women, serving terms of up to six months for drunk and disorderly convictions. At least a thousand of the hospital patients had tuberculosis. It is no wonder that LaFarge admitted, upon first learning of his assignment there, to having feelings that were "pretty much of terror."[37] He and Father Casey were expected to administer to the religious needs of all the Catholics, as well as some non-Catholics, in all the facilities on the island. He described his first evening on the island in his autobiography.

> I arrived at the Work House late in the evening, tired, confused and, as I say, somewhat terrified, and lay down with considerable apprehension for my first night inside the walls of a prison. An electric bulb shone in through the transom on my bed. I had first dozed off in a fitful slumber around midnight when there came a loud knocking on the door. I was told to hurry at once to the hospital tier, that one of the prisoners was out of his mind and dying at the same time. It was my first experience of visiting the cell blocks. With my anxious dread of night awakening, it was quite a rude initiation.[38]

During his eight months at Blackwell's Island LaFarge probably worked harder physically than at any equivalent period of his life. On Saturday evenings at the City Home he heard between four hundred and six hundred confessions of elderly people, most of whom attended *both* of his masses the following morning. "The old folks," he explained "figured that if they came to the first Mass they might as well attend the second, so preaching was rather uninspiring." During his time at Blackwell's he administered the sacrament of Extreme Unction an estimated three thousand times.[39]

Despite the hard work, or perhaps because of it, his health began to flourish. His superiors had made the right decision in sending him there. There was little time for matters of the intellect. His brain, if not his body, got a good rest. A few weeks after his arrival he sent off a brief letter to his mother, much shorter than his usual missives, and apparently sent only because it was her birthday. He apologized for neglecting her and his sister, explaining that his free time was too short for much communication. In the meantime he was composing letters "in his head" that he would write later.

But he did enthuse about his work, despite its being so arduous. "I am getting to like the work here more and more. Though I am kept very busy—going from morning to night—I feel well and find the life agrees with me. There is little mental application or intensity in the work. . . ." After detailing some of his duties and responsibilities, he hinted at the effects of the life on him personally. "Then the sufferers! One forgets all one might complain of in the light of those poor people—especially in the Incurable Hospital."[40]

Never before in his life had he confronted human misery so intensely. It might be too much to say that his life was permanently changed by those eight months on Blackwell's Island, since he had always had a strong humane streak in his character. But it was the first time in a life of intellect and high culture that he gave himself so completely to what his Church would call "good works." The effect was profound and lasting. Still young enough physically to handle the hard labor, he was mature enough to know what it meant to look at the underside of life. The scholar from Newport, Harvard, and Innsbruck was immersed in another world for the first time and he did not run from it. While he would make time again in the future for matters of the mind, he would increasingly apply that mind to people, rather than ideas. As he wrote in *The Manner Is Ordinary,* "Innsbruck and Woodstock were schools of knowledge, but Blackwell's Island was a school of life and death."[41]

Chapter 5

Maryland

On September 1, 1911 Father John LaFarge, S.J., and a fellow Jesuit priest, Father Michael Hogan, traveled by train to Washington, D.C., then took a steamer down the Potomac River to St. Mary's County in Maryland. That county, along with neighboring St. Charles County, had hosted Jesuits since 1634, the first year of English settlement in Maryland. At the time LaFarge was assigned there, the two counties contained twenty-two Jesuit mission stations administered from three main locations — St. Thomas in Charles County, and Leonardtown and St. Inigoe's in St. Mary's County. It was a large area to service, with mostly dirt roads that were "impassable in winter and anything but easy in summer."[1]

Today (more than eighty years later) this is still beautiful, uncrowded land, but the Jesuits are gone, as are nearly all their original buildings. One of their churches, St. Ignatius in St. Inigoe's Manor, however, has been preserved as a landmark building thanks to the volunteer labor of officers and men at the nearby Potomac Air Base. (When the author visited the church a few years ago he picked up the key to the front door from a guard at the base's gatehouse.)

While LaFarge could not have realized it at the time, this trip down the Potomac marked the beginning of his lifelong work among American blacks, whom he usually referred to in those early years as "coloreds" or "negroes" or sometimes "darkies." "Northerners who were assigned to work in the countries," he wrote later," "were sometimes disconcerted at finding that part of their charges would be Negroes. Until I went to St. Mary's County the only Negroes with whom I had come in contact in a priestly way were in the municipal hospitals of Blackwell's Island in New York."[2]

For his first four years in Maryland he served as assistant pastor of St. Aloysius Church in Leonardtown. As a mission priest he moved about over a wide area, ministering to a diverse population of white and black people. Most of the whites were of English heritage, descendants of those English Catholics who began migrating to Maryland in 1634. Intended as a religious refuge for them, the colony had been founded by Cecil Calvert, son of George Calvert, who had been granted the original charter by Charles I. George, however, died in 1632, and so it was left to his son and heir to take over the colony, named *Terra Maria* after the king's French wife, and establish a settlement there. On March 25, 1634, two ships, the *Ark* and the *Dove,* dropped off about two hundred men, women and children at St. Clement's Island in the Potomac. Among the passengers were two Jesuit priests, so there was a Jesuit presence in the colony from its very inception. There was also a small group of Slavs who had come by boat from Baltimore in 1911, the same year that La-Farge arrived. These Slavs would bring him both joy and frustration in about equal parts.

Most of the Slavs were Czechs who had migrated from Pennsylvania, where they had been coal miners, to Maryland, where they took up farming. They were upset at the seating arrangements in the Maryland churches, where whole families sat together in the same pew. By their custom, men, women, boys and girls sat in separate sections of the church. When LaFarge had St. James Chapel built to accommodate them, he "had to place the Slav men separately from the Slav women, boys separately from the girls in the congregation, and the native Marylanders and the Negroes in their own part of the church. However, it all worked out peacefully and they became used to our ways and we to theirs."[3]

It took LaFarge only a short while to become fond of the region and its people. In the long years after he left for New York, he returned for periodic visits to his beloved Maryland Shore. At fist he accepted the segregation of the races without serious questioning. Soon, however, he came to see the wrongness of the practice, although, in those early years of the twentieth century, he felt powerless to change it. But his distress sometimes erupted in his letters home, as when he wrote Margaret about his first Christmas at St. Aloysius. "Then there was a Santa Claus, for the school children . . . It was pathetic to see the poor awkward little colored children hugging their toys—received after the white children's share was given to them."[4]

This sensitivity for the feelings of the blacks was very different from the way he felt about them before coming to Maryland. While still at Harvard he wrote to Margaret of a story he had recently heard about the funeral of a black boy in Boston, told by a woman who employed the dead boy's mother as a servant. He mimicked the black preacher who led the funeral service. "This poor young man is in de clutches of death and every time we feels a pain go through our poor ole bodies it only shows wese in de clutches of death. Now, what we must do brethren. What we must do is to *back up de Lord cogenially*."[5] Humor at the expense of less fortunate people was really never LaFarge's style. That he resorted to it as a Harvard sophomore was more a result of ignorance than spite. Compassion was far more characteristic of his feelings for people in trouble.

While he came to detest segregation of the races in St. Mary's and Charles Counties, he realized the enormity of the problem, and how many years would have to pass before the social patterns and beliefs of his white parishioners could be changed. The dilemma was that if the priest moved too fast to raise the blacks to some degree of social equality, he would alienate the whites, while probably not helping the blacks. He wrote of this in *The Manner Is Ordinary*.

> The plain fact was that the interests, spiritual or temporal, of the Negro in that region could never be handled in any rational and Christian manner save by men of imagination, energy, and a certain imperviousness to the terrific claims of timidity and human respect. No easy formula existed in the past; none exists today, and in all probability there will be none in the future. No matter how tactful and apologetic the pastor might be, he was told that he was moving the Negro "out of his place" the moment he treated him as a human being. He came in conflict at once with an age-old tradition by which the Negroes were not to be considered as persons in their own right but only as persons subject to another's right, as servants.[6]

But not being able to change the deep-rooted racial realities did not mean giving up on improving the lives of the blacks in his care. LaFarge devoted a good portion of his years in Maryland to helping them socially, economically, religiously and educationally, remembering that if changes were to come they would come slowly. He might be faulted for his acceptance of this reality, and writing about it with such resignation, but it must be remembered that white advocates of black civil rights were a small number indeed in the early years of the twentieth century. He published his autobiography in 1954, shortly before the Supreme Court handed down its school desegregation decision in *Brown v. the Board of Education*. Only after that year did the movement for black equality accelerate. Despite his cautious approach to the problem he was still ahead of his time when he wrote in 1954 "The work was to be accomplished not by striking a few heroic poses, not by the bull in the ecclesiastical china shop. It could only be the fruit of patient and determined and planned effort."[7]

Seven years before the *Brown* decision, however, his patience with a dual system based on race was running out. He had just spent a few days resting up at the Jesuit mission in Ridge, Maryland, after returning from an arduous trip to Europe, and learned that a new Catholic church was being planned for Leonardtown. That was fine with him, since it was needed. What was not so fine, however, was a proposal for a new but separate black church nearby. He wrote his objections to this in a letter to the Jesuit provincial in Baltimore, Father David Nugent, S.J., on July 11, 1947.

> I understand there is a plan of building a new Catholic church at Leonardtown. It is certainly very much needed as the present church is old and quite inadequate. Somebody remarked that Father Wheeler had the idea of also building a colored church there and that the colored people themselves have expressed a desire for the same. Such a move, in my opinion, would be a serious mistake. It would involve Father Wheeler and the Society as well as the Archbishop in all kinds of difficulties if the idea of racial separation were to be set up in Leonardtown or elsewhere. The St. Michael's and St. Peter's arrangement has never been too happy. If a separate church were to be set up in Leonardtown there would be complications from outside, Negroes coming to the new white church and being excluded and the usual chain of protests, etc. I am deeply convinced that the period for the separate church anywhere in Maryland is now a thing of the past and that the idea should be buried once and for all.[8]

In the earlier years, however, before formal segregation began to wane, his anger and frustration with the race problem did not take him away from his larger mission, which was to serve all his parishioners, even the ones who insisted on "keeping the Negroes in their places." He eagerly took to his work and his new surroundings, though they were so different from anything he had ever experienced. He put aside, at least for a time, his intellectual pursuits, focusing instead on people and places rather than ideas and knowledge. His letters from these years were the most rhapsodic and idyllic he ever wrote, more Franciscan than Jesuit, if such a comparison may be allowed. His ability to observe truth and beauty in the most ordinary displays of nature and man was acute, and his choice of words in describing them highly expressive. But always in the background was God, the transcendent force behind all things. On

December 3, 1911, he wrote his mother a delightful letter that probably poured from his pen without conscious effort, but which summed up his life until its end.

> The Feast of St. Francis Xavier has brought to my mind his saying that he (in his own words) had taken the resolution which little girls observe, viz. of writing frequently to their mothers. But there is little as yet to write about here. Last First Friday I spent at Newtown, where I was once before for Sunday — such a quaint old place — i.e., the old Church, which somehow reminds me of the saloon of a steamboat, with its low ceiling, neat white paint, and multitude of small windows (new stained glass — one of them, presented by the oyster-men, — being adorned with a little picture of Noah's Ark). The old manor house is a study, — especially at night, when the moon glitters through the little windows in the priest's room, and the stove sends its glare on the ceiling. At dawn I could just hear, — so faint as it were a ghost of a sound, the distant Angelus tolling at Leonardtown across the bay.[9]

A few weeks later, after saying midnight mass at St. Aloysius, he wrote her "I felt as if the benediction of His coming spread far and wide over the countryside, and rested on the poor and lowly, the white and the black. What can Xmas mean to those who have not Christ in Person, as we have? It was not a memory for us, it is a thrilling reality."[10]

In the occasional absence of Father Kelly, the pastor of St. Aloysius and Superior of the six priests stationed at Leonardtown, LaFarge found himself in charge of both the parish and the house, a considerable, if only temporary, responsibility. Why Father Kelly chose him instead of one of the other priests LaFarge did not say. It can be assumed that Father Kelly felt him up to the task.

Shortly after New Year's Day Father Kelly went to Philadelphia to be with his own dying father. While he was gone one of the old priests, Father Finnegan, who was "quite sick," had to be taken to St. Agnes Hospital in Baltimore. The pastor asked LaFarge to accompany him, an assignment he found very agreeable, as he wrote to Margaret after his return.

> I left here with him at 6 A.M., on the boat, arriving in Balto. the same time the next morning, just 24 hrs. on the boat. Except for my anxiety about him, however, the trip was really very pleasant — as the boat is a comfort itself: the weather beautiful, and I had the old gentleman nicely lodged in a $3 stateroom. He was comfortable,

and slept a good deal of the day, and about all night, I arrived at
Balto. fairly well refreshed. We drove out to the hospital in a cab.

He returned to Leonardtown by train. Since the boat could no longer
ply the mid-January, frozen Potomac, all trips had to be cancelled until
the ice broke up. Even Chesapeake Bay was starting to freeze. The train
trip, however, proved as relaxing as the boat voyage. It had been an unexpected freeze, and temperatures dropped as low as ten degrees below
zero. "Father's old fur-coat," he wrote his mother, "which Grant sent, did
splendid work."[11]

As spring came on in 1912 he all but begged his mother and sister to
visit him at Leonardtown. But both women apparently felt the trip would
be too long and tiring. He wrote of his disappointment, urging them to re-
consider, painting a pretty picture of the Maryland countryside that time
of the year. "The country is so wonderfully beautiful now," he wrote, "especially during the glorious weather we have had this week. St. Inigoes
was like Paradise—with the soft balmy sea breezes—the blossoming
plums and cherries and dog-wood—and the blazing green wheatfields.[12]

His letters home dealt mainly with his work or with family matters,
since he wanted to be informed about all his relatives when something
important was going on in their lives. Occasionally he suggested books
or articles Margaret or his sister should read. Except for a few leaves of
absence he remained in Maryland for fifteen years, until the year after
Margaret's death, when he moved on to a very different assignment on
the staff of *America* magazine in New York. One extended leave from
Maryland came in 1917, several months after American entry into World
War I, when he began his one-year tertianship at St. Andrew-on-Hudson
in Poughkeepsie.

Over the years in Maryland his relations with the black population
grew and deepened. He sometimes poked gentle fun at their accents and
cultural ways, and at times he could be exasperated with them. At those
times, and they were rare, he could be uncharacteristically cynical and
sarcastic. But his experiences with them were often filled with surprises
and unexpected adventures. In early September 1912, he described to
Margaret a festival held a few days before.

We had a wonderful colored festival recently—the first of its kind
in *Leonardtown*—though there have been many at other parishes.
It taught me some of the things a Jesuit may be called upon to do—
unexpectedly—such as to start out at 8 P.M.—by moonlight—to
seek a pig. I shall not forget that ride. The objective was a certain

distant farm — Mrs. Carrie Clark's — to inquire *why* Miss Carrie had not sent the absolutely indispensable pig for the morrow's festival. For pig, so says the Medley's Neck colored philosopher, Mr. Big-Foot Price — is a powerful help to a festival — but lamb is no good, it is a kind of drag.

The pig was obtained and the festival proved a large success. La-Farge's "chief office was selling the dinner and supper tickets himself, relieved at intervals by one colored man, who invited one and all to partake. 'Step this way, ladies and genmen, for yah dinner! 50 cents for the dults and 25 for the chilluns.'" LaFarge noted that "they were all wonderfully well behaved — as our country colored folk usually are — and no traces of noise or disorder — just cheerful conversation and a little fun and some *very* proper dancing — in which they always seem to drag their feet about, never to step with them."[13]

Holding dances and festivals was an old Jesuit custom in St. Mary's and Charles Counties as a way of bringing priests and people together. As shown by LaFarge's experience in getting the pig for the feast, they could involve many and trifling tasks. Shortly before war broke out in Europe in 1914, however, there was a movement from the hierarchy to abolish the dances and other entertainments. Distressed, the Maryland Jesuits appealed to the Bishop of Baltimore for guidance. The bishop encouraged their continued practice, as long as they were controlled and orderly, and with a priest always present. "So that settled the question," LaFarge wrote with obvious relief, "and in general the idea of the Maryland pastorate was that the priest should be with the people first, last and always."[14]

A few months after the pig feast he attended a black minstrel show. "It was amusing," he wrote Margaret, "to see real colored minstrels: but they were timid." After the show he made a little speech, urging them to develop their talents. They were pleased, and one remarked later that "'Father LaFarge is a right smart sweet talking man.' Such is the power of flattery. However, they really did well."[15]

Aside from walking, the only land transportation available in the early years of his Maryland ministry was the horse and buggy. Automobiles were around then, of course, but the lack of passable roads precluded their general use in St. Mary's and Charles Counties. Looking back on those years he noted how much time was lost in simply getting around, and the discomforts he underwent. It was hard to decide if the buggies were worse in summer or winter. In the cold weather he could attach a rubber sheet to the top and roll down the isinglass side curtains. For some warmth a hot brick or a small charcoal stove could be placed at his feet.

In the summer "the dust, the green flies, horseflies, and mosquitoes descended upon man and beast alike. And everyone wore long linen dusters to protect the clothing."[16]

But he still felt that the buggy offered some advantages. "The long Drives," he wrote, "offered a chance to meditate, to think out sermons, plan lessons for instructing adults and children, or, if you were of a literary mind you could think out an article."[17] One final advantage was the horse itself, who could find its way home even if the driver fell asleep or daydreamed his way into oblivion. When he first started to drive his Ford a few years later, it took time to realize that the car "had no memory, that holding the wheel was not the same thing as holding the reins. You could not depend on an auto to take you home or to avoid a false turn or keep out of a ditch."[18]

One amusing anecdote about his horse reveals his own occasional absentmindedness, a trait mentioned often in interviews with his friends and relatives. He had said mass at nearby Leonard Hall for boys run by the Xaverian Brothers. He became so absorbed with the school afterwards that he did not return to Leonardtown right away. By the time he left he had completely forgotten that he had come over with his horse and buggy, and had, as usual, tied the animal to a tree. When it came time to leave he walked home without horse or buggy. Just as he was drifting off to sleep that night he remembered his abandoned steed. Reluctantly rising from his bed he "walked the mile to the school, found him angrily champing the bit and pawing the ground with his feet, and brought him home to his oats and hay."[19]

The years at Leonardtown were extraordinarily busy ones, filled with the routines of parish work, including calls upon its sick and dying members. He tried always to be upbeat and charitable with them, despite the frequent demands they made upon his time and patience. As a man he must have sometimes felt put upon, but as a priest he knew his responsibilities to those despairing and desperate people who turned to him as their court of last resort. If he could help it, he seems never to have turned down a summons, no matter how tired he was, the time of day or night, or the beastliness of the weather. On May 10, 1914, he wrote of one such summons to Margaret.

> The other day I returned quite fatigued from a long trip out to Clover Hill Catech. Class, and then all around through the forest to all sorts of queer places.—I looked forward to "early bed"—but just as I began supper, along came Lem Johnson, an elderly and

somewhat muddle-headed colored man, and began talking to someone outside. As soon as I heard the words "Mr. Hayden 'Ates"
(Yates), I knew what I was in for. I had visited the old gentleman
several times before, and now he had another "spell." So after a
hasty supper, out I started again. However it was a lovely night, and
I had a fast horse to drive for the 6 miles of partly bad road.

What a curious scene at the old man's house! A real old-time farm
scene: the house, very neat and prim inside and out; Mrs. Yates,
white-haired, precise, anxious and fussy; old Ford Graves, a highly
respectable little old gentleman who manages poor Hayden's farm,
peering out at me from a corner of the "settin-room" under his big
spectacles,- the little orphan boy, Howard Pridgen, a golden-
haried, angelic-looking little creature, all bewildered and tired, and
a lot of neighbors, all of whom (but one) I knew well. Jeff Tennison (a beautiful simple, pious character, whose wife is dying of
cancer of the stomach.) While he struggles bravely on, never complaining — nor does she — Norma Yates, huge and authoritative,
Perry Abell, the storekeeper, a bustling little busy-body, Dan'l
Woodburn, a typical "Uncle Rube," with a voice like a bos'n, etc.
all sitting around in a kind of conclave, trying to keep up Mrs.
"Ates'" spirits, and render what help they could. As old Hayden
"had no use of his senses," I could only anoint him and absolve him
conditionally. He is better now and I will bring communion tomorrow to him and Mrs. Jeff Tennison.[20]

As he settled into his life in and around Leonardtown, he came to understand the problems of the people and their land. He perceived three
major areas of concern: the deplorable condition of the schools; the low
social standing of and bias against the blacks by whites, including some
of the clergy; and lastly the rural life problem, affecting both whites and
blacks, which doomed most of them to a lifetime of drudgery and
poverty. The public schools, which nearly all the Catholic children attended, offered little in the way of education. Some of the teachers,
though dedicated, had little more than a fourth or fifth grade education
themselves. While there were no regular parish parochial schools, there
was St. Mary's Academy for girls and Leonardtown Hall for boys; but
they charged tuition and not many could afford to attend. LaFarge directed a good part of his fifteen years in Maryland at broadening and improving Catholic education there.

On September 2, 1915, he was transferred from Leonardtown to the
other St. Mary's County mission center at St. Inigoe's Manor, at the

mouth of St. Inigoe's Creek where it runs into St. Mary's River. The Jesuits had been involved in that area for over two centuries. The original manor house, built in 1730, had been mostly destroyed by fire in 1878, leaving intact only one wing, consisting of a few rooms and a chapel. LaFarge shared these primitive quarters with two other priests—Father James Matthews, the superior, and Father Abraham Emerick.

About a mile from the manor house, along a dusty dirt road, was St. Ignatius Church, built in 1790, with a graveyard close by. The church, as already noted, still stands, one of the few original Jesuit buildings not destroyed or replaced in the counties. Both white and black parishioners celebrated mass together at St. Ignatius. The blacks occupied the two galleries of pews running down the sides of the church, while the whites sat in the middle. Each group, however, whether by design or accident, was relatively equidistant from the altar. Mass was celebrated there every other Sunday. On these same Sunday afternoons, one of the priests would then sail to St. George's Island, (about three miles from the mainland) to say mass on Monday morning for the island's Catholics.

Among other entreaties, LaFarge importuned his mother and sister to solicit donations of cast-off clothes for his poor parishioners. They responded a few weeks later with a sizable bundle, which he promptly distributed to the most needy. He told them where the largess went in a letter dated November 16, 1915.

> Thursday I sorted out the articles, and divided them between 7 very destitute families and took them around in the buggy Thursday A.M. You ought to have seen me with seven huge oat sacks stuffed with clothes, behind the buggy, on the seat of the floor. . . . I gave old Mrs. Lukac your black dress, and she nearly kissed my hand off in gratitude; wanted me to take half a dozen turkeys along in recompense. I told her she could give a turkey to our church supper on Dec. 8, by which I hope to raise a few pennies.

The letter went on with more stories of the poverty he found to be the lot of so many of his people, especially the black ones. He needed the help of these same people to keep the mission running and the buildings in usable condition, but hated to appeal to them, "because those who do contribute are people like Jim Carroll, who would pawn their shoes rather than disappoint the pastor. . . ."

His distress at the poverty of the people, however, was often tempered by the quiet, awesome beauty of the land they inhabited. In this same letter of November 16, 1915, he wrote of an old man in the town of St.

James who had not been to mass in years. LaFarge was determined to
bring him back. On the way to the man's house he drove through a long
stretch of lonely woods, with a bare trail winding among the trees.

> Such a trip! It was like fairy-land. Why doesn't anybody ever come
> down here to see what a glorious country this is? The whole way
> was through the woods—about 6 or 7 miles: and such glorious
> woods: trees getting higher as the road sank; magnificent autumn
> foliage—balmy still air, as warm as in September: huge southern
> pines, with their horizontal branches outlined in dark green against
> the intensely blue-sky, fragrant pine needles, immense syca-
> mores;—and then, just as the woods road seemed interminable, out
> on the brilliant blue Chesapeake, like the open ocean . . . No land
> in sight: only a hot haze in the distance. Hundreds of little oyster
> boats scattered about. Absolute silence, except the sound of the sea;
> and occasionally a killdeer or sea-gull's cry, like a child's voice.

LaFarge persuaded the old man to return to the Church. He made a
good confession and received communion. But the priest's labors for the
day were not yet over. He had one more stop to make at the house of a
favorite black couple.

> Stopped in at Clem Beal's and his wife Jenine. She is a very supe-
> rior colored woman: who writes well and reads and studies con-
> stantly: a true apostle. She manages beautifully the colored Cate-
> chism League, Children's Sodality, etc. I expect to lunch with her
> on Wedn.: and her little house is much more attractive than many
> white people's. She loves to read: and would enjoy any odds or
> ends: such as lives of the saints and other instructive things you
> might pick up. I only wish she had more field for her zeal: but we
> are planning quite a campaign among the colored. Beginning with
> a girl called Edith Morgan, one Methodist colored young person af-
> ter another is coming into the Church. They flock to the Sunday-
> School. Old people too come (white): young men and their girls—
> Methodists, Episcopalians. God is blessing our work: but we must
> pray: and oh, so *many* things are needed to make the place decent
> for our Lord.[21]

His last letter to Margaret in 1915 told of the Christmas masses at St.
James, and especially the midnight mass. All the physical hardships of
his missionary life melted away before the beauties of the spiritual and
natural worlds, which to him were one and the same.

The Midnight Mass was beautiful. One old farmer, Mr. Theodore
Hayden, said he could have knelt there all night and couldn't be resigned to Mass being over. The two Slav boys played really beautifully on the violin, with their sister accompanying on the organ.
The inside of the chapel was completed. The old altar of St. Aloysius installed, with two statues from St. Joseph's church, given by
Father Casey, and 75 folding chairs ordered at last moment from
Baltimore by phone. The decorations were lovely. . . . This is *the*
place for Christmas decorations. I doubt if anywhere else in the
world does one find such abundant and beautiful evergreen material. The sanctuary was a mass of cedar trees, running cedar and
holly. The Slavs fixed up a little crib and I used your flashlight,
turned on but concealed in the dark greens to shine like a star on
the little infant.

That night he said two masses without an intermission, alternating
English and Slavic hymns, happily noting that there were a lot of com-
munions. After the masses he drove back to the manor house through a
still, calm, mild night, with a full moon lighting his way. On Christmas
day, however, the weather started to turn bad. By that evening, he wrote
Margaret, there was a "howling storm. Poor Father Emerick was over at
St. George's Island and had a desperate time getting back for his colored
entertainment on Sunday at two. He had to row over to Piney Point, drive
about six miles to Valley Lee, and then auto about twenty-two miles with
Father Matthews to St. Peter's, his colored church. The roar of the sea
here was terrific, like a boiler factory."[22]

The "colored problem" loomed ever larger in LaFarge's mind as the
Maryland years went by, and he saw, with some bitterness, the take-it-
for-granted prejudice of his white parishioners. It would be logical to
read in the pages of his autobiography, written so many years after he
left Maryland, historical perspectives and emotions that he might not
have felt so strongly at the time. This would be a misreading. While he
knew he had to live with what amounted to a caste system while working there as a priest, it still rankled him severely. What to do about it was
another matter. As time passed it became increasingly clear to him that
the blacks could only achieve some measure of equality, not through
beneficent handouts from whites, which they often and rightly resented,
but through education.

To provide this education was not an easy task. It meant more schools
and competent teachers, both expensive to come by. At Blackwell's Is-

land he had found himself in the front line of poverty and despair. In Maryland there was the added ingredient of racism. Through it all he managed to keep his mental balance, if not always his temper. It was another turning point in his life, which would be reflected in the years ahead in his efforts to reduce rural poverty in general for both races, and bring greater social and economic equality to blacks in particular.

Chapter 6

In the Vineyards of the Lord

In the spring of 1916 LaFarge started planning for two new schools to open that fall, one for whites and one for blacks. He needed money and land, then teachers. Although he disliked soliciting from family and friends, he became very good at it. At the end of June he could write Margaret that funds were coming in, which meant he could start seriously looking for land at one of the proposed building sites, the one at St. James, a small town to the north of St. Inigoe's Manor.

Much of the real estate in the vicinity of St. James was owned by William H. Leonard, a merchant who lived and worked on the other side of Chesapeake Bay, in the waterside town of Cambridge. LaFarge discovered that the piece he wanted was actually owned by Leonard and his two brothers, both fishermen, who were usually out on their boats. He decided to go to Cambridge in person to at least meet with William and possibly conclude a deal. To do this most expeditiously he had to cross the bay by boat, a trip that turned into an unwanted adventure. He took the better part of a long letter to Margaret to describe what happened, and also gave a briefer account in his diary dated July 31, 1916.

> Trip to Cambridge, Maryland on the eastern shore in order to purchase property for schools at St. James' from William H. Leonard and Company, who owned most of the land in the vicinity. I drove over to Captain Charlie McKay's early, arriving about 8 A.M. For a long time the Captain couldn't decide about going. I finally left at 12:19, with a high southerly wind in a motorboat and arrived opposite Cedar Point at 1:12 P.M. Left there at 2:20, and arrived mouth of Little Choptank River arriving at Taylor's Island at 6 P.M. We put out again into the Bay, lost our bearings and were obliged to anchor about two miles off the shore until 9:00 P.M. Captain McKay and his boys were mistaken as to direction. It was a stormy night, very high sea and thunder and lightning always threatening. At 3:00 A.M. it was very high northwest wind—totally dark. At 4:00 A.M.—

dawn—we made for an unknown light and from there sighted the
mouth of the Great Choptank River. We went up same and arrived
at Cambridge about 7:00 A.M.

Fortunately for LaFarge, Mr. Leonard and his two brothers were all
available, and within an hour he had finished his transaction. The trip
back across the bay was not much better than the trip over, but at least
this time Captain McKay did not get lost. The winds still blew hard and
the sea was choppy. "The boat was open without any cabin or seats," he
lamented, "except for a couple of narrow planks. On the way over water
and food both gave out."[1]

The school for the white children at St. James opened that September
with fifteen pupils, increasing to fifty-five by the middle of November.
Since there was no actual school building yet, classes were held at first
in a small chapel. A large canvas curtain was let down in front of the altar when the chapel was being used for teaching. Miss Nanny Hebb, a
young woman who had been teaching in the public district school, and
Miss Clementine Clarke, who would later join the Sisters of Mercy in
Baltimore, were the first teachers in the white school.

On January 2, 1917, the school for blacks opened up on land bought
from the Leonard brothers, a five-and-a-half-acre plot. LaFarge's inde-
fatigable optimism was sorely tested when only one student showed up
the first day. But he had chosen the teacher well—Mrs. Jenny Beale, who
had once attended the convent school of the Oblates of Providence, an
order of black sisters. "With unfailing instinct she knew that once the
school was started it could not help but grow. She was placid, imper-
turbable in her manner, with a gentle voice and a fine sense of humor."[2]

In the fall of 1917 LaFarge had to temporarily leave his work in Maryland to make his third probation, or tertianship, as a member of the Society of Jesus. This meant returning for about nine months to St. Andrew-
on-Hudson in Poughkeepsie.

He referred to the tertianship as the *schola affectus,* the school of the
heart. All Jesuit priests were expected to make it about ten years after
their ordinations. "One reviews the early lessons of the novitiate," he
wrote, "in the light of experience and the responsibilities of the future."[3]

The tertianship started with the Long Retreat, a thirty-day-long program devoted to prayer and a review of the priests' lives. LaFarge
emerged from his retreat with a clearer awareness of what his life as a
priest meant, or at least what it should mean. After it was over he wrote
Margaret that he felt a strengthening of his will, where before he "felt

wavering and hesitation." He saw his weaknesses more clearly, "and the means to combat them, and was ready to attack things," which previously he had shrunk from. Most of all he was grateful for his life as a priest in the Maryland missions.

> Looking back, I see a most marvellous Providence of God, for which I am inexpressibly grateful, in letting me spend those six years in the Counties, as well as the year on the Island. It was the most fortunate thing for me that could have happened, for it was that God chose to give me what in many ways I most needed, an intimate, practical knowledge of men—especially the humbler sort, of their daily lives, their economic conditions, their joys and sorrows and temptations, their business relations—as well as a real taste of the missionary life.[4]

While the tertianship was designed to emphasize reflection on past events and preparation for future ones, LaFarge could not neglect his current responsibilities in Maryland, especially those involving his schools. He more than once asked his mother and sister Margaret to keep spreading the word of his need for support. He had two thousand copies of a report on his work printed, and included an appeal for small subscriptions from interested donors. At least once he was allowed to travel to New York City to make solicitations from people he knew there. Just after Christmas he dropped in on two of his sisters-in-law, Grant's wife Florence and Bancel's now returned and recovered wife Mabel, two highly intelligent, sophisticated women. He found them amiable and sympathetic, but somewhat confused about his work. After seeing them he wrote his mother:

> I saw Mabel at Flos's one evening and had a nice talk with them. It is amusing to see them together, as Mabel has her own very quiet way of going on about things. Saw also a number of other relatives. They ask all sorts of questions, and they get the answers to them, too. But they take it all very good-naturedly. One has to be patient, realizing the queer atmosphere in which they live and move.[5]

In general the days for him at St. Andrew's passed quietly, as they were supposed to, since this was a period of reflection, although at times he seemed impatient to be back in Maryland. He occasionally mentioned his health to Margaret, but always to say it was good, even though at times it was not. Earlier in the previous year he had spent five weeks in

St. Agnes Hospital in Philadelphia under the care of Dr. Dennis McCarthy. His only known reference to this hospital stay is a cryptic sentence in his diary. "I was cured of a head trouble that had bothered me for five years."[6] Exactly what this "head trouble" was is not at all clear, but his mother and sister were aware of it, and were always sensitive to his physical condition. In response to a query about his health from his sister, he responded, "I feel well, thanks to the good Lord, and have recovered from the feeling of fatigue that I had after the Long Retreat. The old head trouble never comes back."[7]

In mid-February 1918 he was recalled briefly to St. Inigoe's to replace a priest who had been reassigned. Near the end of that month he sent a very uncharacteristic letter to his mother, complaining about his flock. It was one of the few negative, pessimistic descriptions of his parishioners—whites and blacks alike—that he ever wrote. What provoked this gloomy report is not known, but for whatever reasons, he felt his people had simply gotten lazy.

> I had mass yesterday at St. James' as before. . . . I am afraid that I may have spoken a little severely to them about the necessity of sacrifice in order to keep the treasure of the Grace of God. I showed them how one has to make sacrifices for one's heavenly country, just as the war is teaching us the much needed lesson that we must also make sacrifices if we are to keep our earthly country from destruction. But the idea is so foreign to these folk, who have always led such an easy life, and who look down so intensely on anything like hard labor, as being fit only for a negro. And the negro, of course, is only too anxious "to live like a white man. . . ." The colored population seem to do less and less each year, and there is a general idea that hard work is out of date."[8]

He did not head back to Poughkeepsie until early April, a week longer than he had expected to stay in St. Inigoe's. As he explained, the provincial had let him stay the extra week since it was "so hard to get anyone down to the county for Easter."[9] In one of his few references to then raging World War I, he mentioned that he had delivered two lectures, one at St. Michael's Hall, the other at Leonardtown, "on the Pan-German plan of aggression."[10] How concerned he was about the war, however, is difficult to say, since he rarely referred to it in his correspondence, and wrote nothing about it in his autobiography. One letter, however, to Margaret on Easter Sunday 1917, did suggest that the war might, in the long run, have some benefits for mankind.

As for the war, terrible as it seems, I am convinced that it is provi-
dential, and that great good will come out of it in ways that we cannot yet distinctly foresee. One thing is certain, that it will stave off
the fearfully rapid growth of luxury and reckless hurry which has
been becoming our worst menace. — These alarming events are like
the Passion of Christ. The deeper we progress into the tangled web
of suffering, the nearer we are to the final consummation of the
Resurrection. In the very moment that the full storm of the Passion
broke loose upon our Lord, and He was finally lifted up upon the
Cross, — in that very moment the gates of Hell were broken, and the
eternal Kingdom of Israel was established. The glory of the Resurrection began in the darkness of Calvary. Immediately a time of
suffering is commencing. But at the same time a new era is beginning in the world's history, the dawn of one of God's designs.[11]

On the face of it the sentiments expressed in this paragraph certainly
appear extreme, if not apocalyptic — one world is ending while another
awaits its birth. It also suggests an almost callous indifference to human
suffering, detached and even pedantic — a tradeoff for a better world
ahead. It was Father John LaFarge, S.J., in one of his darkest moods. In
his defense it should be mentioned that his own country had not yet entered the war, although it was within days of doing so. Wartime propaganda on all sides was playing down the slaughters on the eastern and
western fronts in Europe. He had witnessed suffering himself, but not in
the trenches in France or among the horrors in Russia, where as many as
twenty million human beings died during the war. And he could not have
known then that over fifty thousand Americans would be killed in battle
in World War I.

Even in the midst of the war he clung to his goal of improving education in the counties. To attract a teaching order of sisters, his ultimate in
teachers, he had to build them a convent which would cost about six
thousand dollars. If he could not raise the money through donations, he
hoped to get permission to borrow it. In the meantime, the new school at
St. James, where the students were still being taught in the chapel, was
moving along well, and his earlier gloom about his lazy parishioners had
largely disappeared, although he still had occasional complaints. He described Easter Sunday mass to Margaret while traveling by train from
Washington on his way back to Poughkeepsie on April 2, 1918.

There is really very little else of interest to narrate. Easter Sunday
I was at St. Peter Claver's, the colored church, for the early Mass.

It is rather an uncomfortable experience for a new-comer, as one
has to sleep in the Sacristy, and the colored people keep walking in
at all times and unexpected times. They are great at decorating the
altar, and everybody seemed to be bringing in something to put on
it all afternoon and evening before.[12]

Back in Poughkeepsie to finish his tertianship, he continued trying to
find a teaching order of sisters for the white school at Ridge, where he
expected to be transferred to the Church of St. Michael when he returned
to Maryland. The town received its name from the fact that it "over-
looked the two sides of the fifty mile long ridge which runs the entire
length of the southern Maryland peninsula."[13] In mid-April he wrote
Margaret of plans to go to Hartford, Connecticut, to see Mother Josephine, provincial of the Sisters of St. Joseph, to determine if her order could
take up the work. To further his chances of success he made a novena to
St. Joseph, and asked his mother to use her "influence with him for the
same end." He also suggested that his sister "call up the Cenacle, and get
them there to say some prayers for the intention, saying simply that it is
for my school, without necessarily saying what it is exactly."[14]

His efforts to recruit the Hartford Sisters of St. Joseph eventually bore
fruit, but not for another four years. The sisters finally arrived at Ridge
in August 1922, just in time for the fall semester. Before they came he
wondered how they would adjust to the quiet Maryland countryside,
where they would hear "no sound at night save the chirping of crickets
and the occasional yell of a screech-owl."[15] But apparently, as he wrote
in *The Manner Is Ordinary,* it was love at first sight for them. At the time
of his writing this in 1954, twenty-five girls from the Ridge schools had
joined their order.[16]

On Ascension Day, which fell on May ninth in 1918, LaFarge wrote
a long letter from St. Andrew's (five single-spaced pages) to his "dear
children," (all the students at St. James). It was a charming, entertaining
letter, full of stories about his own doings, with an occasional hint about
how they should conduct their own lives.

Week before last I had a long trip in an auto, the longest that I have
ever made that way. We covered 347 miles altogether. Father Mc-
Quillan, who is chaplain of the big Insane Asylum here, very kindly
took me in the machine that he is allowed to use for his work at the
Asylum, an Overland. He was not sorry, I imagine, to get away
from his crazy people for a few days, though he is very devoted to
them, and gives them all sorts of comfort.

The two priests headed east from Poughkeepsie toward the Connecticut line, crossing into that state from New York just past a town called Millerton. He thought the Connecticut countryside looked more prosperous than New York's, remarking that the houses along the road were "finer looking." By ten in the morning they reached Canaan, where they turned south. Coming out of Canaan they drove along a bright blue river, made that color by the dye works along its banks.

From Canaan to Hartford, LaFarge judged, was about thirty miles. They reached Hartford about two in the afternoon, and headed right for the bishop's house on Farmington Avenue. Bishop Nilo was kind and thoughtful to them, showing them through the cathedral and inviting them to spend the night. "With the exception of the new Cathedral at Pittsburg [sic]," LaFarge wrote, "it is perhaps the finest Catholic Church that I have ever seen in this country."

That afternoon he went to see the mother provincial of the St. Joseph Hartford Sisters to talk about the Ridge schools. Unfortunately, there had been a misunderstanding on when he was supposed to arrive, and the mother had gone for the day. He had a good conversation, however, with the mother assistant, "who was ever so much interested in all that I had to tell her."

The next two days took them further south and east in Connecticut, but then they turned north and headed for Massachusetts, crossing the state border at Sheffield. "There," he wrote, "our *other* tire (which had been our reserve tire) exploded with a BANG!, and we were in a fix." Sheffield was a small town and had no auto repair shop. They thought of taking the electric car to Great Barrington, six miles away, to get somebody to come back and fix the tire, but just then "an obliging man came along and agreed to take Father McQuillan up there . . . in his own machine." With the tire repaired they headed north again, reaching the town of Lee at close to 9:00 P.M., where they stayed the night with friends of Father McQuillan. The two men started back for Poughkeepsie after saying mass in the morning in the chapel of a nearby convent. And that, wrote LaFarge, "was the pleasantest of all; for the road this time was fine all the way; the weather was the best, and I myself enjoyed it more, as I now had no headache, as I had most of the way up to then, for I do not care much for auto riding. . . ."[17]

By the end of June he was preparing to leave St. Andrew's, his tertianship nearly over, to return to Maryland and his new post at Ridge. In his last letter to his mother from Poughkeepsie on June 17, he wrote consolingly of her sister's (his aunt's) recent death, which had been expected. With some eloquence he wrote that Fanny's death should not trouble her. "You have long since learned, thank God, to see this life as it really is,—nothing but a place of pilgrimage itself, and a constant packing up for our eternal home in the enjoyment of the Vision of God. . . . We are *not* made for here; what seems to us superficially like the close of *day* is only the close of a long and troubled *night*; for that is all that this life is. Death is not the end, but the beginning.

> It is really the first breaking of the dawn, the darkness and slight chill that comes before the dawn, but also the peace, and the sense that the night is over, and the eternal day of God is near at hand. The more I myself live and meditate, the truer I see to be that way of thinking, that we should look forward in *everything,* and realize that each day should add immensely to our happiness . . . for it brings us nearer and nearer to eternal youth, to the rising of a new day, one hour of which will make up for all the waiting and watching of a life-time. The day is coming, the night is passing, the Bridegroom is waiting for us on the shores of Genesareth, waiting there to share with us the first meal in the House of Our Father.[18]

LaFarge left Poughkeepsie in the early summer of 1918. The tertianship had been a profound experience for him, since he wrote Margaret:

> I finished my retreat at St. Andrew's on Tuesday the ninth. I could hardly realize that I was actually leaving there. At the close of the tertianship it is something like death. The scales seem to drop from your eyes, and you see in bold light all the negligences of the ten months, all the opportunities for self-denial and improvement that one has let slide, and the opportunity will not come again. One has just one lesson to learn there; it is the lesson of the crucifix, and that is not such an easy lesson to learn.

In this same letter, written on the train en route to Washington, he mentioned, without giving a reason, that he had sent in his name to his superiors to become an army chaplain. Although the war would soon be over, the sudden collapse in the fall of the German defenses was not yet predictable. Germany was then mounting a major summer offensive to try once more to take Paris and force the French to sue for peace. By this time, however, more than a million American soldiers were in the front lines in France, and would play a crucial role in stopping the German armies and sending them reeling back to Germany. LaFarge did not expect that his application would be accepted by his superiors. "The school

work is the obstacle in my way," he wrote, "but I leave the whole decision to Superiors." He was right. The order felt he was more needed in
Maryland than on the western front.[19]

In truth, although he obviously felt some call to serve as an army chaplain, the Ridge schools were paramount in his thinking, and he managed
to recruit as teachers a group of four lay women from Alabama who
called themselves the Missionary Sisters of the Most Blessed Trinity.
While not yet a religious order, they lived as nuns and did missionary
work. They began their teaching that fall in the white school at St.
Michael's, but for reasons unknown they did not work out and were gone
by the following June.

He then turned to a group which called itself the Third Order or Tertiary Carmelites, who arrived just in time to occupy the new convent in
the late summer of 1919. He wrote his sister a glowing report about them,
especially their superior, Mother Carmelita.

> The Sisters, the new ones, arrived at last, after all sorts of experi-
> ences. Even at the very end they had trouble, as the bus was delayed
> three hours, by five blow-outs, on the way from Washington! Three
> arrived, Mother Carmelita, Sister Anna Gertrude, who is from
> Providence, and Sister Magdalen. They were certainly tired out.
> The Mother makes an excellent impression. She is apparently
> bright, and with a sweet disposition, and lots of enthusiasm. They
> were delighted with the place, and found it much better than they
> anticipated. Certainly much better than Oklahoma, where they had
> had a terrible time.[20]

Mother Carmelita and her followers, however, lasted less than a year.
Her sweet disposition turned out to be not so sweet after all. "The mother
who had organized the group," he wrote, "was an eccentric. . . . They had
little knowledge of teaching, they seemed to have no idea of the religious
life." When he reproached the mother for her "peculiar conduct . . . She
did not take it very well and remarked with some acerbity: 'I would like
you to understand that I may have a good many faults but I am as strong
as h___ on humility.' "[21]

By November, with the Tertiary Carmelites totally lacking control
over their classes, LaFarge and Father Emerick found themselves doing
almost all the teaching at the white schools at St. James and St.
Michael's. But there were other problems besides the teachers. "The
white school at St. James became uninhabitable because of water in the
cellar, and had to be abandoned."[22] LaFarge was forced to hold classes

in his own small bedroom over the sacristy. Until May 1922, when the St. Joseph Sisters from Hartford finally arrived, there were continual crises at the schools, with LaFarge and his fellow priests resorting to a variety of makeshift solutions to keep them going. In writing about this some thirty years later, LaFarge referred to the period 1918–1922 as years of struggle, in many respects the "hardest years" of his life.

> I felt most helpless and abandoned by everything human. I also struggled with a refractory digestion, not aided by various dietary ventures. I felt deep revulsion at having to seek outside aid for my work. I could appeal to plenty of friends and relatives in Washington, in Philadelphia, and New York, and they were surprisingly considerate and generous once they understood what I was doing. But it was extremely disagreeable to me to pass the hat and talk money to people when I really wanted to do something for their own souls. I shared on a small scale the experience of countless missionaries, foreign and at home, when they try to obtain support for their works.[23]

Despite his burdens, however, his letters to his mother came regularly. She was the lifeline to this other world, the one outside of Maryland and the Society of Jesus. He thought of her often, and even dreamed about her. In early June 1919 he wrote her about a fantastic dream he had had the night before. He wanted to write her about it while it was still fresh in his mind.

> It is raining today, for the first time in a couple of weeks. The farmers are glad, and so am I, as I am very tired after last night. I got to bed at 1:30, and promptly dreamt that you had been taken captive by the Queen of the Bolsheviks, and that you fled from this frightful hag, whose anger meant instant death, in Margaret's motorcar, for 1,000 miles. I wished to rescue you, but you refused all aid, saying that you could handle the whole situation yourself, and the last I saw of you, you were rushing the long-suffering Ford through a tangled forest and across rocky streams, with the angry lady always following behind. It was some relief to wake up, and realize that I had nothing to worry about than to know how to get rid of three gallons of ice cream as yet unsold.[24]

LaFarge also had mystical experiences to go along with his unusual dreams. He felt God's presence everywhere and in everything. More than once he related an incident to Margaret that suggested the supernatural at work on him, even to the point of seeing ghosts and receiving messages from the beyond.

He had one such experience in March 1918, but did not tell her about it until almost a year later. He had preached two masses at St. George's Church, about twenty miles from St. Inigoe's, and had then spent the afternoon rehearsing a play being put on by some parishioners. It was long and unrewarding work. The actors did not know their lines, and LaFarge did not know the play. After the rehearsal, at four in the afternoon, he held devotions in the church, then saw a stream of people who had come to talk to him. Finally, in late afternoon, he broke away and was driven by auto to a family named Burch, for supper and to spend the night. Intending to retire early, he sat up instead discussing the war with the senior Burch, a doctor. At eleven, barely able to keep his eyes open, he crept upstairs to the guest room, where a soft double bed awaited him. He could not imagine, he remembered thinking, that anything could get him out of that bed before morning. But as he was drifting off to sleep a gentle but insistent tapping started on the metallic bedpost at the foot of the bed. At first he paid no attention to it, but the sound persisted. He was determined to ignore it and go to sleep. But as he wrote Margaret months later:

> Then a strange occurrence happened, one of those things which you will remember as long as you live. I felt something coming: I could not say from where; it seemed as if from a great distance, but I was helpless; it was coming with lightning rapidity, and I was powerless: and suddenly, just as if a photographic picture was etched in my mind, or a moving picture thrown upon the screen, I saw with terrible intensity the simple fact that there was a SICK CALL WHICH I HAD NEGLECTED. There it was staring me in the face. That afternoon a colored man had stopped at the church, to have me see his mother. I had agreed to stop there on way down to Burches that evening. There was no escape, for he had distinctly stated that she was NOT EXPECTED TO LIVE THROUGH THE NIGHT. I could wrestle and turn and twitch as much as I liked, but there it was. And the tapping kept up.

> And it was then that I realized the power of the human will. It seems a little thing now, but it looked big at the time. For these things are subjective. I rose, and the thing I most disliked was having to call Combs. But happily he slept lightly, and was up in an instant. We were soon out fixing the car. It was bitter cold, but all sense of fatigue had left, all sense of the cold. It was as if I had had ten hours

of sleep. The moment that I rose the tapping stopped, just a few hurried taps, and it was over, and I never could hear it anymore.

He and Combs, Dr. Burch's son, hurried to the church to pick up the Blessed Sacrament, then drove to the old woman's house. "To my infinite relief," he wrote, "she was still alive and conscious, and all was ready for my coming. I was able to give her all the sacraments. She died a few hours afterward."[25]

One of the major problems faced by the Maryland Jesuits was getting around in decent time to the various missions and schools. Nearly all the roads were dirt, some turning into impassable quagmires when the weather was bad. By the end of the war the counties were so active that LaFarge desperately needed an automobile, both for himself and for the teaching sisters who would soon be arriving. He thought of holding a raffle for prizes donated by the local merchants to raise money for the Ford car he wanted. He even wondered if some prizes could be gotten out of some Newport entrepreneurs, "if the extreme need of the matter could be explained to them." He hoped his mother and sister might be of some help in that department. "The Ford," he wrote, "is to carry teachers all through the year to the schools around the country and then do an unlimited amount of good."[26]

Although an automobile was obtained, LaFarge had only limited opportunity to use it himself. There is a 1920 photograph of him sitting on the running board of a two-seater in his long black cassock, wearing his usual noncommittal expression. His own typical mode of transportation, however, continued to be the horse and buggy, but even that was jeopardized by lack of money to feed the animal properly. He complained of this to Margaret in mid-November 1920.

> I am at present without either horse or other means of conveyance. It makes it hard to get around, to say the least, and I have to beg or steal a ride whenever I can find a chance. My horse fell away to nothing this summer, for we could not afford to buy feed, and he and two other horses were starved out. Poor creatures! It is pathetic to see him now, too far gone to get much back, even if fed. . . . We have a little feed now and I may be able to find a horse to board for the winter, for there is no question of buying one.[27]

A month later he reported that his horse had been sold for a fair price, and that he was going to rent one for the winter.[28] Good fortune, however, struck before the winter was out. In early March, 1921, he received the gift of a Ford from a New York city donor. He wrote Margaret of his luck en route by train from the city back to Maryland. He had been in New York successfully raising funds for the missions when the gift was offered. He was naturally delighted to get it. "It will be a great thing to have one for my own use," he wrote, "and not have to hire that old horse of Wilbur Pembroke's any more."[29] He expected to order it in St. Mary's County. He actually bought the vehicle in Leonardtown on Holy Saturday.[30]

While now blessed with an automobile of his own, it should be mentioned that it was a mixed blessing. LaFarge was a poor, at times even dangerous, driver. He is not known to have had any serious accidents, but stories about his careless driving abound in the family. Many a time, caught up in his thoughts, he would wander off the road and wind up in a ditch or gully, then have to send for someone to pull him out. His absentmindedness is a legend in the family, no doubt a major factor in his erratic steering.[31] Soon after he arrived in New York in 1926 he wisely allowed his driving license to expire. It is doubtful that he ever drove a car again.

At about the same time that he was getting his auto, LaFarge had another one of his small adventures—he was robbed. Some two weeks before Christmas he was coming back from Washington and had stopped at a town called Great Mills, expecting to catch a bus there for Ridge. He had hauled his heavy suitcase to the state road to wait for the bus, only to discover that it had already gone by, which meant a hike back to the town to wait for the next one, some hours away. Rather than lug the suitcase back with him, he left it beside the road. "Nobody here," he wrote Margaret, "would dream of touching it." When he got to Great Mills he sent a man, Tiffany Russell, to carry it back for him. By the time Russell got to the road, however, it was gone. But Russell had seen "four colored persons walking up the road apparently carrying something between them." It was assumed that they had walked off with LaFarge's suitcase.

So began a chase of the four men and the purloined luggage, involving the blacksmith Ryan Matthews and Tiffany Russell (white men) hitching up a team of horses and setting out in pursuit. In the meantime Logan Hopewell (a black man) brought up a car. LaFarge hopped in the vehicle and off they went, finally catching up with the four men, but not finding the stolen article. Much more happened before the mystery was finally solved and settled. Two of the black men had indeed walked off with the suitcase. Their two companions, denying complicity, were supported in their claims of innocence by the guilty ones. The luggage was finally found, although some articles were missing, including a cornet

LaFarge had bought for one of his teachers, and two watches, eventually discovered in the jail cell where the two men were incarcerated.

LaFarge was ready to testify against the two men, seeing how they were criminally-minded characters who had already spent some time in the "pen." He felt that examples should be made of them to do justice to the "native law-abiding negro population, who are anxious to see them get their dues."

At this point, however, a complication arose "in the shape of Mr. Volstead." He explained his dilemma to Margaret.

> There was in the satchel a small bottle of altar-wine, which the aforesaid John Baker did consume, drink, enjoy and regale himself upon. Now to carry, transport, move, or otherwise transfer alcoholic drinks, without a permit given for that particular occasion is against the law, the 18th Amendment, the rulings of the Methodist Church, etc. and lays me open to the Penitentiary, or Federal Prison, or some such very inconvenient place. So if I prosecute Baker, Baker can be a star witness against me. So I fear we shall have to quash the case, as most cases are quashed down here.[32]

Until the summer of 1926, when he got the call from *America,* LaFarge continued his work in the counties. His money troubles never ended, but funds always seemed to materialize unexpectedly. Near Christmas in 1921 he visited Archbishop Michael Curley in Baltimore. He wrote Margaret about the results of this visit with some elation.

> My visit to His Grace Archbishop Curley was most agreeable, though I did not dream I could really get to see him. The little boy who answers the door at 408 N. Charles informed me that there were several priests and some sisters there, and little show for me. But His Grace appeared just then on the stair-case, and told me he could see me at 1:30. When I came back he remarked: Are you the Father LaFarge that wrote that article in "America" on the Negro? I confessed my guilt.

The archbishop told LaFarge that he had sat up the night before reading it, and liked it so much that he had "decided then and there to give me one thousand dollars for my colored work. So he called in Father Connelly, the Chancellor, who handed me a check for one thousand bucks to Yours Truly, who was so stupified [sic] he could only gape, and feebly felt the wheels revolving in his head."[33]

LaFarge's most ambitious undertaking during his last years in the counties was the building of a black industrial arts school, the Cardinal Gibbons Institute, a logical result of his deeply felt need to educate black children. He wrote of this feeling to Margaret on March 13, 1918, as World War I was reaching a climax for the warring powers. "A good many of our colored boys have been sent home from camp, because they could not learn the drill, etc. Another reason for giving them a good schooling when small; for that preternatural stupidity is the result of total educational neglect in their childhood."[34]

The first important step in creating the institute had already come on November 16, 1916. LaFarge recorded the event in his diary as of that date. It was a meeting that took place at St. Peter Claver's Hall, a few miles from the manor house at Priest's Point, where he was then living with Fathers Emerick and Matthew. The three priests met that day with a "large crowd of colored people" from Leonardtown and other parts of St. Mary's County, in response to recently enacted state legislation providing for independent industrial schools throughout the state. A number of white Protestants also attended the meeting. In accord with the legislative enactment, a Mr. Stewart, a Protestant college teacher, called for the establishment of a non-sectarian black school.

The priests spoke against this approach, arguing that the Catholic Church had already been considering the need for such a school, which "would profit infinitely more with the help of a few interested politicians; if we could obtain the services of teachers who could far outclass any that they could think of obtaining, and could also raise far more money towards the fulfillment of the plan."

The Jesuits emphasized that the school would be open to non-Catholics as well as Catholics, and would have a better location at St. Peter Claver's than the one at Morganza being suggested by Stewart. LaFarge noted, probably overoptimistically, that some Protestants in the audience were enthusiastic about their plan. They were invited to join the Catholics in putting it through. Stewart, however, was unwilling to commit himself at the time, "and he and his friends came to the decision not to unite with us but to keep on in their campaign."[35]

Free to go ahead on their own, the Jesuits acquired title to a seventy-to-eighty-acre piece of land just across from St. Peter Claver's for the new school, the property being incorporated initially under the name of St. Peter Claver Institute. Cardinal Gibbons made the purchase possible with an $8,000 contribution. "It was decided then," LaFarge wrote, "that any new institution we started there would be named after him and called the Cardinal Gibbons Institute."[36]

Cardinal Gibbons, however, did not live long enough to see the school completed. He died shortly after making his donation, but Archbishop Curley took up the cause. More funds came in from various, mostly Catholic, sources, including a $35,000 contribution from the Knights of Columbus, and on January 25, 1924, the groundbreaking ceremony was held. LaFarge described it in advance in a letter to his mother. "Ground breaking for the C.G.I. on Friday, Jan. 25th. Admiral Benson will speak, the Band will play, children will sing, and an old colored man from Washington who gave the first money for the school, will dig in, and your youngest near relative will say a prayer. Hope we do not freeze."[37]

The first building was dedicated on October 26, 1924. Additional wings would be added, including a boys' dormitory. After an encouraging beginning, however, the Cardinal Gibbons Institute never really prospered. What started as the first nationally supported Catholic industrial school for black students, soon lost its national character and increasingly became a locally subsidized school. With the onset of the depression in 1931, financial support declined drastically, and on December 31, 1933, the school closed its doors. By then LaFarge had been out of Maryland for several years. In September 1935 he wrote a very discouraging memo on the situation at Cardinal Gibbons, which dealt not only with the collapse of the school, but also with the overall failure of the Church to significantly help the poor people of St. Mary's and St. Charles Counties. He blamed this partly on the lack of cooperation between the Jesuits and the Archdiocese of Baltimore.

> The situation of the Cardinal Gibbons Institute seems to me a *reductio ad absurdum* of the present situation in the Counties. The poor people down there, particularly the Negroes, are stranded between the Society and the Archbishop, neither of which seems to be able to assume the responsibility for the type of effective social and educational program which those poor people desperately need. We owe it out of charity, at least, to these people who have been the spiritual and to some extent the material wards of the Society for some two centuries that something be decided one way or the other in the near future. As it is, those people are gradually being lost to the Faith. Hundreds of them have fallen away already disheartened and dissatisfied with the condition of things in the Southern Maryland parishes.[38]

The Cardinal Gibbons Institute did reopen in 1936, but on a much-reduced scale as a secondary-level day school for local black children. In retrospect, LaFarge saw the school as an important starting point, "a pre-destined seed ground for the development of the Catholic interracial movement in the United States."[39] This was probably an exaggeration, but it was an early attempt to unite white and blacks in a common enterprise, not only to raise money for a black cause, but also to work together to run the institute. Some blacks, for example, sat on the board of directors.

LaFarge's departure from Maryland came in midsummer 1926. His last years in the counties continued to be eventful, filled with tales of his own and his parishioners' activities. The new Ford car in 1921 greatly facilitated his ability to get around (when he was not driving it into a ditch, that is). Also in 1921, electric lights were installed in St. Michael's Church. The Jesuits were keeping up with the modern world. Not so modern, however, as to preclude an occasional reliance on more primitive methods of communication. In July 1924 he wrote Margaret "Recently I purchased a police whistle for Catherine Brown, so she could call her husband, William, when he is working across the creek. She is subject to 'spells,' and as she lies alone, was afraid she might not be able to summon him. It is a practical plan, but seemed to appeal more to her than to William, who is of a nervous disposition, and I think does not like being whistled for."[40]

On April 27, 1935, he received a telegram from his sister Margaret that his mother was dying. She was in her eighty-sixth year. He hastened to Newport and was able to spend her last few days at her side. He described her death in *The Manner Is Ordinary*.

> On Friday, May 1, her last full day on earth, she told us that in the night the Blessed Mother had helped her to obtain relief from pain. She failed so rapidly that day that there seemed little chance she would survive the night. At 6:15 A.M. Saturday morning Oliver and I were sent for. After I had recited the rosary, the Litanies, and other prayers, I left at 9:30 to say Mass for her, returning immediately to the house. Grant arrived from Saunderstown shortly before her death. At 2 P.M. death was imminent. Toward the end she appeared to see something which gave her great joy. Her face shone with a strange radiance, and she was on the point of speaking. At 2:35 she passed away, very gradually, breathing more and more faintly until one final gasp. It was the tranquil passing of a soul united with God.[41]

On the same day that his mother died, LaFarge coincidentally received a phone call from Father Lawrence J. Kelly, the Jesuit provincial of New

York, asking him to stop in and see Father Wilfred Parsons, editor of *America,* before returning to Maryland. LaFarge had been publishing articles and essays in the magazine for a number of years, and the editors had decided they wanted him full-time. It came as a "complete surprise" to him. "It would have been not unpleasant to accept at once," he wrote, "but conditions in Maryland seemed to make it impossible to leave abruptly without upsetting my plans for the schools and for the Institute. Rightly or wrongly I begged Superiors for a bit of postponement. A year later, on July 22, 1926, I received word that I was appointed to the staff of *America,* and departed for New York on August 16."[42]

While he accepted the new assignment without complaint, it was something of a wrench for him to leave his beloved counties and move to New York.

> I had never cared for the city and it took time to get used to it. For some fifteen years I had lived in a community where I could speak to everybody; even if they happened to be strangers, I immediately made their acquaintance. To walk through the streets and see attractive, appealing children, just like the children for whom I had worked in the country, and yet realize that I was totally unknown to them, and had no relation to them—that was difficult. There was no more strolling along the street or road and passing the time of day with everybody whom you met.[43]

Father John LaFarge was about to enter a very different world from the one he was leaving. The move to *America* was another major turning point in his life—he would now be operating in a much larger arena. Over the next thirty-seven years he would make a reputation for himself as an important crusader for black civil rights, an authority on the Catholic liturgy, a principal advocate of the American farmer, and author of nearly a dozen books, a thousand signed articles, and hundreds of unsigned columns and editorials. He would also increasingly interest himself in world affairs and international relations. The scope of his talents was expanded immeasurably by the move from rural, insular Maryland to one of the largest, most sophisticated urban areas of the world. He flourished in his new milieu, transforming himself from a backwoods preacher to an actor on the international stage. By 1938 his reputation had become so considerable that Pope Pius XI asked him to write an encyclical on racism, which was then starting to rage out of control in Nazi Germany.

Chapter 7

Humani Generis Unitas

During his first decade at *America* LaFarge established himself as an authority on race relations and racism. His most important book on the subject was *Interracial Justice: A Study of the Catholic Doctrine of Race Relations,* published by the America Press in 1937. For one thing, it was his first lengthy effort to summarize his understanding and treatment of the problem of race relations in the United States. For another, it was read carefully by Pope Pius XI, who was so impressed with the book that he asked LaFarge to anchor a team of three priests in writing an encyclical on racism in general, not just in America, but wherever it occurred. LaFarge extended and revised the book in 1943 under the title *The Race Question and the Negro.* Since it was the earlier version, however, that prompted the pope to ask him to write the encyclical, this is the edition that will be analyzed in this chapter. The encyclical was titled by its authors "*Humani Generis Unitas*" (Unity of the Human Race).

In his preface to *Interracial Justice* LaFarge made it clear that not just the black was a victim of racism. "One of the most substantial achievements," he wrote, "of recent American sociological literature has been to demonstrate that the Negro-white problem is only one of a multitude of similar interracial problems in this country, and, indeed, throughout the world."[1] Had he limited himself to racism against the Negro in America, it is unlikely that he would have been asked by Pius XI to write the encyclical. By generalizing about the causes and evils of racism, his study became applicable to other examples, namely the anti-Semitism that was infecting parts of Europe in the 1930s.

His approach to the topic of racism is both practical and moral. Writing during the Great Depression, he could stress the self-interest of the producing classes in the United States, the great majority of whom were white, who would benefit from greater economic equality among the races. Given bigger incomes, blacks would be bigger spenders.[2] To achieve some degree of economic equality, however, would mean their gaining greater political, social and educational equality as well. These were all practical goals. But there were also spiritual considerations. ". . . in the *religious field* Catholics cannot be indifferent to the spiritual welfare of one-tenth of the country's population." Even non-Catholic blacks came under the Church's moral teachings, whether they knew it or not. We cannot "be indifferent to these matters when they affect the spiritual conditions of the millions outside the Church, but for whom the Church is no less a spiritual mother, even if she is not recognized as such."[3]

At the beginning of the second chapter he dealt with definitions of the word "race." In then-current anthropological terms, citing a number of authorities in that field, he explained racial differences as a result of environmental differences having nothing to do with intellectual or spiritual superiority or inferiority. In one of his few direct references to Nazism he wrote "The forcible attempt by the Nazi regime in Germany to put the 'race' concept to such a use is the result of political interest and nationalistic mysticism, not of sober scientific investigation."[4]

While blacks have admittedly accomplished less in physical and intellectual achievements, according to LaFarge, this results from lack of opportunities, and is not a matter of racial differences. Athletic skills, for example, are nourished among white boys and girls in their select boarding schools. Were there a black leisure class in America enjoying those same advantages, there would be more good black athletes. Even without the opportunities enjoyed more fully by the white world, "but merely by sheer grit and perseverance, we see today such leaders in the athletic field as Jesse Owens, Ralph Metcalf, Eulace Peacock, Dave Albritton, etc."[5]

As for intellectual differences between the races, they do exist. Again, however, as in the case of sports, these also reflect fewer opportunities. "There appears to be no *rational basis,* and no *factual proof,* for attributing racial mental difference, that is mental difference based upon race as such, upon the supposed inherited traits of a race, to the members of the Negro group in the United States." The inferior education received by most blacks accounts for their inferior mental performances.[6]

Having disposed of the charge that blacks are innately inferior to whites, LaFarge went onto the question of *why* they were held to be inferior in this country. The answer, he believed, was to be found in their previous condition of servitude. "The condition of the Negro as he is now found in this country may be stated in terms either of his past experience or of his present environment. It may be well to cast a glance upon both.

His past experience is that of slavery; his present environment is that of our commercialized civilization."[7]

The slave had been caught up in the capitalist system. He was an investment, and his owner expected to make a profit on his investment. Family life as it existed in Africa was not carried by the slave to America. Slaves could be bought and sold, and families broken up. The social effects were enormous.

The economic results were also staggering. "The low economic status of Negroes at the time of their emancipation was a natural result of slavery. Slaves did not own property. They were property." For support of his contention that slavery was an economic disaster, LaFarge quoted from a speech by Booker T. Washington, who charged that the greatest harm done blacks was depriving them of a " 'sense of self-dependence, habit of economy, and executive power.' "[8]

There were also psychological effects of slavery, imposing upon them "a sense of inferiority or inadequacy." As a result, the development of racial self-respect had been retarded. The inferior status imposed on the slave had been passed to his free black descendants.[9]

Without being ironic, LaFarge did see one benefit coming out of the slave experience—Christianity. It was so like him to see Christianity everywhere, for whatever reasons, as a beacon of hope and a step up the ladder of civilization. "Many Catholic slaveholders" he wrote, "exhorted and warned by the Catholic missionaries, instructed their charges in the elements of Christianity. . . . Slaves attended Mass and other Church services with their masters, and received the sacraments in company with them."[10]

LaFarge often wore blinders when it came to Catholicism and its beneficent effects on its adherents. There were very few Catholic slaveholders in proportion to Protestant ones, and most of those were in Maryland. In truth, Christianity was used more as a weapon against the slave, to keep him obedient with the promise of a better world to come, than as a means of religious enlightenment. LaFarge himself, in *The Manner Is Ordinary,* wrote of a regrettable incident that occurred on one of the Jesuit manors in Maryland in 1838. Some slaves owned by the Jesuits were sold off and carried to Louisiana and Georgia, where they were badly treated. "The Negroes from Maryland," he wrote, "were deprived of ordinary ministrations, and were without priest or church. As a consequence the majority of the descendants of the Maryland ex-slaves drifted away from the Catholic faith and were brought up as Methodists or Baptists."[11]

LaFarge started to get into the moral issues of racism in Chapter Five of *Interracial Justice,* titled "Human Rights." These relate to the existence and nature of God. Here he turned to *a priori,* deductive reasoning, as a scholastic might have done in the thirteenth century.

1. We believe in the first place, as rationally demonstrable, that there is a personal God.
2. This God created the world as a sphere of activity wherein his sons and daughters might perfect, develop, and evolve to their full nature which they derived from their Creator.

As children of God we have a special responsibility toward Him and toward each other. "It determines our attitude towards the material goods of this world, of which we are but stewards, not absolute owners. It also determines our relationships with one another."[12] This last point is crucial to any understanding and application of human rights, which stem from natural law, which is not the same as Divine Law. Natural law is obtainable by man through reason alone. Divine Law can be known only through Divine Revelation. "It was not until the Son of God appeared, as the Great Teacher of mankind, that we learned the simple truths of life and human relationships. Christ spoke not only as the Son of God, not only as the Great Teacher, but also as the supreme representative of the human race itself, who in His own person made all things one, as our Leader, in the practical *work* of achieving those relationships."[13]

Because all men are related to God, all men are related to each other. We are one another's neighbors. The Lord's Prayer, which begins "Our Father," calls attention to that natural unity upon which all human neighborliness is based.

LaFarge was setting up his major premise—that human rights are natural, that "they are something created with man and inherent in him." They may occasionally be suspended in certain situations, but they are always there. No one "can of himself forego his human rights." Nor, by extension, can anyone take those rights away from anyone else.[14]

The United States Constitution is not the source of American human rights, but it recognizes and codifies them. To deny any person equal rights under our constitution is unlawful. Under God's law it is a sin to do so. The logical conclusion of his argument is that racial prejudice is sinful, a violation of God's law. Blacks, along with all other human beings, have the same human rights as everyone else, "*simply as members of the human family.*" (italics added)

From the standpoint of a true believer in God and in God's creation of man, LaFarge's argument is irrefutable. It is this part of *Interracial Justice* that probably appealed most to Pius XI—an attack on racism based on its being immoral and sinful. Take away God and sin, however, and the argument is meaningless; an exercise, despite LaFarge's assertion that the existence of God is "rationally demonstrable," persuasive only to someone of LaFarge's unquestioning conviction. To a non-believer in God, however, something more scientific would be required. Still it was a brave attempt to elevate racism to a moral plane.

At the time LaFarge was writing *Interracial Justice,* legal segregation of the races was practiced throughout the American South and parts of the Midwest. Social segregation without the sanction of law, but with the strong sanction of custom, prevailed in nearly every other part of the country. LaFarge saw no reason to exonerate the northern states from the charge of racism, even though segregation was not legally sanctioned in them, since it ran through almost every important area of work and play. Trade unions, for example, he complained, "traditionally considered as the champion of the oppressed, appear in a novel light where the Negro is concerned, viz., as the question of special privilege, that privilege being the immunity of the white man from being compelled to work 'alongside of' Negroes."

What especially pained him was religious segregation, especially in his own church. He had experienced this abundantly in Maryland, saying mass in St. Inigoe's Church where blacks sat on the sides and whites in the middle. In some parishes, and not only in the South, the pastor refused to admit blacks to mass, reasoning that they could go somewhere else. But there was no consistency to religious discrimination in his church, which sometimes presented the Negro with bewildering and contradictory practices.

> Negroes listen, in Northern churches, to sermons that impress upon the congregation the duty of sending Catholic children to Catholic schools, from the parochial school to the university. Yet if they attempt to comply with this rigid requirement of the Canon Law of the Church, as well as of the natural law of God, they are informed, in many instances, that they are not wanted, and that their presences would amount to a revolution. But in a neighboring town or parish they will find that exactly similar conditions prevail, and yet Negro children frequent the school without any semblance of disturbance.[15]

In theory, he acknowledged, segregation need not be unjust, assuming equal facilities are provided for the segregated race. In practice, however, "segregation, as a compulsory measure based on race, imputes essential inferiority to the segregated group." This imputation "causes a cheapening of the human personality in the mind both of the author and of the object of segregation which opens the way towards violence or exploitation on the part of the one and towards moral irresponsibility on the part of the other resulting in objective injustice, or even in crimes against the human person."[16]

Seventeen years later in the Supreme Court decision *Brown v. Board of Education,* the high court used remarkably similar reasoning in declaring segregation of children in schools inherently unequal, even where facilities were on a par with each other. "A sense of inferiority," the court affirmed, "affects the motivation of a child to learn." In a key paragraph the judges wrote:

> We conclude that in the field of public education the doctrine of "separate but equal" has no place. Separate educational facilities are inherently unequal. Therefore, we hold that the plaintiffs and others similarly situated for whom the actions have been brought are, by reason of the segregation complained of, deprived of the equal protection of the laws guaranteed by the Fourteenth Amendment.

LaFarge astutely realized that merely abolishing legal segregation was not the full solution to the problem. In his mind the only "permanent recipe for happiness in contacts between the races is through the organization of society upon the bases of justice and charity. It is the function of an interracial program to strive for that end."[17]

Race prejudice was not the cause of all racial injustice, but it still carried a "heavy load of guilt."[18] He defined race prejudice, in its most virulent form, as the passing of "judgment of criminality or of essential inferiority upon all members of a racial or ethnic group, with no sufficient intellectual motive for such a judgment."[19]

Several "evil effects" stem from racial prejudice. For one, it can incite to violence. The victim of prejudice is made to feel inferior, losing his self-respect which in turn "brings about a loss of a *sense of responsibility.*" Prejudice also harms those who practice it (another point later made in the *Brown* decision), since it "engenders in the young an entire false idea of their own superiority, while it impairs the faculty of judgment itself."[20]

Finally, prejudice injures the nation at large, and the nation's relations with other nations. "For Catholics," he wrote, "it is particularly disastrous in the field of the missions, home or foreign. The history of the Church's foreign missions has shown repeatedly the ruin wreaked upon the noblest and most self-sacrificing work when the breath of prejudice has passed upon them."[21]

LaFarge was highly critical of prejudiced Catholics, but he tended to defend the Catholic record on racism, arguing that where the Catholic Church could influence the social life of a community, racial intolerance was less severe than it would have been otherwise. He cited as examples Louisiana, Maryland and the Catholic counties of Kentucky, comparing these regions with other parts of the South.

He admitted that there were few Catholics among the antebellum abolitionists. In *Interracial Justice* he quoted from Orestes Brownson, who had written that so many Catholics were anti-black because they were recent immigrants who supported the Democratic party. They were usually victims of discrimination themselves. In a 1955 article in *America* he called Brownson, a Catholic, an "ardent abolitionist."[22] This, however, was probably wishful thinking on his part. Brownson, a convert to Catholicism, was himself at one time a zealous Jacksonian, but by the 1840s had become an equally zealous conservative. There is little evidence that he was an abolitionist at any time in his career. As a movement, abolitionism was pretty much exclusive with white Protestants.

A little beyond the middle of the book LaFarge tackled the sensitive issue of "Social Equality and Intermarriage." In both the 1937 version of the work, and the revised version six years later, he expressed a nearly identical view on the subject. That view began with the certainty that blacks want social equality for themselves. Inconsistent with everything he had written to this point in the book, however, such as the immorality of racism and racial prejudice, and the need for educating whites and blacks to have a better understanding of each other, he unexpectedly shifted to another side of the issue—that full racial equality might not always be good for society or for the individuals involved. It is almost startling to read some of his thoughts.

> I observe that as Negroes advance in education, culture, and social experience they naturally desire such association with persons of other groups who are of like degree of education, culture, and experience, as is necessary to advance the common good. At the same time they appear to recognize as clearly as anyone else and often more clearly, the disadvantages to society and to the individual of the indiscriminate association of persons of unlike condition, tastes and habits.

> Again, if by social equality you mean a disregard of the natural liberty that each man has to form his own intimates and private associates in home, club, private recreation, etc., Negroes as readily as anyone else, recognize such a right to form one's own associates, as part of our American tradition.[23]

In other words, while blacks can aspire to a kind of social equality, they must, and in fact do, acknowledge that because of their different habits they might have to forego membership in social groups that want to remain exclusive. This, however, is more a matter of common sense than a moral issue.

But what if a white person and a black person want to marry each other? On this question he does put forth a moral position. His first step is to raise the question *Will not friendly association between the races lead to intermarriage?*

> The writer has found no evidence to the effect that the establishment of friendly, just and charitable relations between the Negro and white groups encourages any notable tendency to intermarriage. Such indications as there are seem to point in the contrary direction: that in proportion as the pressure of fear and insecurity is removed from the minority group and its status raised by education and improved welfare, spiritual and temporal, the better opportunity is afforded to its youth to find suitable life partners within its own numbers.[24]

The greater social, economic, and educational improvement among blacks, therefore, the less likely will be their inclination to marry outside their race. That there has been illicit as well as legal sexual intercourse between the races is not denied. "The history of the Negro race in the United States, however, shows in a visible and tragic record, that the illicit intercourse between the two groups is derived, to put it mildly, quite as much from the impulse of the dominant race as from any inclination of the minority."[25] Here, of course, he was referring to the white male master-black female slave relationship, that produced so many antebellum mulatto offspring.

He readily agreed that there was no available evidence as to the "deleterious effects from a *purely biological standpoint,* of the union between different races of mankind."[26] He also agreed that the Catholic Church, wherever interracial marriages are legal, does not impose any impediment against them. Where they are prohibited by law, however, as in a number of states, "the Church bids her ministers to respect these laws, and to do all that is in their power to dissuade persons from entering into such unions."[27]

LaFarge strongly opposed interracial marriage, not because of any abhorrence of sex between the races, but because of their effects on family life, especially on the children of such unions. These, taken together, "amount to a moral prohibition of such a practice." Racial intermarriage produces tensions similar to those found in mixed marriages in the field of religion. "The union of Protestant and Catholic, while under exceptional circumstances it can be devoid of any notable strain is apt to affect family conditions far beyond the mere difference of worship on Sunday; and for the sake of the marriage bond itself, as well as for the spiritual good of those who contemplate such marriage, it is subject to a special impediment from the Church."[28]

Should partners in interracial or interreligious marriages live in isolation from their families and the community, tension is more easily contained. But this is seldom the case. "They bring with them into the orbit of married life their parents and brothers and sisters and uncles and aunts and the entire social circle in which they revolve. All of these are affected by social tension, which in turn reacts upon the peace and unity of the marriage bond."[29] When children enter the picture, the problem is compounded, especially if they become victims of discrimination from more than one source.

LaFarge put himself into a difficult, if not untenable, position on the matter of interracial marriage. Given his long history of fighting for interracial justice, it seems anomalous that he was so opposed, to the point of calling it immoral, to its practice. Why he surrendered to intolerance on this issue is not easy to understand. It is easier to comprehend his opposition to interreligious marriages. He was not, after all, pursuing equality for Protestants. If anything, Protestants were the historic oppressors of other groups in America, including Catholics. But he *was* fighting for black equality, and for him to write that interracial marriages were sinful is nearly incomprehensible. If we accept him on the basis of his own words, then we must believe in his sincerity. If we choose to read deeper and less altruistic meanings in those words, then we might consider him a trimmer on the issue, ready to compromise on the most inflammatory of all racial problems. Laws prohibiting miscegenation were still on the books in a number of states until ruled unconstitutional by the Supreme Court in 1967, thirty years after he wrote *Interracial Justice*. We are left, however, with no clear explanation of his attitude on the subject.

On at least one occasion, his condemnation of interracial marriage was used to defend a state law against its practice. In 1948, in the California case *Perez v. Sharp,* the California Supreme Court, in a four-to-three decision, declared unconstitutional the state law prohibiting interracial marriages. In a dissenting opinion one of the judges quoted from LaFarge's book. Had the decision gone the other way, LaFarge's reputation as an advocate of racial justice could have suffered.[30]

An editorial in *America* following this decision, most likely written by LaFarge himself, denied that the Church had any laws against interracial marriage. However, the couples in such a marriage must be extremely prudent. "There are few people who can accept such a burden." The editorial stopped short of calling these marriages sinful or immoral. Presumably by this time LaFarge was backing away from such a position.[31]

Having handled the most sensitive topic in the book, if not to every reader's satisfaction, LaFarge used the last three chapters to sum up the steps needed to achieve interracial justice. Once again, as he did earlier, he stressed education as a principal means of attaining the goal. He agreed that where integration was not enforced, then segregated black schools are better than no schools at all. This, of course, was not the answer in the long run, since black schools were almost always inferior. Black students, in fact, since they were starting behind their white counterparts, should be given even more attention and better facilities. Naturally, this seldom happened where segregation was the rule.

As for the Catholic Church, it could sometimes offer a successful alternative for blacks on every level of education. "In a great number of instances," he wrote, "particularly in the smaller localities, the Catholic schools for Negroes provide plant, equipment, personnel, and curricula far in advance of anything that Negroes can obtain locally under the prevailing dual system. But the Church's efforts were far less than were needed to compensate for the Negro's educational disadvantages."

> The Church needs hundreds, possibly thousands more of such schools as the surest and most immediately realizable hope of spiritual and temporal welfare for millions who must look to the charity of men and women willing to share in loving and unselfish labor their own conditions of separation and social ostracism. And she needs a body of Catholic laymen and lay women apostolic and generous enough to support such enterprises. It is the lack of such support that is now cruelly crippling this Christlike enterprise.[32]

Unfortunately, blacks are excluded from some Catholic institutions on "grounds that are not admitted as valid by Catholic ethics and which do not stand up under actual test."[33] This is wrong and must be changed.

Finally, there is need for more black vocations, which can be fulfilled only through Catholic education. "Missionaries and Negroes alike seem to regard the native-clergy problem, as it exists, largely as an educational one, not for candidates alone, but also for families from whom the candidates may be expected."[34]

In calling for Catholic education for blacks, LaFarge was consistent in his belief that all Catholics should be educated in Catholic schools. For black Catholics, who represented only about 5 percent of the black population (a figure that has scarcely changed at this writing) it was perhaps even more important. Without a significant black clergy, which blacks can relate to, little could be done in making converts to the faith. "For the colored Catholics," he wrote, "the priest of his race *has* a special value as a 'symbol,' which it is impossible to gainsay."[35]

In the concluding chapter, "Interracial Justice and the Church's Work for the Negro," LaFarge once more emphasized the Church's role in bringing blacks into the social and economic mainstream of America. In the last paragraph, however, he cast his net further, to include the whole human race. This passage, earnestly and eloquently written, must have appealed to Pius XI, since it gave LaFarge's message a universal expression.

> Though the foregoing words are spoken of the Negro alone, they apply to all races and conditions of men. Earthly calculation, earthly selfishness and interest will never be wholly satisfied with the catholicity of a universal Church. Forever will this catholicity be opposed, and just so long will society suffer from its own short-sightedness; for by rejecting God's wisdom they have rejected human wisdom as well. But the work of the Church does not live by mere earthly calculation. It is inspired by the Divine folly of the Cross, the vision of the Kingdom in which all tribes and races, Jew and Gentile alike, are united in the love and service of a King who in His own Person broke down the wall of partition and erased the handwriting of human hate and prejudice. In proportion as we further the Christian interracial spirit, we shall hasten the coming of the Kingdom of God on earth.[36]

In 1938, the year after the publication of *Interracial Justice,* LaFarge spent the spring and summer in Europe. The details of his trip will be presented in the next chapter. One episode, however, is given at this point—the writing of the encyclical "*Humani Generis Unitas*," probably the most important writing assignment of his career.

In *The Manner Is Ordinary* he wrote of being summoned to a private audience with Pope Pius XI about a week after arriving in Rome in early June 1938. Shortly before receiving the summons he had been driven out to Castelgandolfo by Father Vincent McCormick, S.J., the rector of Gregorian University in Rome, for a general audience with His Holiness. He wrote of his surprise at receiving the invitation to a private meeting, which took place on June 22.

> A few days later a message from the Vatican was delivered to me in the well-known yellow and white envelope, saying that His Holiness would like to see me privately and appointing a time for the visit. I was mystified, wondering what it could be, and again took the long drive to Castelgandolfo, followed by an apprehensive wait in the papal antechamber. As I stepped into the elevator to go up to the antechamber, the Papal Secretary of State, Cardinal Pacelli, stepped out, but I was in no position to ask him for an explanation.[37]

In his autobiography, LaFarge gave no hint as to the real reason for the papal meeting. He merely informed his readers that the pope had read *Interracial Justice,* and had been impressed with it, calling it "the best thing written on the topic." LaFarge found that the pope's praise of his book gave him a "big lift." "Apparently what had appealed to him in my little effort was the spiritual and moral treatment of the topic, and the fact that I did bring into synthesis the Catholic doctrine and the natural law and the pertinent facts as well as some practical methods for dealing with the question." Pius suggested that he continue his research on the issue, and that if he were ever back in Rome he should come and see him again.[38]

What really happened at this meeting, however, was that Pius XI asked LaFarge to help write a papal encyclical on racism. LaFarge explained this in a confidential memo to Father Francis Talbot, S.J., editor in chief at *America,* on July 3.

> Fr. Maher may have written to you what really did happen at the audience. What happened was the Pope put me under secrecy, and enjoined upon me to write the text of an encyclical for the universal church, on the topic which he considered is most burning at the present time.

He told me that God had sent me to him, as he was looking for a man to write on this topic. He had considered another person—mentioning a *very* eminent scholar—but reflection had convinced him the Fr. LaFarge was more competent. *Dites tout simplement*, he said, *ce que vous diriez à tout le monde si vous etiez Pope, vous même.*[39]

He told LaFarge that he would write immediately to Father Wladimir Ledochowski, father general of the Jesuit Order in Rome, asking him to cooperate fully with LaFarge in carrying out the project. The pope himself met with the father general a few days later, to elicit his support. LaFarge met with Ledochowski on June 27. At LaFarge's request, Ledochowski named two scholars who could collaborate with him on the text, one of whom was in Rome, the other in Paris. LaFarge told the father general that, because of the summer heat, he could not do the work in Rome. It was agreed that he would go to Paris immediately, and start the job there. He left for Paris that same day.

LaFarge had accepted the assignment only reluctantly. As he wrote Talbot, "Frankly I am simply stunned, and all I can say is that the Rock of Peter has fallen on my head. Had I anticipated such a terrific development, nothing would have persuaded me even to go to Rome, much less see the Pope. As it is, there is nothing to do but go through with the whole thing, as Fr. General says."[40]

LaFarge took very seriously the pope's stricture to keep the project secret. Only a handful of priests, including of course his two collaborators, knew what he was doing, and none of them revealed, at least not publicly, their knowledge of its existence. "Naturally," he wrote Talbot, "this will interfere with my literary production, though I will send in a thing or two to avoid suspicion and questions. Please pray for me, pray hard; never have I felt prayers needed so desperately; and get prayers from the nuns; for the task is superhuman, both as to nature and as to rapidity."[41]

He mentioned to Talbot that his audience with the pope had been reported in *Osservatore Romano*, the Vatican newspaper, so that part at least was not a secret. "But what is written here is a grave matter, and if known to the public, as I said, would create more problems than one can imagine. Besides, there is the dread command of the Pope, who said: On dit le secret du Pontife Romain est un secret de Polichinelle. Peut-être. Mais il ne doit être comma ça. Est c'est un *vrai* secret que Nous vous disons."[42]

Talbot responded to LaFarge, assuring him that "innumerable prayers" were being offered for him. He did not, of course, reveal to those who were praying what they were praying for, merely asking them "for prayers for certain people engaged in a most important undertaking for the glory of God." The "certain people" were LaFarge and his co-writers, and the "most important undertaking" the encyclical on racism.[43]

In his doctoral dissertation on LaFarge, "John LaFarge's Understanding of the Unifying Mission of the Church," Father Edward Stanton, S.J., detailed some of the events leading up to the commission to write the encyclical, LaFarge's collaboration with the other two priests during the summer of 1938 in Paris, and the eventual fate of the document after it was delivered to the Vatican. Three translations of the draft encyclical were made—English, French and German. On December 15, 1972, the *National Catholic Reporter* announced on its front page that the encyclical had recently been discovered in LaFarge's papers, nearly a decade after his death.[44]

The report was incorrect. The existence of the document, in fact, was known as early as late 1963. Shortly after LaFarge passed away in his room at *America,* Father Walter Abbott, S.J., then on the staff at *America,* started to prepare a biography of LaFarge. When he went through LaFarge's papers he found the encyclical and a number of letters written to LaFarge during the summer of 1938 by Father Ledochowski, encouraging him to get the job done.

Shortly after starting the project, however, Abbott was given a demanding assignment at *America.* Later, he was sent to Rome to head the Vatican Office for the Common Bible. Since he could no longer work on the biography, he sent the encyclical, along with LaFarge's other papers, to Professor Harry Sievers at Fordham, who agreed to complete the study. But Sievers died shortly afterward. A number of years later, Abbott suggested to Stanton that he use the material that had been turned over to Sievers. Stanton agreed, and went on to use it for his dissertation.[45]

Years after completing his dissertation, Stanton decided to write a full-scale biography of LaFarge (he actually completed about sixty pages of typescript), but before he could get very far he died of a heart attack while jogging. He had, however, used the encyclical for his dissertation. Before incorporating it he wrote to Pope Paul VI, requesting permission to use the draft. On January 28, 1971, His Excellency J. Benelli of the Vatican wrote Stanton "With regard to your wish to use for your doctoral dissertation excerpts from the text on racism prepared by the late Father John LaFarge, I am happy to inform you that you are free to do so."[46]

Eventually most of LaFarge's papers, except for his private family correspondence, ended up in the Georgetown University Library. When this writer could not find the encyclical there he contacted the office of *America* in New York, where he met with Father John Donahue, S.J., who remembered that there was, or at least had been, a carbon copy of the English translation somewhere in *America's* files. But when he searched the files it was missing. He did remember, however, that in 1973 *America* had planned to print the entire encyclical in one of its other publications, *Catholic Mind*. Since the encyclical had never been issued by Pope Pius XI, or his successor Pius XII, the editors of *America* decided to make LaFarge's copy available to scholars in the pages of *Catholic Mind*. This copy was sent to the printer, set up by him in galley proofs, and returned to *America* for any corrections prior to publication.

At the last moment, however, the editors had second thoughts, and decided not to publish the encyclical after all. One of them explained to this writer that they were frankly embarrassed by some of the encyclical's contents.[47] Over the years the carbon copy had disappeared, but the galley proof remained on file. At present the only known extant copy of "*Humani Generis Unitas*" is that proof. A copy of this galley was made at the offices of *America* in September 1993, and most kindly presented to this writer by Father Donahue.

At this writer's suggestion, another photocopy was made and sent to the Georgetown Library. A letter accompanying the copy was also sent, explaining the reasons why it was never published, and why *America* was sending Georgetown a copy at this time.

> 4. After the galleys were returned and read, it was decided not to publish the draft in *Catholic Mind* because some of its comments on racism and anti-Semitism seemed quite outdated by 1973 and liable to discredit the authors of the draft.

> 5. The galleys were kept at *America* and nearly forgotten until Dr. Robert A. Hecht, who was writing a biography of John LaFarge, inquired in the autumn of 1993 whether or not a copy of the draft existed at *America*. He was told there was no trace of the carbon copy but the galleys did exist and xeroxes of these were made for him.

> At the same time, when the editors of *America* learned that there was no copy of the draft in the LaFarge collection in the Georgetown University Library, they decided that this set of galleys should be sent to that collection for the use of qualified researchers.[48]

It is this copy of the draft encyclical that will be described and analyzed throughout the rest of this chapter.

In their introduction to the encyclical, the *America* editors pointed out
that the document would present some problems for the readers if
they made "the mistake of viewing it as intended for contemporary
consumption in 1973 and as embodying the current state of Catholic
thought on its key themes." They warned that there were historical obscu-
rities enveloping the draft. They confessed that they did not know why it
had not been issued by the Vatican. Nevertheless, they felt it was worth
publishing. "It clearly indicts," the *America* editors wrote, "both the ex-
pansionist and anti-Semitic policies and procedures of the National So-
cialist regime in Hitler's Germany and racism in the United States."[49]

It is doubtful that the editors had carefully read the encyclical before
sending it out for typesetting. As the galley was being proofread and cor-
rected, however, some glaring, even shocking, statements appeared in
its pages, especially regarding Jewish responsibility for the crucifixion
of Jesus.

When he accepted the assignment, LaFarge asked that two Jesuit
priests, Father Gustave Gundlach of the Gregorian University, and Father Gustave Desbuquois of *Action Populaire,* assist him in its writing.
The three priests spent the summer of 1938 in Paris at the house of the
Jesuit magazine *Etudes* on the Rue Monsieur, working on the document
almost continuously. They met with each other nearly every day. The
only other person in the house who knew of their commission was the
superior, and he knew very little. In a letter to Talbot at the end of August, LaFarge called the work a "joint martyrdom." He told Talbot that
the writing progressed "as if by a miracle, thanks largely to the team
work among those I asked here to help me."[50] By mid-September the encyclical was finished, and LaFarge set out to hand deliver it to the pope
in Rome. He arrived there on the twentieth, and was told to first submit
it to Father Ledochowski, who would presumably pass it on to His Holiness. His work finished, LaFarge returned to Paris to collect his belong-
ings, then on to Boulogne and New York.

Thus began months of frustration for the three authors of *"Humani
Generis Unitas."* For one thing, by the time LaFarge brought the document
to Rome Pius XI was very ill. It is questionable that he ever saw the encyclical he had personally commissioned. He died on February 10, 1939.

For another, there is evidence that Father Ledochowski was not happy
with the work of the three Jesuits. About a week after receiving the text

he turned it over to Father Rosa of *Civilta Cattolica* "to get the judgment of more than one man about it."[51] By this time LaFarge was back in New York, so was not on the scene to pursue the matter.

Father Gundlach, however, arrived in Rome in October 1, and started to make inquiries about the draft. Based on these inquiries he was convinced that Ledochowski was deliberately sabotaging the project. On May 10, 1939, he wrote LaFarge that their encyclical was dead, for which, with considerable bitterness, he blamed the father general.

> The outline was, after it had lain for a relatively long time in the possession of Father Rosa, either not presented to Fisher Sr. (Pope Pius XI) at all or only at such a time when—in contrast to late summer and early fall of 1938—it was physically impossible for him to deal with it because of the condition of his health. It was not presented evidently to Fisher Jr. (Pope Pius XII) at all, but rather the affair might more or less in passing have been buried in a conversation between the highest gentleman and Pat. (Pater Generalis). The reasons: things which were too delicate to burden the beginning of the new man immediately, who in any case already desired through the greatest possible silence and forbearance to feel out in the first weeks whether any will to compromise would be shown by the other side. I am adding that this attempt appears to have ended negatively, and that people here have also realized this. Our affair in any case in the meantime went the way of all flesh, which indeed is probably more to the views and intentions of Pat.[52]

If Ledochowski did bury the encyclical, and Stanton believed that he did, the question is why? Stanton wrote in his dissertation that the father general "seems not to have liked what he saw in the text." According to Gundlach he lacked an understanding of natural law, upon which much of the encyclical is based.[53] On January 12, 1973, the Boston *Pilot,* referring to the recent story announcing the discovery of the document in the *National Catholic Reporter,* gave a more persuasive political reason for its suppression.

> Pope Pius XII probably would not have been elected after Pope Pius XI's death if the encyclical had been published. The encyclical would have so changed the Vatican's relations with Germany that the election of Pius XII as Pope would have been futile. He was elected partly in hopes of maintaining friendly relations between the Church and Germany.[54]

Had Pius XI lived would he have published the encyclical? According to Robert G. Weisbard and Wallace P. Sillonpor, two recent historians of the Vatican and the Holocaust, he was planning to sign it when he died suddenly of a heart attack on February 10, 1939. "Pius XI," they wrote, "was much more willing than his successor to confront Hitler. . . . His 1937 encyclical *Mit Brennender Sorge* (With Burning Anxiety), issued in German, pilloried those who would exalt and worship the nation or the race thereby perverting the divine will."[55]

After the death of Pius XI, *"Humani Generis Unitas"* was shelved by his successor. Along with other papers on the desk of Pius XI, the encyclical was deposited in the secret Vatican archives.[56] There is some evidence, however, that Pius XII did use parts of it in his first encyclical *Summi Pontificatus* (Of the Supreme Pontificate), issued on October 20, 1939, some seven weeks after Germany's attack on Poland and the outbreak of World War II. In it he wrote of the "evils of totalitarianism and racism." But unlike LaFarge's encyclical, there was no mention of anti-Semitism, and not one word about the Jews. As did LaFarge, the pope stressed the unity of mankind.[57]

Father Abbott was interviewed about the encyclical in Rome in 1972 by a reporter for the *Catholic Transcript*. He told the reporter that Ledochowski "had taken it upon himself to have the original LaFarge version toned down by a Jesuit scholar stationed in Rome. The scholar died shortly after receiving the document with orders to make certain changes. Father Ledochowski since has died too."[58] Actually, the father general of the Jesuits had died in 1942. It is reasonable to state, therefore, that the copy of *"Humani Generis Unitas"* found among LaFarge's papers shortly after his death, was the original wording of the document.

Abbott believed that, if Pius XI had lived, he would have issued the encyclical. He apparently realized that Ledochowski did not approve a strong papal denunciation of Nazi anti-Semitism. But, according to Abbott, the pope told LaFarge "Remember, you are writing this encyclical for me, not for Ledochowski."[59]

That Pius XI would have issued the encyclical is also the opinion of a recent historian of the papacy. J. Derek Holmes has written that ironically, on September 20, 1938, just as LaFarge was delivering the document in Rome, the pope voiced a major protest against racism and anti-Semitism, while addressing a group of pilgrims at the Vatican. "Mark well that in the Catholic Mass, Abraham is our Patriarch and forefather. Anti-Semitism is incompatible with the lofty thought which that pact expresses. It is a movement with which Christians can have nothing to do.

No, no, I say to you it is impossible for a Christian to take part in anti-Semitism. It is inadmissible. Through Christ or in Christ we are the spiritual progeny of Abraham. Spiritually, we are all Semites."[60]

Ledochowski was more concerned with the survival of the German Roman Catholic Church. "He obviously felt," according to Abbott, "that if the document had been issued, there would soon no longer be a Catholic Church in Germany." The attack on the Nazis was too strongly worded. ". . . it would be unwise to invite a head-on confrontation with the Hitler Government and that it was better to work out some 'modus operandi.' "[61] It should also be noted that the father general was an implacable foe of atheistic Communism. In 1938, to him at least, it was the greater danger. Until the Nazi-Soviet Pact one year later, Germany stood as a bastion of anti-Communism.

"*Humani Generis Unitas*" is a curious piece of writing. Looked at more than a half-century later one wonders why people like Ledochowski were so concerned that it would antagonize Hitler, since Germany is never mentioned by name, and since a good deal of the text is a not very subtle attack on the Jews for their crucifixion of Christ.

In their introduction the authors of the encyclical claim they are writing with the authority of the Gospel, "whose guardian and interpreter is the Church. That is why the Church continually intervenes in questions which pertain to social life. In doing so she is only carrying out a sacred duty."[62]

The major problem of the modern world, as they perceived it in 1938, was the secularization of society, which has turned men away from the spirit. "Men were once differentiated and classified, for the good of the social order, by their spiritual and moral qualities, by their professional knowledge. Today, on the contrary, they tend to be classified more and more exclusively by the quantity of capital they possess."[63] Men themselves have been reduced to mere numbers, increasingly controlled by the State. "The result of all this is the modern mass man, who no longer has opinions of his own, no longer his own will, and is merely a passive instrument in the hands of his master."[64]

Men are naturally united with one another under the authority of God. The totalitarian leaders, however, reject this unity, seeking rather to divide men and set them against each other.

> These men enlarge out of proportion the accidental effects, in every case superficial, of blood and affinity of blood in the foundation of social groups larger than the family; and, against all experience and

> still more against the teachings of our Catholic Faith, to crown their
> thought they absolutely reject the unity of the human race and
> would erect insurmountable barriers between communities differ-
> ent in blood and race. They even go so far as to formulate this
> proposition: the human races, in virtue of their natural, immutable
> characteristics, are so different from one another that the most in-
> ferior race is further removed from the most evolved race than from
> the highest species of animal.[65]

Dividing mankind into races based on shared physical characteristics
is legitimate. Attaching labels of inferiority or superiority is not. That is
racism. "Racism has for a long time exerted its baneful influence upon
certain regions of the American Continent, where the consciousness of a
fixed distinction of inferior and superior races has been kept alive not so
much by the circumstances of environment as by the artificial nature of
prejudices. This is exemplified by the unleashing of some of man's
basest instincts in "The so-called lynch law."[66]

Having defined racism, and referring briefly to its practice in the
United States, the Jesuits next turned their attention to the persecution of
the Jews. Nowhere in the document, however, is there any specific mention of their persecution in any country or any part of the world. Their
unjust treatment is condemned. "In the case of the Jews, this flagrant de-
nial of human rights sends many thousands of helpless persons out over
the face of the earth without any resources. Wandering from frontier to
frontier to frontier, they are a burden to humanity and to themselves."[67]

But who are the Jews, and what is the Church's teaching about them?
They were clearly the Chosen People, selected "by Almighty God to prepare the way in history for the Incarnation of His Only-Begotten Son."[68]
When the time came for the Jews to fulfill God's expectations of them,
however, they turned away from Him. In an extraordinary paragraph the
authors showed a startling insensitivity to the very people they were defending against persecution. Had the encyclical been issued in this form,
it would have only added to the ammunition the anti-Semites were using
against them.

> The vocation of the Jewish people culminated in a wholly unique
> and unprecedented historical occurrence which interrupted and
> transformed the history of the world. At a definite moment in time,
> in a definite locality, a member of a certain tribe of the Jewish peo-
> ple, was born from a Jewish Mother through the operation of the
> Holy Spirit, Jesus Christ, whose Person was the person expected

and foretold by the prophets of Israel throughout the ages; whose mission and teaching were the completion of the historic mission and teaching of Israel; whose birth, life, suffering, death, and resurrection from the dead were the fulfillment of Israel's types and prophecies. Extraordinary as was this occurrence, it was linked with another occurrence of a character unknown and unprecedented in history. The Savior, whom God had sent to the people He had chosen after thousands of years of prayer and longing, was rejected by the same, repudiated and condemned as a criminal by the highest tribunals of the Jewish nation in collusion with the tribunals of the pagan authorities who held the Jewish people in bondage.[69]

Because of Christ's rejection by the Jewish people, and his crucifixion at their instigation, the doors of Heaven were opened up to everyone. By his death and resurrection all may be saved. "The very act by which the Jewish people put to death their Saviour and King, was, in the strong language of St. Paul, the salvation of the world." Blinded by materialism and greed "the Israelites lost what they themselves had sought."

> Moreover, by a mysterious Providence of God, this unhappy people, destroyers of their own nation, whose misguided leaders had called down upon their own heads a Divine malediction, doomed, as it were, to a perpetual wandering over the face of the earth, were nevertheless never allowed to perish but have been preserved through the ages into our own time.[70]

Despite the Jewish rejection of the Saviour, however, it was not too late for them to be saved. The sole condition is that they repent what they had done and "accept Him as their Redeemer."[71] Because of the acceptance of the Messiah by the Gentiles, who had not been the Chosen People, the Jews have a historic enmity to Christianity, "creating a perpetual tension between Jew and Gentile which the passage of time has never diminished, even though from time to time its manifestations have been mitigated."[72]

Since the Jews might still be saved, the Church must pray for their salvation. According to the decree of the Sacred Congregation of the Holy Office of March 25, 1928, "The Catholic Church habitually prays for the Jewish people who were the bearers of the Divine revelation up to the time of Christ; this, despite, indeed, on account of, their spiritual blindness."[73]

Having finished scolding the Jews for their spiritual perversity, the authors once again condemned their persecution. Actuated by love, "the Apostolic See has protected this people against unjust oppression and

just as every kind of envy and jealousy among the nations must be dis-
approved of, as in an especial manner must be that hatred which is generally termed anti-Semtism."[74]

Just how much LaFarge contributed to the section on the Jews is not
clear. Stanton believed that LaFarge wrote, or at least typed, the English
version of the encyclical. But even if he had not authored it, he certainly
signed onto the entire document. And it was he who hand delivered it to
Rome.

In partial defense of the three Jesuits, it should be mentioned that the
extent of Nazi persecution was not yet blatantly obvious. Kristallnacht,
the "Night of the Broken Glass," did not happen until that November.
Nevertheless, the sharpness of the encyclical's words against the Jews
for rejecting Christ at this terrible time in their history, is difficult to comprehend. It was probably for the best that Ledochowski, if even for other
reasons, opposed its publication.

Chapter 8

Europe 1938

While writing the encyclical on racism was LaFarge's major project during his European excursion in 1938, the main reason Father Talbot, editor in chief of *America,* sent him there in April was to attend and report on the International Eucharistic Conference held in Budapest, Hungary, that year. This was in the midst of a momentous, tragic period in European history. By the time he returned to America in the fall of 1938, World War II was just a year away, thanks largely to the rise to power of Hitler and the Nazis in Germany, and the appeasement policies of Great Britain and France, who accepted Germany's repeated violations of the Versailles Treaty. Six weeks before LaFarge landed in England, the first stop on his European tour, Hitler had annexed Austria to Germany under the guise of self-determination, in clear violation of the treaty. Two weeks before he headed home in mid-October 1938, the Munich crisis had come and gone, leading to German annexation of Czechoslovakia's Sudetenland. As critical as these events were however, LaFarge was much more concerned emotionally, politically, and religiously, with what was coming to a climax in Spain—the Spanish Civil War. His thoughts during that nearly half-year in Europe, while far ranging, were dominated by both the war in Spain and the writing of the encyclical for Pius XI.

After centuries of rule by monarchs, a republic was proclaimed in Spain on April 12, 1931. Two days later King Alfonso XIII left his throne and went into exile. In June a constituent assembly was democratically elected. While there were some monarchists in the assembly, the overwhelming majority opposed the return of the king to power. In writing a constitution, the delegates were generally able to agree on the first twenty-five articles. Starting with Article Twenty-six, however, dealing with the future of the Roman Catholic Church in Spain, serious divisions arose. The Church and its leadership had enjoyed a privileged status under the monarchy and wanted to keep those same privileges under the Republic. This was not to be. The constitution written and adopted by a majority of the delegates denied the Church special rights, denoting it an association subject to the laws of the country and without special privileges. According to the historian F. Jay Taylor, "Also included within the Constitution were provisions which prevented religious orders, such as the Jesuits, from conducting educational activities and prevented the allocation of any state funds to the clergy. During the next two years the Catholic hierarchy was further alienated by the passage of laws which recognized divorce, secularized all cemeteries, abolished the Corps of Army Chaplains, and permitted civil marriages.[1]

These provisions and laws incited resistance by the Church leaders to the new republic. Cardinal Pedro Segura, archbishop of Toledo and primate of Spain, issued a pastoral letter attacking the constitution and expressing gratitude to the memory of King Alfonso XIII. In response to this letter, over the next few weeks "many supporters of the Republic, fearing the hierarchy as an enemy, created disturbances throughout the country by destroying churches and convents."[2] Over the next five years Spain struggled through economic depression, separatist movements among Basques and Catalonians, widespread unemployment, religious conflict, and growing antagonism to the government by high-ranking officers of the army, who were given the option of swearing allegiance to the Republic or resigning. Many chose to resign, and soon a powerful, discontented group of ex-military men emerged whose goal was the overthrow of the government.

By early 1936 the country was in turmoil. At this point President Don Manuel Azaña dissolved the legislature and called for new elections to be held on February 16. These resulted in victory for a coalition of leftist parties that called itself the Popular Front. This did not solve the political crisis, however, as military and Church opposition continued to grow. At the same time the government increasingly came under the influence of radical leftists, including the Communist Party, which had not been represented in the 1931 assembly.

As the country became polarized between extremists from the Left and the Right, conditions were ripe for a military coup. On July 17, 1936, General Francisco Franco, who had flown from the Canary Islands to assume command of the army in Morocco, crossed the Strait of Gibraltar to Cadiz. This marked the beginning of the Spanish Civil War, which ended when Franco's forces captured Madrid on March 28, 1939. It was one of the bloodiest, most savagely fought wars in the twentieth century.

Throughout the war LaFarge, *America,* and nearly all the American Catholic hierarchy and the American Catholic press supported Franco's Nationalists against the Republican Loyalists, as the opposing sides came to be called.

Only days after the Nationalist uprising, some leftist elements on the Loyalist side started a rampage against the Church, referred to by one historian as the "anticlerical fury." According to José Sanchez in his volume *The Spanish Civil War as a Religious Tragedy,* "It was the greatest clerical bloodletting in the entire history of the Christian Church."[3] Nearly seven thousand priests, as well as some nuns, were killed by the "uncontrollables" among the Loyalists. The great majority of these were killed between July and December 1936. After that the Loyalist government exercised much stricter control over the more rabid elements, and the number of clerical murders after that period, while not totally ending, diminished considerably. For the Loyalist cause, however, the damage had been done. The atrocity stories, some true, some not so true, were publicized abroad, where they influenced decision-making in the United States and the countries of Western Europe.

In addition to the murder of clergymen, hundreds of churches and convents were burned down, often accompanied by the desecration of religious objects, which were thrown to the ground, spat upon, and burned. No simple explanation for the anticlerical fury can be given. Hatred of the Catholic Church by some segments of the population had been going on for more than a century. To many poor people the Church was rich and cared only about its wealthy and powerful supporters from the upper classes. One writer on the Loyalist side, clearly filled with hatred for the Church, wrote of the burnings:

> Those buildings had lasted long enough, their mission was completed; now they were anachronisms, weighty and obstructing, casting a jailhouse stench over the city. The times condemned them to death and the people carried out the execution of justice. These burnings were the *autos da fe* necessary for the progress of civilization.[4]

How many Catholic priests would have supported the Loyalists is impossible to say. As a result of the anticlerical fury nearly all of them, to save their lives, threw their support to the Nationalists as their only hope for survival. The Spanish clergy, especially the hierarchy, saw Franco as a saviour, and Franco played up to this feeling because he needed the Church on his side.

As for Communism, the Church viewed it as a principal enemy seeking the Church's destruction. The Communist threat, however, was probably exaggerated at the time. The Nationalists had strong supporters in the Vatican, who stressed the Communist menace. Father General Ledochowski argued that the fury "was not simply a new and more violent expression of traditional Spanish anticlericalism but was in fact inspired by Soviet Russia as part of a plan to destroy religion everywhere. . . ."[5] LaFarge held strongly to this view himself, both during the war and after Franco had triumphed.

Shortly after the fighting began, Great Britain and France, fearing that the war might spread beyond Spain's borders, declared a strict neutrality and nonintervention policy toward both sides. America was influenced by Britain and France. But American neutrality laws recently passed by Congress applied only to wars between or among nations, not to civil wars. At first the American government tried to persuade its citizens to refrain voluntarily from selling weapons to either side. But on December 28, 1936, an arms exporter named Robert Cuse applied for a license to sell nearly three million dollars worth of aircraft materials to the Loyalists. He had the legal right to do so, and the State Department was forced to issue the necessary permits. It was clear to Secretary of State Cordell Hull and President Franklin D. Roosevelt that the neutrality laws would have to be amended to include civil wars. If not, the United States could not go along with the nonintervention policies of Britain and France.

Both political parties and both Houses of Congress overwhelmingly endorsed neutrality in the Spanish Civil War. On January 8, 1937, at the request of the administration, the Senate voted eighty-one to zero to impose an arms embargo on both sides, followed shortly afterward by a four hundred six-to-one vote in the House of Representatives. General Franco declared himself well pleased by these votes. Not so the Loyalists, who now found most of Europe and the United States following the course of neutrality. Since Franco had greater access to weapons from countries that had not gone along with nonintervention, namely Germany and Italy, western neutrality clearly favored the Nationalists.

The Spanish Civil War raised powerful emotions among many Americans, some supporting the Nationalists, others the Loyalists. In general, American liberals and leftists sided with the Loyalists, while conservatives and the Catholic hierarchy endorsed Franco. With few exceptions Catholic newspapers and magazines also supported Franco, arguing that he was not getting fair and honest coverage in the secular press. Father

Joseph F. Thorning, for example, writing in *Catholic World* in December 1937, charged that American reporters in Spain were unduly influenced by Loyalist propaganda, and were not getting the truth to the American people. This propaganda, he asserted, was disseminated by Russian-financed Communists in the Loyalist government. What was needed, he wrote, was honest reporting not financed by "red-gold."[6]

On the other hand Taylor, in his book on the war, suggested that the Catholic press was not presenting the true story either. It was so strongly pro-Franco, in part at least, because it was getting most of its information from the National Catholic Welfare Conference (NCWC), a Catholic news service in Franco's pocket. The NCWC provided some four hundred fifty Catholic publications with daily news reports. According to Taylor, "A close examination of these dispatches would seem to indicate that factual reporting was circumscribed for the purpose of promoting Catholic interests."[7]

What were the Catholic interests? Far and away the most important was fear of godless Communism. All other concerns stemmed from this transcendent issue. Led by Pius XI, the Catholic hierarchy saw the civil war in Spain in terms of good versus evil. On August 17, 1936, the *New York Times* quoted the pope.

> Satanic preparation has relighted—and that more fiercely—in neighboring Spain that hatred and savage persecution which have been confessedly reserved for the Catholic Church and Catholic religion as being the one real obstacle.
>
> Our benediction, above any political and mundane consideration, goes in a special manner to all those who assume the difficult and dangerous task of defending and restoring the rights to honor God and religion.[8]

Time magazine quoted Pius XI in May 1938, as blessing Franco and telling him, "We send from our hearts the Apostolic blessing."[9] And when Franco finally emerged victorious in April 1939, Pius XII telegraphed him, "Lifting up our hearts to God, we give sincere thanks with your Excellency for Spain's Catholic victory."[10] From the beginning to the end of the Spanish Civil War the Vatican and most of the Catholic hierarchy saw it as a conflict for and against the Roman Catholic Church.

The Church's strong pro-Franco stand brought the American Church into heated debate with some American Protestant leaders who did not see the war in the same good versus evil light as did the Vatican. In early September 1937 a number of Spanish prelates issued a letter justifying the Nationalist revolt against the government. They argued that the Loyalists were ruling arbitrarily and had rigged the 1936 elections against the center and right parties. They also charged that the Communist International, meaning the Soviet Union, had supplied arms to the Loyalists even before the war started.[11]

A group of Protestant clergy and laymen rebutted the Spanish prelates' letter with one of their own, published in the *Times* on October 4, 1937. A month earlier LaFarge himself had entered the epistolary fray, replying to a letter by Professor James T. Shotwell, a Columbia University historian, who stated that the "prelates have neither proved their case nor justified their own." Shotwell was especially disturbed that the Nationalists had sought military help from sources outside of Spain.[12] LaFarge defended Franco's use of non-Spanish military forces in his own letter to the *Times* a few days later.

> Dr. Shotwell asks what right have the bishops to call the war a plebiscite if the Nationalists employ the aid of foreign auxiliaries? Just where the logic in this argument lies is not plain. If a man may defend himself with his own gun, why may he not call on his neighbor to aid with the neighbor's gun? In their entire utterance the Bishops give no angle for suspicion that the acceptance of Moorish, Hitler or Italian military aid means the acceptance of Islamism or the Nazist or Fascist ideologies.[12]

The Protestant letter of October 4, which was heatedly attacked by Father Talbot, was also published in the *Times,* which by then had become a willing and major sounding board for both sides. Talbot, easily more rabidly pro-Franco than anyone else on the staff of *America,* charged that the letter "neither establishes the point that it proposes nor engenders faith in the honesty of its authors or signatories." Talbot went even further, suggesting that the Protestants repudiate their own position and adopt that of the Catholic Church.

> Protestant Christians of the United States, if they are to remain faithful to the principles of Christ, must repudiate the anti-Christ propaganda and practices of the Loyalist government, composed as it is of Communists, anarchists, syndicalists, and atheistic groups in Spain. By such an open letter published over their signatures, they foster atheism and agnosticism.[13]

Even *Commonweal,* noted as a liberal, mostly lay Catholic journal of opinion (also published in New York) took issue with the Protestants' letter. One of its editors, Father John J. O'Conner, accused the Protestants of being "thoroughly hoodwinked" in the matter.[14] *Commonweal* would later change its outlook on the war, much to the dismay and anger of *America's* editors, and would take an official stand of neutrality between the Nationalists and Loyalists—but this would not be until the summer of 1938, while LaFarge was still in Europe working on the papal encyclical.

Not to be outdone by the 150 Protestants who signed their letter, 175 Catholic clergy and laymen drew up their own letter, published in the *Times* on October 14. An article summarizing the Catholic letter appeared on the paper's front page, and the long letter itself was printed inside. The Catholics defended their pro-Franco position by predicting that if the Nationalists were defeated, the Loyalists would end democracy and set up a Soviet-type society, which they had been on the verge of doing when Franco landed at Cadiz with his army.

> Catholics are against war, and more especially against civil war. Catholics hate war, seek for its ultimate abolition, and insist that disputes be settled as far as is humanly possible by pacific means. But when war is brought to them, and when war is the only recourse against an oppressive minority in power, when there is no alternative between liberty and life, then Catholics, as did the Catholics of Spain, must save themselves from destruction and annihilation.[15]

Not all American Catholics, prominent or otherwise, endorsed the Nationalists. Despite the overwhelming support of the hierarchy, a surprising number of American Catholics favored the Loyalists. In a Gallup Poll taken near the end of the war, 39 percent favored Franco's side, but 30 percent sympathized with the Loyalists, despite three years of drum beating against them from the altar and from the Catholic media.[16]

Among prominent Catholic leaders, LaFarge, although less strident than some of his colleagues, was one of the most articulate and outspoken of Franco's supporters, both in print and in private correspondence. His letters and memos written during his half-year in Europe in 1938, while referring to numerous subjects and activities, are repeatedly punctuated with comments about the Spanish Civil War.

LaFarge landed at Plymouth, England, on May 2, 1938, at 5:30 in the afternoon. It was his first visit to Europe in over thirty years. From Plymouth he caught a train to Bristol, then on to Bath, where Robert

Wilberforce, husband of one of his cousins, met him at the station. The next day, in the company of Wilberforce, he toured that interesting and beautiful old Roman town. After another day of sightseeing he boarded the train for London. His first letter to Father Talbot, with whom he kept in regular touch during his tour, is dated May 7. During his few days in London he stayed at the Jesuit house on Farm Street.

> At Farm Street a more cordial welcome was waiting for me. On arrival I found a note from Father Woodlock, who soon came in, and was greeted at once by Father Keating. They were both eager to learn of everything at AMERICA, and talked over old times. Both have been doing everything conceivable to make my stay pleasant, as have indeed all concerned. It seems like an oasis of peace to be here after the hurried days before leaving and the long journey, although the stay at Bath was a great refresher.[17]

There was much English interest in the well-known Father LaFarge, and invitations to meet with him poured in. One of his visitors was Miss Annie O'Brien Christitch, a Serbian-Irish correspondent for *America* in Great Britain. She arranged for him to meet some members of the Catholic Council on International Relations. "They had intended to arrange a lecture for me," he wrote Talbot, "but my stay here is too short, and I am scheduled to speak in Paris on May 17." He was happy to report, though without explanation, that the "feeling about Spain is very strong, and now that the Loyalist regime is crumbling, more and more seems to come to light."[18]

Since LaFarge was planning a stopover in Czechoslovakia on his way to Hungary, Miss Christitch persuaded him to have lunch with Jan Masaryk, the Czech minister to Britain,and son of the famous, former prime minister of Czechoslovakia, Thomas Masaryk. In light of LaFarge's later recommending strict neutrality for the United States during and after the Munich crisis, it is instructive to read what he wrote Talbot about Czechoslovakia several months before it occurred.

Masaryk started the conversation by telling LaFarge of his concern about Hitler. He had argued for hours and hours with Lord Halifax, the British foreign minister, "saying to him that if only he would let me *know* where my country stands with Great Britain, I should then know how to act. If Great Britain is not going to support us, then I shall simply pack up my valise, take a trip to Berlin, and lay all my cards on the table before Hitler. The game will be up, and we shall simply take what Hitler

John LaFarge, Father LaFarge's father, about 1860.

John Frédéric de la Farge, Father LaFarge's paternal grandfather.

John and Margaret LaFarge, Father LaFarge's parents, and his aunt Aimée, his father's sister. Taken at the LaFarge family estate in Glen Cove, Long Island, New York, about 1863.

Father John LaFarge in 1891 (age eleven).

Father John LaFarge in 1888 (age eight).

Father John LaFarge in 1883 (age three).

Margaret LaFarge, Father LaFarge's sister.

Father John LaFarge's family home on Sunnyside Place, Newport, Rhode Island.

Bancel LaFarge, Father LaFarge's brother.

Mabel Hooper LaFarge in 1905. Married to Bancel, Father LaFarge's brother.

University Church, Innsbruck, where Father LaFarge was ordained in 1905.

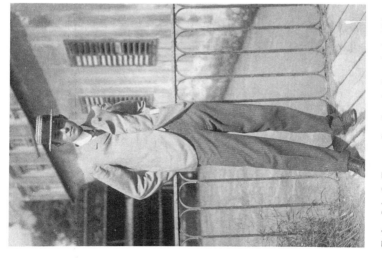

Father John LaFarge at Innsbruck, Austria, in 1901.

Father LaFarge's mother and sister at the family home in Newport, about 1906.

Father John LaFarge soon after his ordination in 1905.

St. Ignatius Church, St. Inigoes, Maryland (courtesy of Georgetown University Library).

Margaret Perry LaFarge, Father LaFarge's mother, about 1920.

chooses to leave us. . . ."[19] Masaryk very much wanted LaFarge to see for himself the situation in his country.

> Dr. Masaryk wanted me to see the President and the Prime Minister when I go to Prague, though I could not see what *I* could do about it all, and told him so. I guess, however, they are all so worried that they welcome anyone who can say a good word for them. He said that when I get to Prague a representative of the Govt. would call upon me and learn my wishes about any place I wanted to see. They have already given me a free pass over all the railways in Czechoslovakia and promised me an automobile to take me around the eastern part, if I wish to go. But I fear time will be too short for anything but a hurried glance at the land of Huss and St. John Nepomuk.[20]

LaFarge mentioned in his autobiography that during his luncheon with Masaryk he needled the Czech, as far as he could do so politely, on the mistreatment of Slovaks by the Czechs. He found Masaryk "extremely on the defensive" on that subject. After the abandonment of Czechoslovakia by Britain and France a few months later, LaFarge would repeat this point in an article calling for calm in the face of the German annexation of the Sudetenland, the western end of Czechoslovakia inhabited largely by German-speaking people. Somewhat incongruously, in the same article, he used the occasion of Munich, not to judge what had happened there, but to call for a "free Russia," who would help maintain stability in Eastern Europe. By a free Russia he of course meant one free of atheistic Communism.[21]

After about a week in England, LaFarge moved on to Paris, where he stayed at the Jesuit house at 15 rue Monsieur, headquarters of the French Jesuit magazine *Etudes,* more or less a French version of *America.* In his first letter to Talbot from Paris he explained that he was so recently arrived that he could report only a few general impressions. "One impression, however," he wrote, "I already have, as I had in London, that we need feel no anxiety as to our attitude on Spain, as long as we keep our eyes upon the main ball, which is the encouragement of the Spaniards in their resistance to the Reds."[22]

Two days later he added a postscript to Talbot that dealt almost solely with Spain. He gathered that sometime during the coming summer there would be a showdown "between the two elements that are difficult to reconcile in Nationalist Spain; the Traditionalists and the Falangists." He described the Falangists, an extreme faction of the Nationalist Party, as harboring ex-radicals on the one hand and German Nazis on the other. If the latter dominated the Nationalist ranks, then he feared the Spanish Church would be subjected to the same strongarm methods it was suffering under in Germany.

The Traditionalists, also part of the Nationalist party, who included a number of Monarchists, wanted to create a Catholic Corporate State. The hope of the Traditionalists, he wrote with obvious approval, "is to model the new Spain on the new Portugal, and to construct it on a federalist basis. While they would demand a uniform recognition of the Spanish language, the regional languages, such as Basque or Catalan, would be tolerated." As for Franco, his personal inspiration seemed to be the Portuguese leader Antonio Salazar, "whom he immensely admires." Franco had "with him the army, and it is through the sentiment of the army that he hopes to maintain the liberty of the Church in Spain." He reported that Franco had recently sought aid from France in a direct appeal to the French foreign minister Georges Bonnet.

> Franco recently made a powerful appeal to Georges Bonnet to stand with him and aid Spain. His argument was unique, and I think, very significant. It is, he said, to France's own interests to have a free and really Catholic Spain, and not a country which shall be at the mercy of Hitler and a breeding-ground for Hitlerite ideologies. Bonnet completely agreed with him; saw the logic of his arguments; but could do nothing, since he is dependent upon the Communists for his votes. Thence it comes about—as is evidently happening with regard to many other phases of the nearby international situation—that the Communists by their intransigence are playing into Hitler's hands.[23]

Except for Franco's impending victory in Spain, LaFarge could see few moral bright spots in the Europe he was surveying in the spring of 1938. Only the Church seemed to be holding to its principles. To him the Church was the "center of everything in Europe." Incredibly, there appeared to be a developing *rapprochement* between the German Nazis and the Soviet Communists. "Curiously enough," he wrote Talbot, "Jan Masaryk, the Czech Minister in London, told me he believed Hitler and Stalin would come to unite."[24] LaFarge was impressed with Masaryk's prediction (if not with Masaryk himself), and would pass it on when he returned to New York in the fall.

After one week in Paris LaFarge boarded a train for Germany, a journey he did not face with anticipation. At this point there is a three-week gap in his known correspondence with Talbot. He did, however, describe these three weeks in some detail in *The Manner Is Ordinary*. As his train approached the German border, he wrote, his "spirits at the same time sank correspondingly at the ever-nearing prospect of Hitlerland."[25] When the train did finally cross the German border at a town named Perl, there was only one passenger besides himself—"a sad looking Polish lady who was returning to her home country."[26]

At this point he had to switch trains. He descended to the platform and was told to go to the waiting room until a customs official checked his baggage.

> A couple of other gentlemen then appeared who viewed with suspicion a copy of *Portugal,* by Gonzaque de Reynold, but returned it to me after careful inspection. They then confiscated a little French travel book I had picked up on a walk and were disturbed because I carried an Italian grammar. They took it as evidence that I had been in Rome at the time Hitler was there. I explained that I was not *from* Rome but was *going* to Rome, and they let me pass. Only after I was again safely on the train did I recall that happily they had not spied the map of Czechoslovakia I had absent-mindedly taken with me in the satchel, the last thing you'd want to carry in visiting Hitler's Germany. Oddly enough, they paid no attention at all to my typewriter, which I had been lugging along.[27]

His first stop in Germany was Coblenz, in the Rhineland, where he was to stay with an old Innsbruck classmate he had not seen in decades, Reverend Doctor Heinrich Chardon, pastor of the Liebfrauenkirche. (He would briefly come back into Chardon's life after World War II when he revisited Coblenz.) It had rained during much of the train trip there, but by the time he reached Coblenz the sky had cleared. Chardon met him at the church door, since May devotions were just ending and parishioners were streaming out of the building. The pastor introduced LaFarge to some of his congregation, who were full of sympathy when he told them he had just come from Paris. They were incredulous that he had survived his stay there, since they had been told by the Nazi propaganda machine that the streets of Paris were running with blood, that there was a terrible revolution going on, and that people were being murdered by Jews and Bolsheviks. LaFarge assured them that the streets of Paris were not running with blood, and that calm and order prevailed in the city. When he said this one of the parishioners yelled " 'Potztausend!' meaning "Look at the stuff they have been handing out to us here."[28]

LaFarge found the deep, oppressive presence of the Nazi regime everywhere. Its control of the press and radio was nearly complete. The churches were still open, but had to toe the line or face retaliation. Each day the pastor and his curates had to fill out dozens of forms accounting for the movements of every member of the parish. One afternoon he was driven out into the countryside. In one village he "watched the Hitler Jugend, little kids marching in a listless, wooden fashion up and down in front of one of the old village churches, in charge of a pastyfaced young man who looked even more depressed."[29]

When LaFarge commented that the churches were allowed to hold services, he was told that Hitler permitted the churches to function for propaganda reasons. It made it seem abroad that Hitler loved religion. But any government official seen or filmed at a service or procession would receive a note a few days later informing him he was no longer employed. LaFarge was appalled at what he was seeing and hearing. "I was so used to the Germany of old, where you always engaged in conversation with your neighbor, that I could not get used to the averted glances and the silence that met you on any kind of conveyance, or to the tight-lipped, dead-pan SS guards on the city streets." It had become a society in the grip of totalitarianism. He feared greatly for the safety of his friends, whom he left behind a week later, to head for Prague. "It was with a heavy heart," he wrote, "that I purchased my ticket to Prague and said good-bye to Dr. Chardon on that May morning."[30]

When he arrived there on May 21 he found the people of Prague "in the midst of the general fear of an immediate German invasion."[31] The crisis atmosphere, however, temporarily abated during his brief stay. "The Republic remained upon the map that spring and summer," he wrote, "but fell from it like an autumn leaf when September blew its political gale. I am thankful that I saw Czechoslovakia at least once, before it passed from history as a free country."[32]

From Prague he went to Budapest, Hungary, to attend the International Eucharist Congress, his primary reason for coming to Europe in the first place. On the way he stopped at Bratislava, the homeland of his St. Mary's County Slavs, which reminded him of his interest in rural life. He found Budapest crowded with pilgrims. Fortunately, he was invited to stay at the villa home of old friends, the Baron and Baroness de Hédry. He found the Congress immensely interesting, but it also filled him with dark foreboding for the future.

> In view of the frightful events that followed in all eastern Europe, one can only look back with terrible nostalgia to those few magic

days of the Budapest Congress. A city and a nation, and delegates from many lands, poured out their hearts in solemn adoration to the Eucharistic King, with all the dignity and splendor they could muster. Ominous presage of the future was Hitler's forbidding all Germans and Austrians to attend. One sensed the gathering background of totalitarian hate during the mysterious night procession, when the Papal Legate, Cardinal Pacelli, later Pope Pius XII, carried the Sacred Host in a spotlighted glass chamber at the prow of a steamer swiftly moving down the dark Danube and symbolically limned against the huge mass of Buda's mighty rock.[33]

Posting his article on the Congress to Father Talbot, he left Budapest on May 31 heading for Rome, but first passing through Yugoslavia. Stopping briefly at Zagreb and Ljubljana, he entered Italy via Trieste and Venice, a city he had last visited thirty-four years before when he was still a student at Innsbruck, and where he had been shown around by the two Scots ladies. He wrote Talbot about his stay in Yugoslavia.

One passage through the Reich was enough for me, greatly as I longed to see Innsbruck and Vienna. On the other hand, I have always wanted to see Yugoslavia, and judged if I missed this chance it would not return. The choice was amply rewarded. I spent a couple of days in Zagreb and a night in Ljubljana (Laibach). They are wonderful old places, full of curious bits of past history and of Jesuit glory in the olden days, as well as a most interesting people. They don't get many U.S. visitors, and were bubbling over with questions. Father Poglajen, editor of the Jesuit monthly *Zivot*, is one of their biggest young men, and expects to come to New York next year. He has a keen mind and is a regular fellow.

That the city of Ljubljana is habitable—for much of it is built in a former marsh below the surrounding hillside—is due to the famous Fr. Gruber, who was professor there in the olden days, and constructed the canals, the Gruber canals, which drain the city. Later he became General of the Society in Russia, as all well know from the familiar portraits.[34]

He reached Rome on Saturday night, June 5. While there he stayed with the Jesuit Fathers at the Fondamenta Nuove. A priest from his own province in New York, Father John J. Killeen, S.J., was living there at the time. He offered to guide LaFarge through the labyrinth of Rome during his stay.

On Monday he visited Father General Ledochowski. He wrote Talbot about the meeting the next day. "Monday Father Rector here took me to the Curia, where I first saw Father Maher and Father Killeen. Father General then received me, and talked to me for nearly an hour." This, of course, was before either man could know that LaFarge would soon be assigned the task of writing the encyclical on racism. At this first meeting LaFarge was somewhat in awe of Ledochowski. "It was fortunately one of his good days," he wrote Talbot, "and he was most lively and spoke most entertainingly and has the wonderful gift of making you feel at once entirely comfortable and at ease. Indeed, I had to pinch myself a few times to realize that I actually *was* talking to the A.R.P.N. [Superior General of the Society of Jesus] himself, the object of so many consultors' letters and generally for us such a mysterious figure."[35]

During the conversation Ledochowski strongly urged LaFarge to visit Spain on the way back to Paris. LaFarge immediately wrote Talbot requesting permission to go, explaining that he could make a short visit there "without great inconvenience and practically without cost. Bernard Fay, who is one of the leaders of the pro-Franco group in France, has offered to motor me to Santander in July, for a meeting which is to be held there, which he believes will be of great interest."[36]

At this point LaFarge knew nothing about the encyclical. When he was finally given the assignment there was no time to go to Spain. He had to start working on "*Humani Generis Unitas*" as soon as possible. The war in Spain, however, continued to claim much of his attention.

After three momentous weeks in Rome, culminating in the meeting with Pope Pius XI, he headed for Paris, with a brief stop in Geneva on the way. Back in the French capital he found his "French friends in a state of political optimism. As for Hitler, they explained to me, there was really nothing to worry about. France, I learned, was amply protected by that wonderful institution called the Maginot Line."[37]

On June 24, LaFarge and *America* were stunned and furious when *Commonweal,* an early supporter of Franco, shook up its editorial staff and decided to declare a policy of neutrality on the Spanish Civil War. An editorial in *America,* probably written by Talbot, berated *Commonweal* for its change in position, and renewed its support for Franco.

> . . . the solutions offered by General Franco and the Nationalists are immeasurably superior to the solutions offered by Señor Negrun, his predecessors, and the Loyalists of the future, if any remain. . . . It is an established fact that the leftist factions, since the establish-

ment of the Spanish Republic, were being driven toward a Social-
ist state as a transitional approach to a Soviet state.[38]

As for LaFarge, it is fair to say he was becoming obsessed with the
war in Spain. In early July he started drafting an article that would be
published in *America* at the end of August. As usual, his major concern
was the stake the Church had in Franco. The draft version follows the
printed version closely, but was written about six weeks earlier.

> At the present time, General Franco is endeavoring to restore order
> in Spain. Critics of Franco point to grave abuses, to serious injus-
> tices, committed in this process of restoring order. Some evidence
> of this sort of thing has been submitted to me already, for whatever
> it may be worth; if I hear more of the same kind I shall not be sur-
> prised. Even such peaceful affairs as schools and parishes are lit-
> tered with memories of injustices committed by good men, teach-
> ers and parish priests, who tried to restore order when order was
> needed. The memory of such injustices remains, sometimes rankles
> ineffaceably. The very nature of the Communist assault is such, in
> its diabolical ingenuity, that it arouses such frantic hatreds, such fu-
> rious resentments, that any reaction against those assaults is apt to
> go to extremes. Add to this the temperament of a people whose
> range of emotions, like those of medieval man, range over a much
> wider gamut than those of the northern and soberer races.[39]

In the last sentence quoted above he implied that southern Europeans
are more emotional than northern Europeans, a dubious proposition, especially in light of the terrible bloodletting of World War II, fought mainly in Europe's northern regions. Admittedly, LaFarge agreed, Franco was
no angel, nor were some of his henchmen. But he was striving to restore
order in Spain. In fact, he was "the only force for order in Spain at the
present time."[40]

As for the charge that he was getting help from Hitler and Mussolini,
that did not mean he would steer Spain in the direction of a totalitarian,
anti-Christian state. He had not "sold out to the 'totes,' " as some tourists
who had visited Nationalist Spain had recently claimed.

Little by little, he believed, the voice of reason about Franco was being heard in France.

> One by one leading men are making clear that you can see good in
> Franco; that you can endorse the essential soundness of his posi-
> tion; that you can, as you must in all reason, admit the necessity and

to say legitimacy of an act of self-defense for Spain's Catholics, menaced in July, 1936 with the total destruction of their nation without thereby being an emissary of Mussolini or Hitler.[41]

The article was published in *America* on August 20. Talbot called it "one of the finest statements that we have yet had and it will completely collapse the 'Commonweal.' " He reported to LaFarge that *Commonweal* was "suffering greatly because of its neutrality editorial. They were violently attacked by practically every Catholic paper, but the harm was done to the Catholic cause, since they had been quoted with favor by the liberal non-Catholic papers."[42]

Before returning to America LaFarge made one more trip to Rome, ostensibly to consult with Father General Ledochowski about "some of the social and political developments I had investigated."[43] In reality, as indicated in the previous chapter, he was hand delivering the encyclical. The father general had offered to let him return to New York from Paris. It was LaFarge who insisted on taking the document to Rome himself. He arrived in Rome on September 20, returned to Paris a few weeks later, and headed back to America on October 15.

While in Rome for the second time that year he heard (on the radio in the Jesuit residence where he was staying) the speech delivered by Hitler in the Sportspalast, attacking Czechoslovakia in general, and Prime Minister Eduard Benes in particular. Years later he recalled how his "bones quaked" at the sound of Hitler's "frantic screams of fanaticism, and the crowd's roar of 'Sieg Heil! Sieg Heil!' " Over and over the voice rose and fell in volume. He called the speech a "rhythm of passion." In retrospect he saw in the shouting the impending voice of war.[44]

The war, however, did not come until a year later. LaFarge's concern that fall was getting aboard a ship before it broke out, as it seemed it might do any day over Germany's demands on Czechoslovakia, and the possibility that Britain and France might fight Germany to save that small country. Back in Paris he nervously awaited the outcome of the Munich Conference that might decide for peace or war. One afternoon, while sitting with some Jesuits in their recreation room, the telephone rang in the next room, the office of the superior. A few minutes later the superior told them there would be no war. " 'M. Daladier and M. Chamberlain have conferred with Hitler and Mussolini in Munich and all will be well.' " "My passage home," he wrote, "was now assured."[45]

The deal among the four leaders gave Hitler the green light to dismember Czechoslovakia, starting with the immediate annexation of the

Sudetenland, then, on March 15, 1939, most of the rest of the country. Hungary and Poland took the opportunity to seize some disputed lands from the hapless and abandoned Czechs, and the Slovaks were persuaded by Hitler to proclaim an independent Slovak Republic. Czechoslovakia disappeared as a nation from the map of Europe as quickly as it had appeared after the First World War.

LaFarge had nothing to say about the Munich crisis in *America*, but the magazine did run a short piece on its "Comments" page that called war in Europe over the Sudetenland an unjust war. "Not one of the nations involved in the dispute had a clear right to fight. The aggression of Hitler, taken in terms of the future, might constitute a basis for a future just war of defense on the part of certain nations. But the extent of these aggressions to date, though menacing, though condemnable, though sufficient to arouse the most intense anger, would not justify the resort to arms on the part of any nation."[46]

LaFarge summed up his six months in Europe and his return home in *The Manner Is Ordinary*.

> The steerage trip back to New York was anything but comfortable, especially as I was not a good sailor; but this was made up for by the greetings on my return. Shortly after my arrival in New York I attended a welcome dinner where I prophesied that Hitler and Stalin would get together in the not too distant future. All my studies that summer and my conversations had convinced me of the complete compatibility of Nazism and Communism, and the prophecy was thoroughly borne out by the Ribbentrop-Molotov pact. My trip to Europe had cost me thirty pounds in weight, which probably I could miss, and a rich harvest of experience. It afforded me a copious background for the understanding of the years that were to become a tragic part of the world's history.[47]

By the early weeks of 1939, it was becoming evident that the Nationalists were going to win the Spanish Civil War. *America* stood on the sidelines, none too quietly cheering Franco on, clearly delighted with his impending victory. The titles of articles appearing in the magazine reflected its partisanship. On January 28, for example, C. F. Carsley published one titled "Democracy in Spain under the Hammer and Sickle."[48] In February Gault Macgowan wrote, "Festering Barcelona as the Stooge of Stalin."[49] When Franco finally triumphed *America* called for his immediate diplomatic recognition by the United States government. On April 1, Joseph B. Code published "The New Spain Merits—Demands

Recognition by the United States."[50] And on May 20, *America* printed Daniel Sargent's "Madrid: The City That Was Drugged."[51]

Years after Franco had installed a repressive regime in Spain, LaFarge maintained that he, *America,* and the American Catholic press and hierarchy had done the right thing in supporting him. Writing in his autobiography in 1954 he did acknowledge "that there were certain political problems in Spain," but he was optimistic that the Spaniards could work these out by themselves.[52]

As for the Spanish Church, it did indeed prosper under Franco, who restored both its privileges and its properties. Civil marriages, for example, had to be repeated in church to be valid. The Church was given a key part in education and had the right to censor literature. It was also given a large, tax-free subsidy from the State. Under the Concordat of 1953, the Catholic Church was declared the only recognized religion in Spain. This was a long way from the days of the "anticlerical fury."

All this had come at a fearful cost to the Spanish people. While the often quoted figure of a million deaths as a result of the war is probably inflated, the number six hundred thousand was calculated by Hugh Thomas in his history of that war. He estimated that three hundred twenty thousand died in battle on both sides, about two hundred twenty thousand from disease, perhaps another one hundred thousand by murder and execution. The executions continued after the war ended, with accused Loyalists being shot nearly every day in such cities as Madrid, Barcelona, and Seville.[53]

Had the Loyalists won, the Church certainly would have suffered, and probably suffered badly. On the strict grounds of survival and self-interest the Church and LaFarge were no doubt right in supporting Franco during the war. To continue supporting him after he installed one of the more repressive regimes in modern times is another matter. In the years ahead LaFarge and *America* would occasionally criticize Franco for some of his political excesses, but they would never really abandon him.

Chapter 9

The Catholic Interracial Movement

Father John LaFarge is best known, and rightly so, for his leadership in the Catholic interracial movement. From the time he came to *America* in 1926, until his death in 1963, he devoted more of his time and effort to the movement than to any other cause. Historically, his most important single contribution was the founding of the Catholic Interracial Council of New York (CICNY) in 1934. In the long run, however, it was his continual, almost day-by-day picking away at racism in America that far exceeded the memorable founding of CICNY.

In writing portions of this chapter the author has utilized two doctoral dissertations about LaFarge and the interracial movement. The first is by Marilyn Wenzke Nickels, "The Federated Colored Catholics: A Study of Three Variant Perspectives on Racial Justice As Represented by John LaFarge, William Markoe, and Thomas Turner," completed in 1975 for the Catholic University of America. The second is Martin Adam Zielinski, " 'Doing The Truth' ": The Catholic Interracial Council of New York, 1945–1965," also written for Catholic University. It was completed in 1988.

LaFarge explained that the CICNY emerged from two principal sources—the Cardinal Gibbons Institute in Maryland and the Catholic Laymen's Union (CLU) in New York.[1] LaFarge was the major force behind each of these groups. The Cardinal Gibbons Institute, as mentioned earlier, had started initially as a Catholic industrial arts school for black boys. Most of the money to build the school, and a boys dormitory, came from the Knights of Columbus. LaFarge called it the "first national project undertaken by Catholics on behalf of the Negro."[2] Dedicated on October 26, 1924, the school struggled to stay alive from its very inception. Unfortunately, through a combination of administrative failures, and the onset of the Great Depression following the stock market crash in 1929, it was forced to close as a boarding school on December 31, 1933, although it did reopen as a day school in 1936.

While disappointed that his hopes for the school were not fully realized, LaFarge did see some good coming from the effort. He wrote of this in *The Manner Is Ordinary*.

> Finally, the extraordinary amount of hard work and close thinking that had gone into the problem of keeping the Institute alive were turned into channels that were undoubtedly not picturesque and not as immediately and physically tangible as a school, but in the long run would open the door of opportunity not only to the colored boys and girls in Southern Maryland but advance the whole situation of the Negro and other racial groups in the United States. From this point of view the Institute was emphatically not a failure but was, as I see it, a predestined seed ground for the development of the Catholic interracial movement in the United States.[3]

One reason LaFarge expressed optimism despite the failure of the institute, was the fact that the board of directors of the school was multi-racial. One of the directors, Dr. Thomas Wyatt Turner, taught biology at Howard University in Washington, D.C. Turner was also president of the Federated Colored Catholics of the United States (FCC), one of whose purposes was to support the Cardinal Gibbons Institute. Another was "to promote the cause of Catholic education among the black population, and to raise the status of black Catholics in the Church."[4]

As was the case with some other black Catholics, Turner felt that not enough was being done to bring blacks into the faith, or to make them feel comfortable when they did come in. LaFarge strongly agreed with Turner on this point. From the time of emancipation of the slaves, until well into the twentieth century, the Catholic Church had moved only slowly in attacking racial discrimination. In 1868 in Baltimore, a Church council did express sympathy for blacks, but only for their spiritual condition. The council called for more priests to go into the South to work among blacks, but few answered the call. Much more attention was being paid during the closing decades of the nineteenth century to Catholic immigrants from Europe—Poles, Irish, Italians, and Germans.

Further Catholic attempts were made in future years to help blacks, mainly in educational and spiritual matters, but little was attempted to end racial discrimination. Jim-Crow laws were strongly enforced throughout the South, and even in some parts of the Midwest. *Brown v. Board of Education* in 1954, for example, ordered an end to school segregation in

Topeka, Kansas. When LaFarge put in his years in southern Maryland, segregation was still part and parcel of the social scene. He deplored it, but found his hands tied when it came to making changes.

Not until 1919 did the American bishops, in a pastoral letter, condemn racial hatred, but not racial segregation. In 1943 the bishops did issue a statement calling for improved economic, educational, and housing opportunities for blacks. But it was not until 1958, four years after the *Brown* decision, that the bishops, as a group, finally condemned racial segregation. Not until five years before his death, therefore, did LaFarge have the imprimatur of the American bishops for the work he had been doing for several decades.

Individual bishops had occasionally raised their voices and pens to condemn racism. Archbishop John Ireland of St. Paul, Minnesota delivered a sermon attacking it in 1891. Other bishops spoke out before and between the two world wars. Some priests made known their opposition to racism and segregation. According to Father Stanton, however, of all these men "LaFarge was, without question, the most productive writer and the most energetic and effective organizer of programs calculated to enable Negroes and whites to live in harmony with each other.[5]

While working on his dissertation about LaFarge, Stanton communicated with Roy Wilkins, then executive director of the National Association for the Advancement of Colored People. An excerpt of this letter appears in his dissertation. The letter speaks for itself.

> No one who worked with the late Father John LaFarge will ever forget the man. He chose for his special project the improvement of race relations by means of the application of the tenets of religion to specific situations. . . . Some of us went to speak informally and to confer at the New York meetings of the Council. We came to speak, but we stayed to learn at the feet of this selfless man. The meetings became valuable to us personally. He was not one to pray and preach and trust to a later harvest. Meticulously he ran down all the threads. He sought understanding of the complex factors in race relations. . . . He left his imprint indelibly on the pattern of race over the nation. . . . He was unquestionably ahead of his time. His church and his Society of Jesus can thank him for his prescience, for it placed those who heeded him in the vanguard of the army of change in present-day race relations concepts.[6]

In addition to attacking racism and segregation, LaFarge was also ahead of most of his colleagues in the Church in pushing for black con-

verts to the faith. To his occasional dismay, he saw the Church dragging
its feet in this area as well. Writing in 1989, the black bishop John Ruard reflected on this situation, which he felt had not changed much during the last century or so.

> American Blacks did not take to Catholicism earlier for a very good
> reason. John LaFarge, the Jesuit historian who wrote in the 1920's
> and 30's, and whose work is still around, said the reason we have
> so few black Catholics is *not* that any deliberate effort was made to
> keep them out. In the early years in America, the Catholic Church
> was an immigrant church and concerned mainly with European im-
> migrants, protecting the faith of immigrants, fighting the onslaught
> of Protestantism, which saw them as a foreign invasion. There was
> little time or energy to think of the Blacks. More precisely, Father
> LaFarge said, no bold or innovative steps were made to invite
> Blacks in.[7]

LaFarge's initial approval of Turner's FCC stemmed in part from his
feeling that the organization would seek and make converts. The FCC had
its beginning in 1917, when Turner invited some of his black Catholic
friends to his home in Washington, D.C. They met specifically to discuss
the role of blacks in the Catholic Church. By 1919, after numerous meetings and discussions, a "Committee for the Advancement of Colored
Catholics" had been formed. This committee eventually evolved into a national organization. It was fully endorsed by Bishop Emmett Walsh of
Charleston, South Carolina, who was also secretary of the National
Catholic Welfare Conference. LaFarge belonged to this group, as well as
the Northeastern Clergy Conference on Negro Welfare. His anti-racism
tentacles were spreading far and wide.

The FCC held its conventions in different cities. The earliest included
New York, Cincinnati, and Baltimore. At the fifth annual convention in
Baltimore at the end of August and early September, 1929, a young Jesuit priest from St. Louis, Fr. William Markoe, S.J., pastor of St. Elizabeth parish in that city, offered its newsletter to the FCC as its official
journal. The offer was quickly accepted and the journal was named the
Chronicle, with Markoe as its first editor.

Despite its early and rapid growth as a predominantly black organization, the FCC did not come close to achieving its goal of black equality
in the United States. LaFarge blamed the federation for this failure since
it did not seek more support and membership from the non-Negro population, nor did it do much to bring more blacks into the Catholic Church.

LaFarge made this criticism in his 1956 book *The Catholic Viewpoint on Race Relations.*

> Year after year, at the Federation's conventions, eloquent speakers renewed their demands for recognition and protested against manifest injustices and discriminations. Church authorities, high and low, were repeatedly called upon for redress. But the tone remained one of demand, and the more repeatedly the demands were uttered, the less attention and interest did they create. As one prominent member of the organization commented: "We spent a great deal of money, time and energy talking *about* people whom we should have been talking *to*." In spite of good intentions, the net effect of Negro solidarity proved to be a tremendous obstacle to integration in Catholic life. A separatist organization was not in a very strategic position to protest against separatism.[8]

LaFarge felt very strongly about bringing blacks into the Church. Conversion, along with education, were among his main solutions to the race problem. His successful efforts to organize the CICNY in 1934 were in accord with his thinking. Mixed race organizations were necessary to educate both whites and blacks on the harm to everyone of racial prejudice. Before racism could be ended, attitudes, and especially white attitudes, had to change. This could not happen if the races were kept apart from each other. He had put up with segregation in Catholic schools in Maryland, but by the time he reached New York in 1926 he was ready to roll up his sleeves and push for integration in all the institutions of the Catholic Church.

Not all black leaders agreed that interracial groups were needed, including Turner, who steadfastly argued that blacks were better off in all-black organizations. His own FCC split on the issue, causing dissension and hard feelings.

On September 3, 1932, four thousand black Catholics attended mass at St. Patrick's Cathedral in New York, after which they held their eighth annual meeting of the FCC. Before the meeting ended, Turner had reluctantly agreed to change its name to the National Catholic Federation for the Promotion of Better Race Relations. Father Markoe informed Turner two weeks later that the *Chronicle* was to be renamed the *Interracial Review*. He had no compunctions about doing this since his order owned the publication. According to Nickels in her dissertation on the FCC, "Markoe had initiated a controversy which was to split the Federation permanently. The old Federated Colored Catholics of the East and the new National Catholic Interracial Federation of the Midwest both lost momentum and eventually disappeared. Only the future Catholic Interracial Council of New York, under the leadership of Father LaFarge and composed of several members of the older Federation, was to survive into the present, publicized in the pages of the new *Interracial Review*.[9]

The collapse of the FCC gave LaFarge his chance to construct a new interracial group, which would bring blacks and whites together under the same organizational roof. He was much assisted in this by the Catholic Laymen's Union (CLU), which he had helped organize several years earlier. It consisted of twenty-five black business and professional men in New York.[10] LaFarge was the group's chaplain and mentor. Other organizations also helped, including the executive committee of the Cardinal Gibbons Institute, headquartered in New York. Although the institute had temporarily closed its doors at the end of 1933, its executive committee was still in place and could go to work immediately for the CICNY.

Of special help to LaFarge was the institute's executive secretary, George K. Hunton, who moved over to become executive secretary of the CICNY. According to LaFarge, Hunton did yeoman service for the council. In 1945, while submitting Hunton's name to New York Governor Thomas E. Dewey as a possible appointee to a new state anti-discrimination committee, he wrote the governor "Mr. Hunton is a member of the New York Bar, a graduate of Holy Cross College and a man of unimpeachable integrity and reputation for his prudence, his ability and his great adaptability in meeting difficult and intricate situations in the racial field."[11]

Hunton was indeed a major figure in interracial activities. In her dissertation Nickels wrote that Hunton's "years with the Catholic Interracial Council are a legend all their own."[12] An important source of information about LaFarge and the council are Hunton's memoirs.[13] Shortly after LaFarge's death Hunton reminisced to the writer Walter G. Murphy about his longtime friend and colleague. He recalled "that he, Father LaFarge, and other leaders of the interracial movement were derisively known as the 'flag wavers on Vesey St.,' the site of the council's old headquarters in lower Manhattan."[14]

Hunton credited LaFarge for his own newfound interest in racial problems. In 1955, on the occasion of LaFarge's fiftieth anniversary of his ordination, Hunton wrote that he first met LaFarge in late August 1931, when he was being considered for the post of executive secretary of the Cardinal Gibbons Institute. Until then he had little interest in, or knowledge of, blacks. He left the meeting "completely changed in attitude, convinced by the persuasive, hopeful and challenging picture that this great priest had painted."[15]

With the agreement of Father Markoe, Hunton took over the editorship of the *Interracial Review* in early 1934. At the same time publication of the journal was transferred from St. Louis to New York. "From a lowly parish chronicle," LaFarge wrote with considerable satisfaction, "it had developed into a monthly magazine of distinctive character and general national interest."[16]

On Pentecost Sunday, 1934, the Catholic Laymen's Union sponsored an interracial mass-meeting in New York's Town Hall. More than six hundred people, about evenly divided between blacks and whites, attended. Prominent clergy and laymen were there, including the editors of *Catholic World* and *Commonweal,* members of the Cardinal Gibbons Institute board, and Msgr. Michael J. Lavelle, representing Cardinal Hayes, archbishop of the New York archdiocese. Out of this meeting arose the Catholic Interracial Council of New York. In accord with LaFarge's thinking on bettering relations between the races, its board members included both blacks and whites. By 1963, thanks largely to the efforts of Hunton, there were sixty additional councils in cities throughout the United States, including those in such Southern states as Virginia, North and South Carolina, Texas and Louisiana.

In his dissertation on the CICNY, Zielinski wrote of the goals of the council and its principal organ, the *Interracial Review.* All the members of the review were also members of CICNY, so there was no conflict or cross purposes among them. According to Zielinski, one goal of the journal was educating the laity, "which reflected the thinking of LaFarge. Rather than subscribing to the theory that racial tension was the result of prejudice, LaFarge thought that tension could be traced in many instances to ignorance."[17]

Writing to a missionary priest in 1942, LaFarge emphasized this aspect of "what we call the Interracial Program, from the very strict sense of the word, and that is the type of work which I am directly interested in promoting. This work is directed systematically against race prejudice. It is an educational work aiming at the white people and operating by the usual means of an educational program. It is directed at the clergy over the heads of the laity who receive the direct impact."[18]

Another aim was interracial justice as part of social justice. In the October 1934 issue of *Interracial Review* LaFarge included social justice in the larger concept of Catholic Action.[19] There was a third theme that ran through the CICNY program. Again, quoting Zielinski, "This was the strong anti-communist stance which both John LaFarge, the CICNY, and the *Interracial Review* maintained throughout their history."[20]

LaFarge worried a great deal about Communist inroads among American blacks. Acts of racial injustice gave the Communists opportunities to falsely pose as protectors of blacks. "Communist civil rights agitation is a perfect means of capitalizing upon certain types of human misery," he wrote in *The Manner Is Ordinary,* "but its goal is not to secure civil rights for the Negro or for anyone else. It aims simply at exciting greater and greater bitterness and confusion, until a situation is created where the Communist party can step in and take charge."[21]

As an example he referred to the Scottsboro case in 1931, involving nine young black men falsely accused of raping two white women in Alabama. The Communists moved in quickly, raising large sums of money, "so that the case could be used as a powerful instrument for world-revolutionary propaganda."[22] Not only could they use the episode to propagandize, but in openly associating themselves with the young men, they were inhibiting their chances of acquittal. ". . . all available sources of information," he wrote on December 13, 1935, "confirm my belief that the temper of the Alabama courts, juries, and people is such that the boys' chances of freedom is [sic] utterly destroyed if those sponsoring them are suspected to be in any way affiliated with the Communists, or sympathetic to the Communist cause."[23]

While most educated blacks rejected Communism, the Communists especially went after blacks because, as a downtrodden minority, they were vulnerable. "But the Negro group," he wrote in the *Interracial Review* in March 1936, "whether in this city or throughout the United States at large, is judged by the Communists to be such a fertile field for the very reason that the colored people are for the most part at the bottom of the social scale."[24]

Communism, to be successfully thwarted on every level, he wrote to a fellow Jesuit in April 1936, "required greater social justice for all groups." In fact, the best and "only practical way to fight Communism was by removing from our society the inequalities and exploitations and injustices which make it possible for Communists to agitate. But for this it is necessary for us to have a well-defined philosophy of our own on all the fields in which we meet Communism. . . . Consequently, the first step to be taken in our opposition to Communism, is to have something concrete to oppose to it. This we look for in Revelation, and in the Encyclicals of the Pope."[25]

The two most important encyclicals were those of Leo XIII, *Rerum Novarum,* "On the Condition of the Working Man," and Pius XI's *Quadragesimo Anno,* "On the Reconstruction of the Social Order," issued in 1931. Pius XI, he wrote, "was solicitous not only for remedial charity but also for preventive charity." Help must come before the poorer classes turn to Communism, not after.[26]

Eliminating injustices against blacks, therefore, would serve the dual purpose of improving their lives and keeping Communism at bay. For good or for ill, much of LaFarge's thinking on social justice was closely entwined with the issue of Communism, which he considered a major, deadly atheistic enemy of the Church.

The CICNY aided black college students, presumably the black leaders of the future. LaFarge was distressingly aware, however, that several Catholic colleges and universities, including Fordham, Holy Cross, Georgetown and Notre Dame refused to admit black students. In 1934 he had a bitter experience with Fordham University in the Bronx, a Jesuit institution, when it turned down a black applicant, Hudson J. Oliver, Jr. Oliver had recently graduated from St. Francis Xavier High School in New York, also Jesuit run. His father was a doctor, and served as president of the CICNY. Both his parents were converts to Roman Catholicism. "They are," LaFarge wrote to the father provincial at Fordham, "people of the highest education. Mrs. Oliver is one of the four or five most educated and influential colored women in New York City; and entirely white in appearance. The boy is almost white and can easily pass as such."

The younger Oliver had applied to Fordham for admission, but was told that his application would have to be reviewed by a committee. LaFarge investigated and learned from the college registrar that his application had been rejected. "No reason, I am informed, is being offered." LaFarge was outraged, and expressed his anger to the father general of the university. For him it was a most uncharacteristic outburst.

> No possible explanation can be given to his parents for this inconceivable conduct on the part of the Fordham authorities. If it were in the South, it would be another matter. If it were even the border cities, such as Baltimore or Washington, there would be some plea on the part of "custom." But there is none such here. Columbia, N.Y.U., C.C.N.Y., etc. take colored students. Not many apply: but there are some. Yet his parents are convinced: a) that a Catholic education is a sacred duty: b) that the boy will lose his faith and morals if he goes to a secular school. He will; they practically

invariably do, i.e. the colored, because they are preyed upon intellectually by communists and atheists.

In LaFarge's opinion the reverend rector of Fordham had "committed
a very grave mortal sin." He threatened to "denounce Fordham in public, either in word or writing, or both." If he did not, he must abandon all
his "colored work forever," for blacks would pay no further attention to
him. This would end most of his usefulness among them.[27]

Generally LaFarge was cautious in his open attacks on segregation. Father George H. Dunne, S.J., in his 1990 autobiography *King's Pawn*, criticized LaFarge for his restraint. Dunne claimed for himself the credit for
being the first person in the order to label segregation sinful in print. In
1945, over the objections of other Jesuit priests, he published an article
in *Commonweal* titled "The Sin of Segregation." He compared his own
boldness and courage in publishing this article with LaFarge's prudence.

> Its publication marked a milestone in the struggle for complete
> emancipation of the blacks. It was the first time anyone had bluntly
> labeled segregation sinful. Fr. John LaFarge, for example, who was
> properly recognized for his efforts in support of the black people in
> this country, had argued in favor of desegregation, but always on
> the grounds of expediency. A "prudent" man, he stopped short of
> calling segregation what he privately admitted it was—heresy. I ar-
> gued that segregation was not only an offense against democracy,
> it was also an offense against God.[28]

Technically, Dunne was right. As early as 1934, however, in the Fordham case, LaFarge did equate segregation with sin, at least in the case of
a Catholic university. Dunne was a well-known, outspoken maverick.
But unlike LaFarge, he was not responsible for running a large interracial society. LaFarge, although equally fervent, had to be more circumspect in his public statements. While Dunne, or someone like Dunne,
might consider him overly restrained, LaFarge had to accent the honey
over the vinegar approach. Considering his achievements in the field of
civil rights it is hard to fault him on this.

LaFarge, had, in fact, openly condemned racism as immoral earlier
than Dunne, as shown in his 1937 book *Interracial Justice*. It was his ultimate argument against its practice. Seven years later the Swedish soci-
ologist Gunnar Myrdal published his epic study of American racism, *An
American Dilemma*. LaFarge reviewed the book for *America* in February 1944.

Overall it was a favorable review, but he did have some fundamental criticisms. One was his objection to Myrdal's suggestion that birth control might be practiced to alleviate some of the problems caused by racism. LaFarge opposed birth control under any and all circumstances. He was also disturbed that of the fifty-three people who contributed to the study not one was a Catholic. Finally, he was piqued that Myrdal made not one mention of the Catholic interracial movement.

He agreed, however, with Myrdal's central thesis that the dilemma was the discrepancy between the American creed and its practice. Both men saw this as a moral issue, with LaFarge stressing its religious nature and Myrdal seeing it as a violation of America's guiding political philosophy.[29]

It is not known whether LaFarge carried out his threat to publicly denounce Fordham for turning down a black applicant. It is unlikely that he did so. What is known is that Hudson Oliver, Jr. was not admitted, nor were any other blacks until several years later. Father Frank Carnavon, S.J., who attended Fordham from 1935 to 1939, remembers no blacks in the college during those years. He recalled, in fact, an incident in the spring of 1939, when it was suggested to the graduating class that some surplus class funds be used to establish a scholarship for a black Catholic student. The class voted the motion down. According to Carnavon, it was not until sometime during or shortly after World War II that blacks were admitted to Fordham.[30]

While exclusion of blacks from some Catholic institutions of higher learning would continue for awhile, one such institution, the College of the Sacred Heart, Manhattanville, then in New York City, but now in Purchase, New York, took a bold stand against segregation in the spring of 1933. Under the leadership of its president, Mother Grace Dammann, R.S.C.J., the student body at the college drew up an eight point resolution attacking racism against blacks. These soon came to be called the Manhattanville Resolutions.

The all-female student body had been aroused that spring by a series of talks by George Hunton, who was still executive secretary of the Cardinal Gibbons Institute. He lectured on Catholic social action and civic responsibility. The resolutions were drawn up by three students at the college, then thoroughly debated by the entire student body. They were adopted at a meeting of the college's Catholic Action Forum on May 3, 1933. They included resolves to "maintain that the Negro as a human being and as a citizen is entitled to the rights of life, liberty and the pursuit of happiness . . .To be courteous and kind to every colored person, remembering the heavy yoke of injustice and discrimination he is bearing. . .Not to speak slightingly or use nicknames which tend to humiliate, offend, or discourage him." The students also resolved to remember that blacks are members of the Mystical Body of Christ. In the last resolution they promised to "become increasingly active in some form of Catholic Action looking to the betterment of his condition, spiritually and materially."[31]

While coming across as somewhat naive and patronizing when read today, the Manhattan Resolutions were a sincere and honest attempt by a group of Catholic college women to do something about racism against blacks. LaFarge was well aware of the resolutions, since he had been closely advising Mother Dammann on the matter. He probably had a strong hand in framing them. It is not surprising, therefore, that *America* quickly and enthusiastically endorsed them in its issue of June 10, 1933.

> If the spirit in which these noble resolutions were conceived becomes prevalent among the younger generations of Catholics in this country, the most difficult of America's problems will be solved. Best of all, it will be solved on the only lasting basis, that of true social justice.[32]

Despite Manhattanville's "noble resolutions," however, the college did not admit its first black student until 1939 or 1940. She was readily accepted by her white classmates, but a storm of protest arose from the alumni. Mary LaFarge, wife of one of LaFarge's nephews, was attending the college at the time. She remembers that some of the protests were "vicious in tone." She also remembers that they died down rather quickly.[33]

Ironically, the third annual meeting of the CICNY in April 1937 was held at Fordham, still several years away from accepting blacks in its own student body. Twelve Catholic colleges and universities sent student delegates, all of whom were white. By this time a college program had been drawn up by the CICNY. One point in this program called for the formation of interracial clubs in the colleges, "based on the Manhattanville resolutions and engagement in some form of interracial justice. One of the hopes of such a college program was that the education for interracial justice would create a climate of opinion in the schools so that the colleges would allow the admission of black students if they previously had been refused.[34]

In *The Catholic Viewpoint on Race Relations,* LaFarge laid out three guideposts for the Catholic interracial movement. The first explained that the Church's ministry, both "spiritual and cultural, to the people of a racial minority is bound to be frustrated and to defeat its own end of gaining souls and forming good Christians—and honor to Church and country—unless it vindicates the entire, integral dignity of those to whom it ministers." It must be concerned not just with blacks or any other race, "but simply with human beings who share the needs and problems common to all mankind."

Secondly, no progress could be made "without creating a new climate of opinion." This could not be done by direct attacks on the old climate, but by persuasion, enlightenment and education, which he defined as "public relations for the truth." When people see the truth they will change for the better, and interracial justice and brotherhood will emerge. But it must come from the people.

> The spiritual citadels to be captured are not the bishops and chanceries of the Church. These have long since declared their official position. It is the mass of the Catholic people, on the religious side; just as on the civic side the basic task is the education of the community at large.[35]

Writing in the May 1936 issue of *Interracial Justice,* LaFarge affirmed "The Church, as the Church, knows no prejudice, injustice or distinction of races. Where such trouble exists, the blame is on the members of the Church who fail to live up to her principles."[36]

The final guidepost was the necessity of uniting the races in a common effort, a subject LaFarge referred to over and over in his writings, letters and conversations. Once again he pointed to the "disappointed experience of the Federated Colored Catholics," who tried to go it alone in an all-black group. The blacks, he insisted, must work together with whites. "The Negro, in short, can hardly achieve full recognition in society by his own unaided exertions, however dramatic and heroic." Racial justice demands interracial cooperation. "It means, furthermore, the cooperation of the laity with their clergy and their bishops along with thoroughly generous lay initiative, and the cooperation of Catholics with men of good will outside the Church.[37]

While powerfully inspired to end racism, LaFarge knew it could not be done overnight, especially in the South. Confrontation produced only anger and passion, putting an end to reasoned dialogue.[38] Although occasionally exploding into anger himself, as when Fordham rejected the black boy in 1934, he usually moved forward with caution and, where necessary, was willing to make compromises. He wanted interracial councils to be set up "in every large center of the country that shows a mixed racial composition." When he wrote these words in 1948 there were only eight councils nationwide.[39] He was proud of the fact that by 1963 there were sixty around the country, including a number in the South.

He was very sensitive, however, to the special situation in the South, where even by the late 1950s *de facto* segregation was still widely practiced. He showed this sensitivity in a letter rejecting an article by a Jesuit from Kansas titled "A People in Pain." The article contained a strong condemnation of Southern racial practices. LaFarge wrote a lengthy letter to the author explaining why he could not publish the article in the *Interracial Review*.

> We do not think we can use it for *Interracial Review* because we have made it a policy not to say harsh things about the South or Southerners. We rather lean back on that matter, placing our emphasis in the main on delinquencies in the North and letting others belabor cases of prejudice or discrimination down South. We have taken the policy of encouraging the fine element among the Southern white people and featuring rather the positive than the negative side. The magazine has quite a circulation in the South and we find that that attitude is appreciated. Publishing from New York, it doesn't go down so well in the South to be lecturing them.[40]

While LaFarge wanted the interracial councils to have whites and blacks working side by side, he insisted that they be *Catholic* whites and blacks. In *The Catholic Viewpoint on Race Relations* he wrote "We want always to keep our Catholic integrity. The inner life of the Council would suffer if we were to admit non-Catholics to membership." He added, however, that "we can and should cooperate generously with non-Catholics of good will in our outward relations: inviting them to consult with us on our plans, working with them on committees that bear real fruit."[41]

As previously noted, he was well aware of the poor showing his Church had made in earlier years in helping blacks, and of the very small percentage of blacks who were Catholic. As a first step in bringing more blacks into the Church, he knew that he and the Church had to win their confidence. Too many white priests and bishops were, or at least appeared to be, indifferent to the black's plight. As a result much of the black press was hostile to the Church. One of the CICNY's goals was to change that attitude. Writing in the *Catholic Home Messenger* in April

1964, Walter G. Murphy explained "In New York the Catholic Interracial Council soon helped to reverse the tide. Expressions of hostility
against the Church began to disappear from the Negro press, while the
silence of the Catholic press gave way to a healthy interest in racial
matters."[42]

A large part of the problem, therefore, as LaFarge saw it, was winning
a more active cooperation from the clergy. Blacks had to be shown that
the Church was working to end segregation in its own house. Such segregation was particularly intolerable to LaFarge. In a March 1951 letter
to the Most Reverend Vincent S. Waters, bishop of Raleigh, North Carolina, he repeated thoughts he had published in an article that had appeared in the *Fides Press* just a year before. The article had been
reprinted in publications worldwide, including the journals of the Brooklyn and Chicago interracial councils, both of which had large circula-
tions. It dealt specifically with racial segregation in Catholic parishes,
condemning such segregation, but recognizing that in some instances
change could not come instantly.

Blacks, he wrote Bishop Waters, accepted segregation, but only "for
want of anything better." It was certainly not something agreeable to
him. Integration had to be brought about as soon as possible but consistent with his thinking, it had to be done cautiously, or more could be lost
than gained. "In other words," he wrote, "I commend the courageous, but
prudent, steps that are being taken by many bishops in this country to
make clear that this is *not an accepted Church policy,* but merely temporarily tolerated, in certain instances, in order to avoid greater evils."
He summed up his reasoning near the end of the long letter.

> The nature of such steps, the degree to which a war against the pol-
> icy of compulsory segregation may be prudently pushed, will rest,
> of course, with the varying conditions that exist amid the different
> regions and in the different dioceses of this country and is a matter
> that lies within the judgment of the respective bishops. Undue haste
> can do as much harm as undue timorousness.
>
> It is my belief that many of these problems will be solved by the
> nature of our rapidly changing times. But I should like to see the
> Catholic Church in this country a bit ahead of the times, rather than
> to seem to be always following. At the same time it seems to me
> that prudence and tact can prevent our losing the precious fruits of
> the invaluable work that is already being accomplished in our
> Southern colored missions.[43]

Three years later, shortly after the *Brown v. Board of Education* decision, he started pushing harder for an end to segregation in his Church.
Writing to Bishop O'Boyle in Washington, D.C., he urged him to try to
move things along faster. By this time he was clearly frustrated with the
slow pace of integration within the Church. He had recently returned to
New York after having spent a few days in St. Mary's County in Maryland talking to some of the clergy there. "The attitude," he wrote the
bishop, "seemed to be that they were waiting for further directions from
the Archbishop."

> I was wondering whether the present or the near future might not be
> an opportune time for such indications to them, if Your Excellency
> were to find it suitable. The point could be made that Catholics
> should now take the lead. It would seem urgent for the county clergy
> really to start to prepare the people's mind. Even if the school ques-
> tion were to be tabled still for a time—and as I see it, it can *only* be
> for a time—the distressing situations in the churches—whatever ex-
> clusivism or discriminations are practised—can hardly be expected
> to endure any longer.
>
> It is hard to expect much from the older clergy, but some of the
> newer men, starting in with fresh vigor and under favorable aus-
> pices, ought to be able to take the lead. Personally I believe it is up
> to them to show some real initiative, and not wait to be pushed by
> higher authorities into the front line.[44]

He wrote this letter ten days after the *Brown* decision. In a postscript
to Bishop O'Boyle he wondered whether "a joint public declaration on
the significance for Catholics of the Supreme Court decision could not
be made by the archbishops of Baltimore and Washington. I have no idea
whether such a proposal would be feasible, but I thought you would not
mind my mentioning it."[45]

As he entered his eightieth year a sense of urgency to win blacks to
the Catholic Church seemed to grow in him, along with a continuing concern for black welfare in general. At the same time he was thinking more
in terms of blacks doing more of the job themselves. Writing to a fellow
Jesuit in December 1960, he noted that major changes were taking place
in the black world. "My experience with Catholic Negroes here in New
York has been their intense interest in the African situation. A lot of the
emergence of Africa, like the emergence of the sit-down movement in
the South, has given the Negro a new image of himself. That image may

become distorted, chauvinistic, anti-Christian, or it may become profoundly Catholic."

He saw a "deep and urgent need for a real interracial spiritual program for the Negroes themselves." Twenty-six years after arguing against the all-black membership policy of the Federated Colored Catholics, La-Farge's pendulum had started to swing the other way. While still advocating interracial programs and organizations, he realized that the civil rights movement of the sixties was giving blacks a new picture of themselves and their worth. They were now better positioned to take the lead in their own struggles. But it was still important that they be brought into the Church, for the "Church alone has an adequate answer to the problems of the American Negro."

> The question of the conversion of the American Negro to the faith is crucial at the present moment. The Church has missed the opportunity through timidity, shortsightedness, and certain definitely mistaken policies. I know that some priests engaged in this apostolate feel this very definitely. We must work fast if the Negro people are not to be lost to the faith. The present moment seems to be our last great opportunity.[46]

LaFarge was honored over and over for his ecumenism, his reaching across religious boundaries to work with people of other faiths in common causes. Until the end of his life, however, he maintained an unquestioning, guileless confidence that in the final analysis the Church was the only real hope for solving the major social problems of the day. This was not a contradiction. He would seek help when and where it was available, but the best hope was to bring everyone into the true faith.

Three months before his death LaFarge found himself doing something he had never done before—participating in a mammoth demonstration for civil rights. He was one of the two hundred fifty thousand marchers in Washington, D.C. on August 28, 1963, when Dr. Martin Luther King, Jr. delivered his "I have a dream" speech. By this time much of the Catholic hierarchy was supporting at least some forms of civil rights activism. In mid-July Cardinal Francis J. Spellman, archbishop of New York, had a letter read in all the 402 parishes under his jurisdiction in support of racial justice. Archbishop Patrick O'Boyle of Washington, D.C. was invited to give an invocation at the Lincoln Memorial. In an interview in the *Catholic News,* LaFarge explained "that the march was not a case of civil disobedience but within the tradition of the American people. He encouraged people . . . to participate in the march."[47]

In late July LaFarge addressed an emergency meeting of the National Catholic Conference for International Justice in Chicago. He was blunt and incisive in his call for action.

> We cannot escape a sharp confrontation of issues. We are faced with yes or no to the question of taking part in public demonstrations. Are we prepared to witness publicly to our belief, as did the early Christians? To witness even if it means scorn, suffering and physical hardships? This is our challenge, and I see no honorable way of evading it.

He asserted that Catholics can have "no hesitation about taking part in the march."[48]

His reaction to the march was one of exhilaration, briefly pulling him out of his darkening mood on civil rights. He wrote of the march in *America* on September 14, 1963 (probably his last published piece of writing). He was especially pleased that so many Catholic groups were involved.

> Sustaining this immense outpouring was a twofold certainty: that the demonstration's aims were completely reasonable, in line with the nation's oldest and best traditions; and that these aims were certain of fulfillment. The certainty was born of American pride in our country and its heritage. As in ancient Israel, their hope was in the God of justice and love. Henceforth, nothing could stop their progress until the "dream" so eloquently hailed by the final speaker, Doctor Martin Luther King, should finally be realized.[49]

One year after LaFarge's death, Rev. Thurston Davis, S.J., spoke about his trailblazing work in civil rights.

> We who have come here this morning know perfectly well that what was symbolized by the March on Washington—the march on the hearts, minds and wills of people all over the land—has only begun. Fr. LaFarge's glory is that he was its pioneer, the one who persistently went ahead of all of us to mark out the trail of that march. And if he were here, he would be the first to say that we have only set our foot on that trail. We have only begun our protest. We have only made the first small beginnings of a peaceful but effective revolution whose effect will be to cancel out three hundred years of error and prejudice.[50]

Davis's upbeat-downbeat assessment of LaFarge and interracial justice dovetailed LaFarge's own ambiguity about the pace of civil rights toward the end of his life. LaFarge had clearly been more optimistic a decade earlier. At the end of 1953, when the Supreme Court agreed to hear five school segregation cases that were ultimately bound together as *Brown v. Board of Education of Topeka, Kansas,* he happily saw segregation as a dying practice. Writing in *America* on December 12, 1953, he boldly declared that it had outlived its time. It was doomed. "In the modern world," he wrote, "under the rapidly changing conditions of ever more industrial life, no amount of legal backing can indefinitely prolong the life of this policy."[51]

Ten months later, after the decision had been announced, he was even more optimistic. Writing again in *America* he reviewed the current situation in the segregated states, especially the southern ones. Compliance had been spotty, ranging from Georgia and Mississippi moving to abolish all public schools, to Washington, D.C., where integration was moving rapidly. No matter what the problems, however, he believed segregation would soon be a thing of the past everywhere.

Just a few weeks before his death on November 24, 1963, he wrote reviews of three books on black civil rights. The first was on the Black Muslims by Louis E. Lomax; the second on Lincoln by William O. Douglas; and the third based on interviews with James Baldwin, Malcolm X, and Martin Luther King, Jr., written by Kenneth Clark. It was a pessimistic review. It appeared posthumously in the *Saturday Review of Literature.*

> Each of these eloquent writers testifies, in this own way, to the painful fact that 100 years after Lincoln's Emancipation Proclamation the situation of the Negro in this land of hope, democracy, and liberty is still in a good deal of mess. It is in so much of a mess, in fact, that it takes an adventurous spirit like John Howard Griffin, the white man who disguised himself as a Negro for a time, to give other white men something of the idea of what it feels like to be a Negro in the U.S.A.

In the review of Lomax's book on Black Muslims, LaFarge predicted that this group, with a potential to become violent, will eventually have to come to terms with "human facts." Nevertheless, he saw some good coming from their movement as a way of shaking up the white world in a display of all-black unity. "But the reality of their protest is also evident," he wrote, "as is the driving power of their appeal to moral force and racial unity. Such a collective demonstration is needed in order to prove to the white world the impasse into which uncompromising white racism is leading us."[52]

In his last years, therefore, LaFarge was considerably less critical of all-black organizations, although he sensed the potential danger for violence in them, which he strongly opposed. He clearly favored the civil disobedience tactics of Martin Luther King, Jr. over the militancy of the Black Muslims. He probably would have deplored the "long hot summers" of the last half of the 1960s. But just as probably he would have recognized their inevitability, considering the failure of white America to end segregation in practice, even though the courts had ended it in law.

Near his death, therefore, he was an eighty-three-year-old priest who had given a large part of his life to a cause that he feared was hitting a brick wall. His own background and attitude cried out against violence. Yet, how else to get it done? It was a dilemma that, in a way fortunate for him, he did not have to resolve.

Chapter 10

Catholic Action and the Farmer

LaFarge strongly believed in the Church's mission in the temporal world. Catholic Action, participation by clergy and laymen in the apostolic work of the Church hierarchy, was needed to defend the poorer and weaker classes against their exploiters. If the gap between rich and poor became too great, the poor would listen to the tempting, siren call of Communism.

He was once asked by a Catholic chaplain at Columbia University in New York to explain how Catholics could achieve a synthesis of the two prime aspects of Catholicism—the inner contemplative life and apostolic activity.[1]

In his reply LaFarge stressed the primacy of the spiritual side of the faith. The temporal role, however, was also very important.

> On the other hand, the Christian (or Catholic) has a genuine mission to the world, even in its temporal condition. . . . He has not the mission to prescribe techniques or "solve" social and political problems. But he *is* called upon to spread the leaven of moral and religious principles by which the solutions can be found, and to train men and women in the knowledge and practice of these principles. Such a mission of the Christian extends into a threefold area; the religious, the civic and social. . . . It is guided by the understanding of *man,* as he is in his daily life; particularly as a member of a family; who is obliged to seek his supernatural destiny as a member of a natural as well as a supernatural community, and is subject to the humble conditions of housing, employment, wages, ownership and partnership, etc; in his social life, and to the manifold responsibilities of citizenship in his civic life.[2]

In a 1948 letter to Evelyn Waugh, the English novelist and convert to Roman Catholicism, LaFarge wrote that to influence the world in a fruitful way, the Christian must first detach himself from that world in his inner being—"for ours is a battle between light and darkness, between the powers of evil and the powers of redemption." Some people, he acknowledged, can live only an inner life. They flee the world and find peace and quiet in the cloistered life. These men and women are important members of the struggle against evil. ". . . without these desert seekers and desert dwellers those who battle in the marketplace would fight in vain. But on the other hand the cause of Christ demands that others shall descend into the city, shall penetrate public life and, in short, fulfill the real papal idea of the much abused expression 'Catholic Action.' "[3]

Among the major documents that contribute to our understanding of the Christian's mission in life are the "great encyclicals of recent decades."[4] Specifically, he referred to two major papal encyclicals—*Rerum Novarum* (The Condition of Labor) issued by Pope Leo XIII in 1891, and *Quadragesimo Anno* (On the Recent Reconstruction of the Social Order), proclaimed by Pius XI in 1931, exactly forty years later.

In *The Manner Is Ordinary* he warned that a world revolution might occur if social injustices were not removed. "I was convinced," he wrote, "that the problem of social disorder which had 'betrayed' the Old World would, if neglected, prove an abundant seed-ground for Communism even here in the United States."[5] The task, as he saw it, was to move quickly on the problem of social reconstruction.

> That meant a fundamental renewal of religious life in its totality, and particularly in its communal aspect, the renewal of communal religious worship as it was practiced in the earlier ages of the Church and was recommended by the leading liturgical scholars of the present time.[6]

He wrote that it was easy to put forth these convictions in 1953, but before the year 1931, when Pius XI issued *Quadragesimo Anno,* the earlier warnings of Leo XIII in *Rerum Novarum* "had been largely forgotten."[7] He did not think the working classes in the United States were on the verge of revolution, since the inequalities between rich and poor were not as glaring in this country as in Europe. Still he felt the idea of a world revolution would appeal "to certain elements in the American mind: to those who felt themselves disinherited, and particularly to the discontented minority groups, the American proletariat, whether they were rural workers or racial and religious minorities."[8]

The two encyclicals had stressed the primacy of the Church in helping cure the ills of society. They emphasized that the best way to keep the masses away from Socialism and Communism was to give them justice. The Church and its ministers had to work through the faith to give the workers great economic equality. Among other remedies, they advocated the formation of trade unions to give workers stronger negotiating positions with their employers. Pius's encyclical quoted favorably from Leo's "The workingmen's associations should be organized and governed so as to the best and most suitable means for attempting what is aimed at, that is to say, for helping each member to better his condition to the utmost in body, soul and property."[9] The right of private property, however, was loudly confirmed. In this, the social-minded popes were pro-capitalist, strongly opposed to Socialism and Communism, but just as strongly opposed to the oppression of the workingman.

It was the Industrial Revolution and its consequences for the masses of landless workers that the popes were responding to in these encyclicals. LaFarge, however, rarely commented in print on the condition of the American factory worker. This does not mean he was not concerned about him. At the weekly meetings of *America's* editorial board, he regularly contributed to discussions about labor. Another editor, however, Father Benjamin Masse, S.J., was the staff's labor expert, and it was he who was assigned the articles and editorials to write on that subject.[10]

LaFarge drew upon the two encyclicals intended to benefit factory workers and instead applied them to the American farmers, most of whom were technically capitalists themselves, owning their own land and farming it for a profit. He was especially concerned with black farmers, whom he earnestly believed should stay on the land and resist migrating to the cities and factories in the north. It is impossible to escape the feeling that LaFarge thought the cities corrupting, while the country fostered a higher morality.

He saw confirmation of this during the middle of World War II when race riots rocked Detroit. "The racial disorders," he wrote in *America,* "are part of the price the whole country pays for the wrecking of our small rural economies, our reckless industrialization, our inability to harmonize, as yet, the interests of the city and country, producer and consumer."[11]

Catholic Action on the farm was more difficult to apply than it was in the city. He admitted that proportionally few Catholics lived on farms. Nevertheless, it was important that he try. He sometimes expressed a simplistic, almost naive belief in the purifying effects of the soil. But at the same time he could be realistic about life of farming. It was a hard, uncertain life. The demographic trend, he understood, was clearly from rural to urban areas, and those who did stay on the land needed all the help they could get if they were to stay.

> The work in St. Mary's County had helped me to realize how closely the life of families and thereby the salvation of souls was affected by welfare and adjustment within the rural community. I became painfully aware of the gap between the city and the country, which in many respects is greater in the United States than it is abroad.
>
> The rural question was particularly important in the case of the Negroes, and confronted me in working for the development of the Cardinal Gibbons Institute. A generally depressed state of rural life made the special problem of the Negro all the more difficult, as he contended not only against purely racial obstacles but obstacles which he shared with the entire white rural population.[12]

In 1927, the year after he joined the staff at *America,* he started to write regularly about rural life, stressing the importance of keeping those few Catholic farmers on the land. "Even though rural life is largely non-Catholic," he wrote, "its preservation is important for the preservation of the Faith, since experience shows that when rural life perishes from a country, the Faith always suffers."[13]

He viewed the farming regions as potential harvest grounds for making converts to the Church. "Except for immigration," he wrote in 1930, "the countryside is the source of potential Catholics."[14]

In the spirit of fostering a better life for rural Catholics, LaFarge enthusiastically endorsed the work of the National Catholic Rural Life Conference (NCRLC), which concentrated on the farmers of the Midwest. The conference, founded in 1922, held annual conventions in one or another midwestern city. LaFarge began attending these annual meetings soon after coming to New York. In 1930 he attended the conference in Springfield, Illinois.

By this time the country was sliding into the deepest depression in its history. It would not bottom out until 1932, by which time the gross national product was only about half what it had been in 1929. Some 30 to 40 percent of the working force was unemployed when Franklin D. Roosevelt was sworn in as president in March 1933. About five thousand banks had closed their doors since 1929. Most of these were small banks in rural areas, but their total impact on the farm population (a much higher percentage of the total national population than it is now) was devastating. Farmers by the tens of thousands, unable to meet mortgage payments, had their farms sold out from under them.

Violence erupted in the Midwest, as farmers fought to hold on to their land by threatening judges holding foreclosure proceedings, intimidating auctioneers trying to sell off foreclosed farms and equipment, and organizing "strikes" to deprive towns and cities of farm produce until they agreed to pay higher prices. Uncooperative farmers who tried to get their milk and other food to market sometimes had their trucks stopped by angry farmers and their milk cans emptied on the ground. While these acts of intimidation were not widespread, the fact that they occurred at all reflected the desperation of these people.

With the advent of the New Deal on March 4, 1933, and the "First Hundred Days" of Roosevelt's first term, legislation aimed at getting the economy spiraling upward once again was hastily passed. For the farmer this meant passage of the Agricultural Adjustment Act, which subsidized him for growing less food, thus enabling him to sell what he did grow for higher prices. One of the ongoing problems of the farmer since the end of World War I was overproduction, resulting in surpluses on the market and low prices for his produce. While this law was held unconstitutional by the Supreme Court two years later, it was repassed by Congress in a different form.

The act did not end the depression for the farmer, but it did ease his situation. Nevertheless, the decade of the 1930s was the worst in American agricultural history. The farm segment of the economy did not really recover until World War II, when the demand for food to fight the war rose dramatically.

Among Roosevelt's cabinet appointees in 1933 was Henry A. Wallace as secretary of agriculture. A midwestern progressive, Wallace had long studied the problems of the farmer. Until coming to Washington he had edited his family's venerable magazine, *Wallace's Farmer*. He knew as much about agriculture as any person in the country, but he was something of a dreamer, as LaFarge discovered in his only meeting with him in Wallace's Washington office.

Wallace had asked LaFarge to come and discuss "some plan he had in mind." They talked for about two hours. Wallace told LaFarge that he wanted to start "a pioneer settlement project in the United States." He was looking for "a group of men and women endowed with the religious spirit of the early pioneers, with their sense of idealism and self-abnegation." He believed that Catholics knew the secret of such a life. Every day for a half-hour, he confided to LaFarge, he read such Catholic books as Thomas à Kempis's *Imitation of Christ,* and the works of St. Theresa of Avila and St. John of the Cross. He also demonstrated familiarity with "Catholic pioneering in the past, the work of St. Benedict and his monks, St. Bruno and his Carthusians, the great Jesuit missions of Paraguay, and so on. . . ." Aware of LaFarge's interest in and knowledge of both farming and the Catholic Church, he "wondered if it would not be possible for such a project to be started in some way under Catholic auspices."

LaFarge offered no immediate comment on the proposal, but wondered to himself how it could be carried out. To his knowledge nothing came of his conversation with Wallace, but he was glad to note that "our Rural Life Conference seemed to have made more impression on the public mind than I had suspected."[15]

LaFarge was no doubt pleased and flattered that Wallace thought so highly of Catholics and their special qualifications for pioneer life. Up to a point he agreed with the secretary, but only up to a point. Writing in 1945 to a priest in England he commented on Catholics and Catholic Action. "Catholics," he wrote, "have some principles clearly fixed, and in constructive work of organized Catholic Action, you can rely on them to a much greater extent than you can the others." This did not mean, however, that Catholics had any unique authority or expertise in political or social matters.

> One of history's painful conclusions about which you can probably say much more yourself is that being a Catholic does not by any means give us the quality of rightness in purely political matters. Even if we are completely orthodox theologically we may have very poor ideas of government. I become impatient when I hear people speak of the Catholic solution for all social questions. I see solutions of social questions which Catholics can approve of, which a Catholic in a negative sense, namely, that they are solutions of economic or social matters which are not ethically unsound. But to convey the impression that our faith gives us a magic key which we can apply to every problem of social security or international organizations or what not is a dreadful delusion.[16]

LaFarge probably did not have his 1933 conversation with Secretary of Agriculture Wallace in mind when he wrote the above paragraph. Wallace's thinking about Catholics, however, was one he clearly rejected. Catholics might be able to take the high ground on some moral issues, but they were not divinely more suited than non-Catholics to working out social or economic programs as Wallace suggested. La-

Farge did endorse Catholic Action in areas where Catholics, both clergy and laymen, could use the Church to stimulate, both by example and by inclusion of non-Catholics, social progress. The Cardinal Gibbons Institute, for example, did not educate only Catholic blacks, although it was under Catholic direction and was considered a Catholic school. The institute's board of directors, however, "was mixed in every sense of the word: it included white and colored Catholics and Protestants, men and women, local southern Marylanders, Baltimoreans and Washingtonians, and people from other parts of the country."[17]

During the 1930s LaFarge attended nearly all of the annual meetings of the NCRLC. It was a gathering he looked forward to, even though, with travel time and attendance at the sessions, it took about a week out of his busy life. He had the special ability, however, to keep up with his reading and writing on trains, later planes, and in church rectories, where he usually bedded down while away from New York.

The ninth annual conference met in Wichita, Kansas, in October 1931. The depression was heating up and the farm situation was becoming more desperate by the day. The conference all but ignored this reality and instead concentrated on finding ways to keep young people on the farm by removing burdens that sat upon the countryside. This, he wrote in *America,* would be preferable to any "attempt to heal the rural home by putting an end to its very existence, either by destroying its actual inmates, by birth control and similar practices, or by destroying its material basis, through abolition of home ownership."

Religion was a necessary ingredient to supply spiritual uplift and to inspire a Catholic way of life. He raised this question in the *America* article "Can the Church do anything to lift the economic burden that rests upon the rural home, and upon the agricultural process itself?" His answer revealed his naiveness on the role of religion in American government and politics. He began by pointing out that most agencies working to help the farmers were secular, whether private, state or federal. "Yet many of the non-religious agencies," he wrote, "recognize the impossibility of solving even the bare economic problems without the aid of religion."[18]

How religion, and which religion, was to work with secular programs for the farmer he did not try to explain. If he meant the Catholic religion he was simply ignoring facts. Federal subsidies to farmers for reducing the number of acres they planted, rural electrification programs, and the Tennessee Valley Authority to provide power and control flooding (all designed to help the rural segment of the American economy) could have nothing to do with religion. Except for Indian reservations in the nineteenth century, the federal government had never significantly subsidized religious groups. In his more candid moments LaFarge understood this fact. He also realized that the Catholic Church, despite his wishes, was a minor force among most rural people. In some regions it did not exist at all.

In the fall of 1932, for example, he spent a working vacation in his old Maryland stamping grounds; the Great Smokey Mountains in North Carolina; New Orleans; Dubuque, Iowa; (for the annual Rural Life meeting) Prairie Du Chien, Wisconsin; Memphis, Tennessee; and St. Louis, Missouri. On one excursion through the North Carolina mountains in the company of another priest, he visited "Father Toup's extraordinary mission in the Laurel Creek Valley, amongst an absolutely Protestant population. On another trip," he wrote his sister Margaret, "I happened into a meeting of the Bailey Clan, some 300 in number, who, as the young man who introduced me around informed me, 'probably never did see a Catholic priest afore in their lives.' They certainly looked that way."

The largest number of North Carolinians, he discovered, were Baptists. The Presbyterians had been seeking converts to their religion among them for twenty-five years, and so far had made only three. It was so hopeless that they were pulling out of this missionary field. One day he sat on a hillside under a growth of white pines, "and heard the local Baptist revivalist, as he thundered forth from his church the remarkable pronouncement that 'St. Peter was the first Pope; St. Peter, he was a Babbtist; and tharfor, Bretheren, the first Pope was a Babbtist.' "[19]

There were however, Catholic communities in the Midwest where there were better chances of enlarging the faith, either through conversions, or by bringing in bands of Catholic immigrants. One midwestern priest LaFarge greatly admired was Father Luigi Ligutti, whose parish was in Granger, Iowa, a small prairie village not far from Des Moines.

Most of Ligutti's parishioners came from Ireland. They were miners, but they worked at mining only about half the year. As a result they were poor and lived "in miserable shacks amid loneliness and poverty." Father Ligutti came up with the idea of starting a farming community where they could work the rest of the year for themselves. This meant acquiring land. He assisted them in obtaining long-term loans paid off by selling the produce from their gardens. The whole effort was a grand success. "The parish," LaFarge wrote, "became more or less a rural show-place and a model of what could be done in the way of part-time farming." In 1939 Ligutti was persuaded to take the job of secretary to the NCRLC.[20]

Some of LaFarge's visits to prairie country stood out in his memory. In 1936 he attended the conference in Fargo, North Dakota. "More than five thousand persons," he wrote, "gathered for the four-day session in Fargo, with its riot of displays and visual material."[21] Earlier, in 1929, he visited Shelby County in Iowa, which had been settled in 1872 by German Catholics joined later by some Irish immigrants. The towns of the county were "centers of a uniformly Catholic rural population, well integrated and progressive." The pastor of Panama Parish, Father Martin A. Schlitz, had helped to transform a "monotonous countryside" into a sylvan paradise. "An enthusiastic gardener and tree lover, Father Schlitz had established a parish park, reforesting the Church property and the park itself with Japanese junipers, hard maples, Lombardy poplars, decorative shrubs, etc."[22]

These prairie success stories, LaFarge suggested, stemmed in large measure from Catholic unity and cooperation. He was quick to point out, however, that successful farming was not a monopoly of the Catholic Church. Other religious groups could show the same enterprise and support for one another. He had high praise, for example, for the Jewish Agricultural Society, and the Jewish Agricultural College in Doylestown, Pennsylvania, "said to be one of the most efficient and practical agricultural schools in the United States."[23]

In 1937 LaFarge met with a number of Catholic Rural Life leaders in St. Louis. Their goal was to draw up a manifesto on rural life, which the group finally promulgated two years later. It ran to 213 pages in printed form. LaFarge called it "a sort of bible of the Catholic Rural Conference movement."[24]

Despite his occasional disclaimers of Catholic superiority in social planning, he did obviously believe that his Church offered an effective vehicle for rural cooperation. The manifesto stated that "while co-operatives are not proposed for all conceivable economic and social ills, nevertheless soundly established co-operatives will be potent agencies for the protection of the farming group."[25] And the more Catholics involved in working the land, the better for them and their neighbors. He quoted the general aims of the manifesto.

1. To care for the underprivileged Catholics living on the land.
2. To keep on the land Catholics now living there.
3. To increase the number of Catholics living on the land, not as a back to the land movement, but to offset a false urbanization and encourage the practical rural indoctrination of country youth.
4. To convert the non-Catholics living on the land.

The fourth point was especially audacious, since it was an outright challenge to Protestant leaders to hold their own people to their own faiths. LaFarge, however, dismissed any difficulties that might arise from his goal of proselytizing non-Catholic farmers. This statement, he wrote, "never seemed to raise any objections among the many non-Catholics, both clergy and lay, who have attended our meetings and generously cooperated with us."[26] Lacking solid evidence to the contrary, it is difficult to refute LaFarge's word on this. But considering the large amount of anti-Catholic feeling in the country in the twenties and thirties, especially in the rural areas, it is not unreasonable to express some skepticism.

In 1948 LaFarge received the conference's first annual award for contributions to the cause of rural life betterment. He was typically modest in mentioning this achievement. "They were most generous in conferring upon me through the hands of the Most Reverend Bishop Treacy of LaCrosse the first of these annual rural life medals, though I contributed only a small addition to the pioneer work of the Conference's originators."[27]

By the early 1940s, LaFarge's usual optimism about the future of the American farmer was giving way to a more pessimistic outlook. More and more farmers were being displaced by increasing mechanization. More machines meant fewer farmers. Those forced off the land would have to come to the cities and take factory jobs. It was a process, he admitted, that could not be stopped. But he deplored it anyway, showing once again that he valued rural life over urban life. Rural living promoted a higher morality. City living tore morality down. The threat to the farmer of greater mechanization had taken a long time to penetrate "the vast mass of our dispersed Catholic thinking," he wrote in *America*. "But the penetration has begun. The rural apostolate faces certain conditions in which technological progress plays a disturbing part. . . ."[28]

Acknowledging the inevitability of the industrialization of agriculture, however, did not mean giving up his fight to save the family farm; at least not yet. For him the family farm was both a symbol and an inspiration of stability and goodness. "The natural, and therefore *in the long run* the most effective, unit for producing the varied foodstuffs needed for human living is the small, not the large, agricultural unit," he wrote near the end of 1942. "Agriculture is a biological, not a mechanical process."[29]

As for blacks, it was even more essential that they remain on the farm, but he feared they were vanishing from the land, at an alarming rate, even though they were peculiarly at home there. It "offers him special opportunities," he wrote in *Interracial Review,* "for independent, self-respecting living." He felt blacks had an extraordinary penchant for adapting to rural life. The National Catholic Rural Life Conference had an "unwavering interest in keeping the Negro on the land."[30]

By the middle of World War II he was taking the government to task for its neglect of the farmer—a neglect he claimed was responsible for food shortages. But the problem long preceded the war. "It was obvious," he wrote, "that we are now reaping a threat of starvation after generations of neglect of a sound farm and rural-life social and economic policy." The small farmer had been hurt by "indifference to his welfare by our industrial and capitalist economy. This neglect has driven many off the land, which becomes unproductive."[31]

From the perspective of a half-century later it is evident that LaFarge overstated the case for the small farm—both for its superior productivity and its higher morality. He often saw what he wanted to see, even when it was not there. Small farms, self-contained and away from the corrupting influence of the cities, bred goodness and stability, he was certain. It was part of his creed. The reality of rural life, however, was frequently very different. All too often it was harsh, lonely, and precarious. Even by 1940 many farms did not have electricity or indoor plumbing, despite intense New Deal efforts through such federal projects as the Tennessee Valley Authority and the Rural Electrification Agency. Nor, if the Kinsey Report issued shortly after World War II was accurate, were farm boys any more morally sound than their city cousins.

The food shortages that LaFarge complained about during the war were inevitable, but not because of the decline of the small farm. Farmers, in fact, did a prodigious job of feeding America and its allies during World War II. Some thirteen million Americans served in the armed forces during the war. The government's demand for food was insatiable. Thousands of men and women left the farms to work in war plants, many never to return to the farm. For the first time in a decade they had steady work for decent wages. It was neither reasonable nor realistic for LaFarge to blame government policies for food shortages during those chaotic and perilous years.

LaFarge never lost his interest in, or concern for, the farmer. Following the war, however, other issues caught his main attention. For example, he increasingly immersed himself in international affairs, especially after the start of the Cold War. He went to Europe in 1947 and again in 1951.

His interest in civil rights remained steady, even though he felt discouraged by the lack of progress during the last years of his life. And amidst all his activities as writer, editor, civil rights proponent, foreign correspondent, anti-Communist crusader, Church liturgy reformer, and general intellectual factotum, he maintained a never diminishing interest in his own large family; sometimes to the distress of some of its members, but more often to their benign tolerance.

Chapter 11

Family

When LaFarge came to New York in 1926 to join the staff of *America,* he took up residence at the magazine's headquarters at 329 West One Hundred Eighth Street. He would die in that same building, really two connecting brownstones, thirty-seven years later. As is the case with many priests, his nuclear and extended families, including in-laws, meant a great deal to him, especially after his mother's death in 1925. After moving to New York from the Maryland Shore he was much better positioned to visit relatives in and around the city. Despite his many writing and editing assignments at *America,* he kept up a steady correspondence with family members. Some of these letters have been retrieved by the writer from relatives, some from the LaFarge family collection at the New York Historical Society, and a few more from the Georgetown LaFarge papers.

All of the surviving relatives contacted, related either by blood or by marriage, remember him with affection. In an interview, Phyllis LaFarge Johnson, one of his grandnieces, granddaughter of his brother Bancel, said that he was "terribly interested" in the family. He wanted it to be a practicing Roman Catholic family, sometimes deluding himself that they were all more or less in the fold, when all too often some were not. Phyllis called him "one of the two or three spiritual people" she had ever known. She called him "brilliant," but said he never flaunted it. When you were with him you felt in the presence of someone with a "quality of greatness, an inward greatness."[1]

He was often at hand when a family member experienced a crisis in his or her life. On these occasions he was quick to offer help, advice and prayers. These were usually welcomed. Sometimes, however, his relatives found him intrusive, but seldom told him so for fear of hurting his feelings. Once in a while, however, they *did* let him know that his attentions were not appreciated.

Once such rebuff happened in the spring of 1962. He had received a letter from his nephew Bancel, one of his brother Bancel's four sons. "This is the most painful letter for me to write," his nephew began, "for, as of March 23, my marriage to Hester has ended in divorce by common consent, without bitterness or recrimination." Bancel carefully explained that he and his wife had waited until the children were grown and on their own before parting. "As for myself before God, that is a matter of conscience. I have been a good provider. I have been an unsatisfactory husband, but I have little qualms as to being a good father to my children." He ended by regretting that he had to becloud his uncle's "later years." But he asked his forgiveness and "perhaps his blessing."[2]

LaFarge responded by sending a consoling letter to Hester, whom he assumed was the injured party. He wrote that "no matter how tangled are our skeins, the love of our Creator for his children will always find a way to disentangle them; provided we continue in spite of our obstacles and quietly to ask His help." He concluded by advising her to "pray often the Lord's Prayer."[3]

Hester was scathingly resentful of his letter, and let him know in no uncertain terms that it was most unwelcome. She insisted that she had never led him to think that she had any religious beliefs. "I was trying to make it clear that I was an agnostic and have surely done so," she wrote. "How can you suggest to me that I say the Lord's Prayer?" As for who was to blame for the breakup, she stressed that it was a mutual decision, and she resented LaFarge's assumption that she was more emotionally dependent on Bancel than he was on her. She assumed that LaFarge was distressed because marriage is a sacrament. "This should not enter into an appraisal of Bancel's and my affairs as neither is a member of the Church." Finally, she wrote angrily, "To expect a man of sixty-two, whose children are married, to be bound to a woman he does not love for the rest of his life shows the old order at its worst—the old group tyranny and cruelty against the individual."[4]

It is not known how LaFarge reacted to her anger, since no further correspondence on the matter has been discovered. But it is doubtful that he brooded about it for long, if at all.

In any case, both Bancel and Hester were misleading in their letters to LaFarge. The divorce was not as amiable as they pretended. What Bancel could not bring himself to tell his uncle was that he was in love with another woman, whom he married one week after the divorce became final. According to their son Ben, Bancel was afraid to tell LaFarge the full truth of the affair. As for Hester, she was putting up a good front for

LaFarge, but in truth was deeply hurt. Ben agreed with the writer that his mother probably vented her anger at LaFarge as a way of sounding off at her former husband. LaFarge just happened to get in the way. Hester died two years later. Ben believes that she deliberately starved herself to death.[5]

Despite the occasional religious black sheep, LaFarge was proud of his family. Once, in response to a question from one of his grandnephews on the meaning and destiny of the family, he became quite reflexive.

> I do think that our tribe, which now has so many ramifications, has pretty consistently clung to certain values, that are not to be despised in the present world. Perhaps I could describe these as a really great cultural sense, which, as far as my generation is concerned, is an inheritance—I use the term culturally, not biologically—from both sides of my own parentage of, the Rhode Island and Philadelphia, on Mother's part, and the French, on Father's. And those who have later entered the stream have kept to this main current. It is a family—using the word in a wide sense—that does bravely and unashamedly hold very high the things of the mind and the spirit; love for imagination, for learning in one form or another, for the finer things in life, for travel and intercourse of minds, and for certain precious traditions.

> Coupled with that is a tradition of affection, and a certain demonstrativeness, which comes to us, I imagine, from the French. But not wholly, for there was much of this in the Perrys and Sergeants as well. LaFarges have done foolish things, they have made blunders and possibly made enemies. But they have not, as a rule, done mean or narrow or harsh things. One of the grave and wonderful experiences of my later years is to know how strong and how universal is the appeal of the good, the noble, the generous among all our number, even if the actions might not always measure up to the sentiment.[6]

Since LaFarge was the youngest of his parents' seven surviving children by six years, it is not statistically surprising that he outlived all of them. The first to go was his sister Emily, who married W.R. Claxton and settled down in Philadelphia. Seventeen years older than LaFarge, he remembers her as a strict disciplinarian. In *The Manner Is Ordinary* he wrote that she had two principal methods of punishing him for his misdeeds. One was to lock him up in a large closet until his "tantrum" was over. "At this dramatic moment 'a small bird' would appear with a chocolate cigarette, and on agreeing to be good, I was allowed to come out of the closet and consume it under Emily's watchful eye. The second, more dreaded punishment, was to be almost suffocated on the bed with a pillow."[7] Emily's marriage to Claxton was a bad one. After bearing four children they were separated. She died in 1919 after falling on ice and severely injuring her head.

Oliver, who had gone to Alaska for the gold rush of 1898, was the next to pass away. LaFarge described his brother as "handsome, jovial and blessed throughout his generous life with hosts of friends."[8] When he returned from Alaska in 1899 he settled for a number of years in Seattle, first going into insurance and real estate, then into banking. Eventually he returned to the East and became a vice-president of the General Motors Acceptance Corporation. He and LaFarge were very close to each other. For a few years Oliver headed the executive committee of the Cardinal Gibbons Institute. A talented, if mostly part-time, artist he gave several exhibits of his work in New York. He died of a stroke in 1936 at the age of sixty-seven.[9]

Bancel and Christopher Grant (known simply as Grant) both died in 1938. Bancel was probably LaFarge's favorite brother. He did more to help him in his youth than anyone else, with both financial and moral support. Bancel himself had a very hard life. While a freshman at the University of Pennsylvania, where he was studying medicine, he lost an eye during a laboratory experiment that went wrong. He left to recuperate but never returned. Instead he went into his father's studio to study art. Of Bancel's artistic talent, his grandson Ben wrote, "We in the family have always believed that his public work was uninspired and rather mediocre in execution. This was perhaps mainly because he wasn't very skillful in drawing the human figure, but it may also have been because he was doing the kind of painting for which his father had been so famous—including allegorical scenes."[10]

Bancel married Mabel Hooper in 1898. Their marriage produced four sons over the first four years—Bancel, Edward, Henry and Thomas, in that order. After quarreling with his father in 1900, he and his family moved to Paris, then later to the French countryside. In 1907, Mabel had a severe mental breakdown, leading to her confinement in a Swiss sanitarium for more than a year. Eventually making a reasonable recovery, she and Bancel returned to the United States in 1915 and bought a dairy farm in Mount Carmel, Connecticut, which continued to be operated as a farm until Mabel's death in 1944. Also a painter, she and Bancel used some of the farm buildings as studios. Ben compared her work with his grandfather's.

> Everyone in the family agrees that my grandmother was a more
> gifted painter than he, but we also believe that she goaded him into
> undertaking the kind of public mural painting for which his father
> was famous and for which he himself had so little talent. Whether
> or not that's true, they exhibited their work together four times —
> in Paris, Boston, New York, and at Yale. One New York reviewer
> judged her to be the better painter. Yet she painted nothing but
> flowers, and only in watercolor, presumably in order to avoid com-
> peting with him — a classic case of a woman denying herself for her
> husband's sake.[11]

It distressed LaFarge that he could not be at his brother Bancel's side
when he died in August 1938. At that time he was in Paris working hard
on the racism encyclical for Pius XI. Father Talbot, however, his editor
in chief at *America,* visited the family shortly afterward, then wrote to
LaFarge assuring him that Bancel had been spiritually cared for just before the end. His letter is dated August 18, 1938.

> You will be consoled to know that Father Downey, of Mount
> Carmel, had been to visit Bancel several times, usually at the call
> of Mrs. Bancel. Some days before death Father Downey was called.
> He was asked to give the final blessing, for there was imminent
> danger of death. He told me that he was alone with Bancel who at
> the time could scarcely mumble any words and had been unable to
> speak distinctly for more than a week. When Father Downey en-
> tered the room Bancel lifted his hand to him. Father Downey
> grasped his hand and said a few words. Bancel meanwhile was
> mumbling, attempting to express himself. Suddenly, as if with a
> tremendous effort, in a voice that could be heard outside the room,
> he almost shouted: "Father, I am very happy that you have come to
> see me." The members of the family marveled that Bancel had the
> strength to speak in such a tone. As far as I know, he did not speak
> aloud after that.[12]

During World War II Bancel's youngest son, Tom, lost his life at sea.
Commander of the Coast Guard cutter *Natsek,* he and his crew of thirty
drowned when the ship went down in a severe storm in the North Atlantic, not far from Newfoundland. The body turned up on the Newfoundland coast about six months later, and was temporarily interred on
the beach where it was discovered. LaFarge felt he should go and bless
the grave, but could not get away at the time. More than a year later he
welcomed the news that a Father Hennebury had blessed the grave.[13]

Only Tom's body, and that of one of his crew, washed ashore. In late June 1993, his daughter Phyllis and her son visited the site where the body had first been buried, outside the small town of Big Brook, along the cold, rugged northwest coast of Newfoundland. "The land is a desert of rock," she wrote the author, "the blasted heath of Macbeth." A man named James Diamond had found the body while walking along the shore in early June 1943. He was looking for any thing of value that might have washed up during the winter. According to Phyllis, "it was no good . . . to go scavenging until late May or early June because the ice had not broken up enough until then. In other words, my father's body had been buried in the ice on the shore for months in all likelihood."

Phyllis was able to talk to Diamond's son, who was sixteen at the time his father found the body. He remembers his father returning from his walk. Young Diamond had just finished spading his garden. He told his father he was going into the house for something to eat. " 'No you're not,' " Diamond Senior said. " 'We have a job to do.' " "They carried the boards and tools they needed down to the shore, built the coffin and dug the grave. 'We were done before dark,' the son told me." After the war Tom's remains were brought back to Newport and reburied in the family plot.[14]

LaFarge was especially attached to Bancel's and Mabel's children and grandchildren. When Mabel died in 1944 he sent a long letter to her son Bancel, who was then a captain in the army overseas. Bancel could not get home for the funeral. LaFarge wrote him of a two-day visit he had with Mabel just ten days before she died. "I had a delightful visit with your mother on September 18th and 19th," he wrote. "I was on my way to Newport for a short vacation. I came to Mount Carmel in the afternoon on September 18th. It was a glorious day, still warm and summery." Other friends and relatives were there as well. LaFarge described it "as agreeable an afternoon as I have ever had there."

Within a week, however, Mabel started to fail. Her son Henry telephoned LaFarge to tell him about her weakening condition. LaFarge could not get away from New York in time to see her, but he kept in close touch with her pastor, Father Daly, who gave her the last sacraments. "These," he told me, "she received when she was still able to speak and with tremendous joy and peace and resignation. She was really triumphant in receiving them."

LaFarge said the funeral mass for her at St. Columba's. He was very touched by the large assemblage of friends and relatives who came to the mass. He wrote Bancel of her exceptional faith, which was to LaFarge, of course, gratifying.

> Your mother was certainly most prepared, as was your father. There
> was a strange similarity in both terminations of their lives. Every-
> thing in the house was left, even in the minutest matters, in complete
> order. Everything was attended to, arranged, and planned. She told
> Aileen Tone that she expected she might go off any time—this was
> when she was perfectly well,—and to be sure to do three things: to
> practice intense prayer, frequent confession and frequent Commu-
> nion. It was a very holy ending of a very holy life.[15]

Grant, the second brother to die in 1938, was the first born of the La-
Farge children. An accomplished architect, he and his partner, George
Lewis Heins, a classmate from the Massachusetts Institute of Technol-
ogy (and the husband of his father's sister Aimée), were the original architects of the Cathedral of Saint John the Divine in Morningside
Heights in New York. They worked on the cathedral from 1892 to 1907,
the year that Heins died. By that time only the apse had been completed
according to their original design, which was for, more or less, a Ro-
manesque, pre-Gothic style. After Hein's death, certain of the church fathers who had been urging a switch to a more traditional Gothic style,
saw an opportunity to dissolve the contract, and persuaded the church
board to drop Grant as the principal architect. Although urged by friends
to sue for breach of contract, Grant accepted the decision without protest,
but it was a severely damaging blow to his pride, reputation, income, and
creative inspiration. LaFarge commented in his autobiography on how
seriously his brother was affected by losing the commission, and how at
least part of the blame for losing it fell upon Grant himself.

> . . . Grant's hasty temper and his absences from the scene at criti-
> cal moments did not promote his case nor strengthen his moral
> claim. Yet from the day he was notified of the non-renewal of the
> contract until his death, he never discussed the matter, and only
> very rarely did any of his friends or family realize how severe a
> blow he had absorbed. From an economic standpoint it was terrific,
> for the work on the cathedral would have been a lifework, and from
> a professional point of view it was still more bitter.[16]

Grant married Florence Lockwood in 1895, a union far from made in
heaven. The Lockwoods were a distinguished family, numbering among
their close friends the Theodore Roosevelts. Florence was a beauty and
an intellectual, but while she is described by more than one source as
brilliant, the same sources called Grant only clever. He was consistently
unfaithful to her, and for many years it was a marriage in name only.

They quarreled so loudly in company that friends ceased inviting them, as a pair, to their homes.

They owned a summer house in Saunderstown, Rhode Island, on Narragansett Bay, which was severely damaged during the hurricane of 1938. By that time Grant had suffered two heart attacks. Florence was taking care of him more from pity than from love. By this time they were living in near poverty. He suffered the third attack, which finally killed him, two weeks after the storm. Not a religious man, Grant pleased LaFarge, but confounded two of his sons, the writers Christopher and Oliver, by agreeing to see a priest a few months before he died. Apparently the experience did not go well, as he wrote to LaFarge in Paris while he was preparing the encyclical. "Your friend, Fr. Clark," he wrote his brother, "came to see me, and he made me rather angry, though I realize that he was only stupid. But I don't like a sinuous approach, which he tried. I suppose he thought he ought to be clever and that's not his line." He asked LaFarge to come see him as soon as he returned from Europe, as he had a lot of questions to ask.[17]

What those questions were LaFarge would never know, as Grant died very shortly after his return to New York, before he could travel out to see him in Saunderstown. Instead he had to content himself "with the sad consolation of officiating at his funeral Mass in the Church of Saint Joseph in Wickford, Rhode Island."[18]

Two of Grant's sons, Christopher and Oliver, achieved considerable literary success. Christopher, trained as an architect, abandoned that profession, choosing instead to write poetry and fiction, sometimes combining the two, as in his poetic novels *Beauty for Ashes* and *Each to the Other*. Christopher died in 1956, Oliver in 1963.

In 1960 LaFarge received a puzzling letter from the Catholic novelist Taylor Caldwell, who had just published her most popular novel, *Dear and Glorious Physician*. She told LaFarge that in 1946 she and Christopher were both invited to speak at a book and author's meeting in Baltimore. She bitterly described what happened at that meeting, charging that Christopher had grossly insulted her from the podium. She wrote that she did not know Christopher personally. They had never met, and she could think of no motive for the attack.[19]

Caldwell had referred to Christopher as LaFarge's brother. When he replied to her curious letter he wrote that he was Christopher's uncle, not his brother. He obviously believed her story, since he set about trying to explain Christopher's behavior. He wrote that his nephew "had been badly shaken by the death of his very lovely first wife, Louisa Hoar;

made an unsuccessful re-marriage, and had his health impaired by his experiences in World War II."

Although he had not seen Christopher much in the last years of his life, he understood that in his final days he "was spiritually a considerably changed man." LaFarge believed that the many prayers offered for him during his lifetime had their effect in bringing him a degree of religious faith, which he did not have as a young man. "Please do not think too hard of the LaFarge clan, despite your experience," he asked her. "Rather, do pray much for the Catholic members who are raising families of wonderful Catholic children. Three who are non-Catholics have entered the Church of late."[20]

This author discussed the episode with Christopher's two sons; neither could account for his father's behavior, which if it really happened the way Caldwell described it, was entirely out of character for him. One of these sons, Grant LaFarge, a doctor in Santa Fe, agreed with the writer that Caldwell might have mistaken Oliver for Christopher. For one thing, the brothers resembled each other. Additionally, Oliver was acerbic, sometimes drank too much and told people off, and was still in the military, stationed in Washington, D.C., in 1946. He was also bitterly anti-Catholic. It is more than possible that he was Caldwell's *bête noire,* and not Christopher.

Grant has a complete set of his father's diaries. He obligingly went through the year 1946 at the author's request, and could find no mention of Taylor Caldwell.

> Thus, I remain baffled by this incident. That Taylor Caldwell could have misidentified the speaker as Father John's *brother* (Grant) clearly puts the identification of my father as the perpetrator in doubt, at least in my reading of the materials you sent me, and in my own knowledge of my father, to say nothing of the 1946 Diary. What Taylor Caldwell described was heinous, and recalled roughly 14 years after the fact. I don't think Christopher was capable of such a diatribe (he had been trained, too, as a formal debater at Groton), though I have a hunch that Oliver could well have been, and I base that on some of the vituperative exchanges that I have heard in the past from him. Oliver was, indeed, a complicated man, though I was fond of him.[21]

LaFarge's near obsession for keeping his family members in the faith, or bringing those in who were out, displayed itself in a bizarre incident involving Oliver, winner of the Pulitzer Prize for literature in 1929 for his novel *Laughing Boy,* about a young Navajo Indian couple whose lives were blighted by the white man's world. In addition to writing fiction for a living, Oliver was an authority on the American Indian. For thirty years, until his death from emphysema in 1963, he was president of the Association on American Indian Affairs, a major Indian welfare group. During World War II he served as official historian of the Air Transport Command, rising to the rank of lieutenant-colonel by the war's end.[22] LaFarge was interested in his nephew's work from a humanitarian standpoint, but also as a Jesuit, since the order had a number of missions on various Indian reservations.

Oliver's first marriage was to Wanden (pronounced Wandeen) Matthews in 1929. After producing two children, a son and daughter, they were divorced in 1937. Wanden had been baptized Roman Catholic, but they were married in an Episcopalian ceremony. As it turned out, no baptismal certificate was ever found for Oliver. In Santa Fe in 1936, while his marriage was already foundering, Oliver met Consuelo Otille Baca, a beautiful, dark-haired woman thirteen years younger than he. They fell in love with each other and married two years after his divorce from Wanden became final.

Because Oliver was a divorced man they could not marry in the Church, which distressed Consuelo, a devout Catholic, for whom the sacraments were now denied since, according to the Church, she was living in sin. This presented no problem to Oliver, who had long since rejected the Catholic Church. Marrying Consuelo, however, even outside the Church, threw him willy-nilly into that Church. The Bacas were Catholic in the deep Spanish way: mysteries, sacraments, saints, superstitions—all of it. When his son by Consuelo was born she insisted that he be baptized. Oliver reluctantly agreed, and even attended the ceremony at the Cathedral of Saint Francis in Santa Fe, made famous by Willa Cather in her novel *Death Comes for the Archbishop.* He and Consuelo lived in Santa Fe for the last seventeen years of his life.

Belatedly discovering Consuelo's plight, LaFarge stepped into the picture. From January to November 1954, he maneuvered to persuade the archbishop of Santa Fe to nullify Oliver's marriage to Wanden, so that he might marry Consuelo in the Catholic Church. The combination of Father John, whom he admired and respected, and Consuelo, his beloved wife, proved too much for Oliver to resist. To make matters harder for him there was a third collaborator in the plot, his former wife, Wanden, who cooperated fully with LaFarge to provide necessary information that would win the nullification.

The whole episode is documented in a series of letters in the LaFarge family papers in the New York Historical Society. LaFarge first wrote to Wanden, then living in Colorado, to ask her help in getting her marriage to Oliver nullified. He posed in this letter certain questions which he hoped she could answer. What he needed was proof that she was a Roman Catholic who had married outside the Church. If sufficiently documented, this might be enough to invalidate the marriage in the eyes of the Church, thus enabling his nephew to marry Consuelo in a Catholic ceremony. It would make an even stronger case if it could be proved that Oliver himself was a baptized Catholic.

In response to LaFarge's letter, Wanden wrote:

> Dear, dear Uncle John, of course I want to help! I think it is most important that Oliver's marriage be regularized according to the laws of the Catholic Church, if it is in any way possible.

She wrote that as a child she was taken to "Roman Catholic Churches for services many times." As a teenager she "went alone to Midnight Mass on Christmas Eve in Paris to the Church of San Sulpice and *not* for cultural reasons, but for religious ones." Until she was about twenty-two she continued going to various Catholic Churches to pray at least twice a month, "entirely on my own volition and always alone . . ."[23]

On the strength of Wanden's letter, and documentation from other sources, LaFarge was able to make a case for nullification before the archbishop of Santa Fe. He assured him that Oliver was a baptized Catholic, and that his parents, though Florence was Protestant, were married in a Catholic ceremony. "My brother Grant," he wrote, "was a believing but non-practicing Catholic, making the usual promises, but who failed to keep them, largely through the influence of his wife's bigoted parents."[24]

He and Wanden had been married in an Episcopal ceremony. According to LaFarge, at the time of this marriage in 1929, "Oliver professed complete disbelief." This was undoubtedly true. LaFarge's next claim about his nephew, however, is much harder to accept. "Later he repented of his disbelief," he wrote the archbishop, "and professed at least fundamental principles. This repentance is, I am convinced, sincere . . ."[25]

While LaFarge was eager to obtain the nullification, and was stretching some points to achieve that end, he is not to be entirely faulted for exaggeration in some of his claims. Oliver, who had done nothing to initiate the proceedings, was grudgingly cooperating with his wife and uncle, telling them things that, if not outright lies, were misleading deceptions. On March 6, 1954, for example, he wrote his uncle "I do deeply appreciate your continued interest in the problem of our marriage, and so, most emphatically, does Consuelo." He told LaFarge that he was trying to track down his baptismal certificate, but so far without any luck.[26]

On the very next day he wrote his brother Christopher that while their other brother, Francis, had been baptized Catholic, so far there was no record of his own baptism, which was a "relief" to him. "I should be very much annoyed if it could suddenly be shown that I was R.C. after all."[27] As it developed, LaFarge was premature in telling the archbishop that Oliver had been baptized. No record of his baptism was ever found, which made it essential that Wanden prove her Catholicism to the archbishop's satisfaction. One of them had to be Catholic, married outside the Church, for the marriage to be subject to nullification. This Wanden was able to do, writing LaFarge that she was baptized Esther Cary Matthews in Stockbridge, Massachusetts in 1902 or 1903.[28] This baptismal record was tracked down, and in January 1955 the marriage of Wanden to Oliver was officially nullified by the archbishop of Santa Fe. Oliver and Consuelo were now free to be married in the cathedral by Father John LaFarge, who made a special trip to Santa Fe to perform the ceremony. Consuelo was jubilant, writing LaFarge of the wedding plans and her emotions:

> Pete (Oliver's brother Francis's wife) and Franny arrive on the 16th. We just had a letter from Franny, giving us their dates. What a celebration! Also thank you for your prayers at Christmas and your dear note. You give me courage.
>
> It's a heavenly thought that soon I will be able to offer not only mass but communion too for you.[29]

Oliver's sardonic note to Christopher was in sharp contrast to his wife's joyous note to LaFarge.

> Uncle John finally got us a dispensation—to my regret. I sit and watch the Church catching up with Consuelo, and it rouses every drop of Roundhead blood in my veins. Well, we'll talk about it some time. Anyhow, Uncle J lands here next Tuesday, performs the ritual on Thursday morning, and that afternoon we throw a joint birthday party for Mrs. Baca (76) and Uncle J. (75) To this affair will come both the Archbishop and Uncle Vidal, who has arranged for his flock to put on a dance for us in the living room—for free! Very warming. They asked me what dance I'd like, and I suggested one with four dancers, extraordinarily pretty. It happens to be a

phallic when you get into it far enough, but that's not at all apparent to the uninitiated observer, and none of the godly will suspect
that those two demure and graceful girls are, in a mystical way, being screwed. I don't know if they'll do that one, but I hope they will.
It's really charming, and the songs are cheerful and catchy.[30]

Vidal Gutierrez (Uncle Vidal to Oliver) was an elder of the Santa
Clara Pueblo tribe in New Mexico, with whom Oliver had a very close
friendship; so close, in fact, that he was adopted into Vidal's family. At
the time of his Catholic marriage to Consuelo, Uncle Vidal was in his
nineties. He would live to be over a hundred.

There is a postscript to this whole affair. Oliver, to please his wife
while he still lived, accepted the nullification of his marriage to Wanden,
his Catholic marriage to Consuelo, and his second wife's devout Catholicism. What he could not accept was burial as a Catholic himself. Without telling Consuelo, he had left instructions that he be buried Episcopalian. Consuelo had no inkling that this would be his last request of her,
and she was stunned. In her distraught condition she might have ignored
his order, but she did not. Oliver's body would not be carried from
Bishop Lamy's cathedral of St. Francis to its final resting place. He was
buried, just a few months before his Uncle John's death in 1963, from
the Episcopalian Church of the Holy Faith in Santa Fe.

His brother Grant's death in 1938 left LaFarge with only two living
siblings, his sisters Frances and Margaret. Frances married a lawyer
named Edwards Childs. They had two daughters, the youngest of whom
died at age nineteen. The other, also Frances, never married. She became
a professor of history at Brooklyn College, Brooklyn, New York.

His sister Frances was living in Mount Dora, Florida, when she died
suddenly on February 28, 1951. She had gone to mass the previous Sunday, received communion, and seemed well. By Monday afternoon,
however, she felt sick and called the doctor. He came and reassured her
about her blood pressure, but told her to rest. "Tuesday she was quite un-
well," LaFarge wrote Margaret, "they had two nurses to look after her;
still she seemed as if she might pull out of it. Tuesday night she became
unconscious, and died about 7:15 Wednesday morning, February 28."[31]

The body was first brought back to New York. LaFarge said a funeral
mass for her at St. Ignatius Church. In addition to a large number
of friends and relatives, fifteen priests assisted. Her remains were then
taken by train to Cleveland, where her deceased husband was buried,
with LaFarge and her daughter Frances accompanying them to their

final resting place. After LaFarge returned to New York he wrote to Margaret about their sister.

> Frances' inner life was not very articulate—you remember she never found it quite easy to express herself. But it was nonetheless very deep and real. She had a wonderful, simple, and loving piety, which showed itself, like her charity, in all sorts of beautiful, unexpected ways. She bore a hard cross, or rather many hard crosses, uncomplainingly and sweetly, over a lifetime. I feel sure that her holy and loving soul went very straight to God, and that we shall all feel the results of her prayers.[32]

Margaret, the only LaFarge offspring, besides himself, never to marry, was LaFarge's closest sibling. She and his mother visited him twice in Europe while he was a student at Innsbruck, and returned again in 1905 for his ordination. After their mother's death in 1925 she was by far his most regular correspondent, sending him lengthy, handwritten (at times almost indecipherable) chatty letters from the house on Sunnyside Place in Newport, where she lived alone after her mother died. She was his only real connection to his old home and Newport. LaFarge hoped that the house would remain in LaFarge family hands indefinitely, but two years after Margaret's death it was sold. It still stands, but at this writing it has been divided into three separate apartments.

In her letters to her brother Margaret usually inquired about his health (she worried about his health), and included a mine of information about the doings of family and friends. On July 18, 1936, for example, she wrote "Many thanks for your letter. I was glad to receive it for I was anxious about you in the great heat. Here it has not been at all uncomfortable, only one day that I should consider really hot and every night cool."[33]

She had the LaFarge love of nature, and could describe things she saw and liked with considerable skill. At the end of November 1942, an empty coal barge was hurled up in a storm on the rocks off Bailey's Beach in Newport. Their sister Frances was visiting her at the time and they decided to view the scene in person. She sent a photograph of the rock-bound barge from a local newspaper, along with a description of the sight.

> I thought the enclosed would interest you. Frances and I were taking a little drive and just as we got to Bailey's Beach this is what met our vision. It was like a picture of Turner's. A tremendous sea,

rather blue than gray with the north wind blowing back the foam
against an angry sky towards the southeast—long funnel shaped
clouds moving rapidly. The barge (coal: but empty) is just in on a
narrow passage of water between rocks off the old Lippett place. It
is a very long barge—the end is hidden by the waves.

In this same letter she wrote of going to a surprise golden jubilee party
for friends named Brad and Emma Norman. Although Frances had not
been invited, she took her along anyway. The Normans not only did not
mind, they "said her coming was the nicest surprise of all."[34]

Unlike LaFarge's correspondence with his mother, however, there
were few of what might be termed "intellectual" exchanges between
them, either in his letters to her or in those to him. Apparently Margaret
did not wander far from Newport during the last decade or so of her life,
which is not surprising since she was moving into her eighties by then.
She died on May 25, 1956, at the age of eighty-seven. She was up and
around her house just two days before her death, but on the evening of
May 24 she was seized by a severe pain in her stomach. The doctor came
and injected her with morphine, which calmed her down for a few hours.
But by the next morning she was in agony, but did not want to leave the
house. The doctor returned and insisted that she go to the hospital, which
she agreed to on the condition that she could return home as soon as possible. But she expired a few hours after her arrival there. The doctor later
explained to LaFarge that she had been suffering from a stomach tumor.
"The actual cause of death, however, was heart failure brought about by
the distress that she had from this obstruction."[35]

She was waked at home, in the same parlor where LaFarge's mother
had been laid out thirty-one years earlier. The day of the funeral "dawned
sunny and beautiful." LaFarge celebrated a solemn high mass for her.
"We placed Aunt Mar," he wrote a niece, "in the plot in St. Columba's
cemetry in which my mother rests. . . ." At the gravesite he was able, for
the first time, to avail himself "of the new permission to use the English
language at the obsequies both in the church and at the graveyard . . .
Everyone joined in the alternate verses in English, which we never had
before."[36]

Not a demonstrative man, LaFarge wept at Margaret's funeral. He
would miss her keenly, but was glad she had not suffered long at the end.

> I shall of course miss Aunt Mar intensely, as she has always been
> so near to me and I have kept a constant intercourse with her
> through letter and telephone all through the years, but nevertheless

it is an immense relief, first of all, to know that she did not have to
linger on with a long and painful illness in a state of mental as well
as physical collapse; secondly, it was my own constant prayer, as
it was hers, that I might not have to go before she did. It would have
been very distressing for her. It was always a comfort to her to think
that I would survive her and be able to offer the Holy Sacrifice for
her after her departure. So happily this prayer has been granted. It
will take us all some time to realize that she has actually gone. She
played so large a part in our lives.[37]

LaFarge lived seven more years after Margaret's death. They continued to be productive years right up until the end, when he expired peacefully in his room at *America*. For the last two decades of his life he found
himself caught up in the tremendous events that followed the outbreak
of war in Europe in 1939. After Pearl Harbor, as did so many of his fellow Americans, he had to adjust to the spectacle of the United States and
the Soviet Union embracing each other to defeat their common fascist
enemies. It was not an easy adjustment, but one he knew he had to make.

Chapter 12

World War II And After

When war broke out in Europe in early September 1939, LaFarge called for American neutrality. "Europe's circumstances," he wrote in *America,* "are not the same as America's. Since they are not ours, since the onslaught on the social order does not come to America in the guise of military aggression, we should be fatally mistaken if we drew a false conclusion and sought to defend the social order by means quite unsuited to the combat."[1]

The first six months of the war were called by some people at the time the "Phony War," since the major combatants—Great Britain, France and Germany—seemed unable, or unwilling, to use their forces to conduct serious offensive operations. Some pundits were predicting that the war would peter out and there would be no winners or losers, except Poland, which had already been divided between Germany and the Soviet Union. In his eagerness to justify and insure American neutrality, LaFarge was able to view the war as a result of injustices done to Germany after World War I, especially in the matter of colonies, which were stripped from Germany by the Versailles Treaty in 1919. He even suggested giving those colonies back to Germany.

> Granting the *present aims* of governments, to which their peoples give at least implicit consent, a readjustment in the distribution of colonies is a simple matter of justice. If Great Britain, Belgium, Portugal, Spain, Italy, the Netherlands and France are entitled to colonies, particularly their respective slices of Africa, there seems no cogent reason why Germany's slices should not be restored to her.

With some foresight, but also with surprising insensitivity to the native peoples of Africa, nearly all of whom lived under the control of the aforementioned powers, LaFarge wrote that at present these colonies

191

were "too deeply woven into the political and economic texture of the world to permit such overnight abolition."[2]

When overnight divestiture of African colonies did take place in the late 1950s and early 1960s, much chaos and intertribal conflict resulted, and is still resulting decades later. LaFarge was prescient in this observation. But as for returning Germany's colonies to her, that was an emotional, irrational and irresponsible suggestion, which can be explained only by his passionate desire for a quick restoration of peace. It was also right in line with the appeasement policies of Britain and France from the mid-to-the-late 1930s, with the difference that those countries had finally abandoned appeasement and gone to war.

Several weeks later, in another article on stopping the war, LaFarge returned to one of his favorite themes—peace through religion. Any uniting for peace in Europe and the world, he argued, any hope that any federation of states after the war could achieve lasting peace, could happen only if it drew its strength and inspiration from religion. That most world leaders would view such a suggestion as hopelessly naive probably did not cross his mind.

> This is another way of saying that any international structure must have a moral basis. You cannot erect a federation upon crowds of atheists or near atheists. Without religion the peoples who engage in a peace contract are mere hordes, at the mercy of their political exploiters. They lack that moral cohesion which distinguishes a true people from a mob. They also lack that charity which is necessary if international justice is to be fulfilled.[3]

The most logical, indeed only, effective religious leader for such a movement was the pope. Whether LaFarge really thought the leaders of the European powers—officially atheistic Russia, Anglican Britain, anticlerical France, Nazi Germany, and Fascist Italy—would turn to the papacy for leadership in their international relations is unclear. His own faith in God, the Catholic Church, and the papacy was so strong that he was sometimes perplexed that everyone did not see it the same way. The League of Nations, he wrote at the end of November 1940, failed because it did not seek the religious support of the Vatican. The pope, as the successor to Saint Peter, was "the keeper of justice for the whole world."[4]

The "Phony War" ended abruptly when Hitler, concerned that France and Britain were about to occupy Norway and establish bases there, invaded that country and Denmark on April 9, 1940. Denmark wisely capitulated without resistance. The Norwegians fought back, but were soon overrun and forced to surrender. On June 9, 1940, Norway sued for an armistice.

In the meantime, Hitler launched a major invasion of the Netherlands and Belgium. It took only five days to defeat the Dutch army. German parachute troops dropped near Rotterdam and The Hague on May 10, capturing vital Dutch bridges and airfields. On May 14 the Dutch surrendered. The German armies then swept through Belgium and on into northern France. The vaunted French Maginot Line, built between the wars to protect France against a German invasion from the east, was not even tested. The line had stopped where the border between France and Belgium began. Swinging through Belgium the Germans simply skirted the line and, led by their tanks, broke through the thin French defenses in the Ardennes. The German *blitzkrieg,* spearheaded by tanks and dive bombers, proved unstoppable. Within six weeks, on June 25, 1940, France had surrendered.

A last-ditch French stand along the Straits of Dover coast, along with a German pause to regroup, enabled the British to evacuate the greater part of its expeditionary force from Dunkirk. Some three hundred thirty-eight thousand men, two-thirds of them British, made it back to England. Hitler was now supreme in parts of Eastern, and most of Western Europe. Great Britain, for the moment at least, stood alone in opposing him.

LaFarge sympathized with France, but felt that she had brought many of her troubles on herself by abandoning religion. After the French surrender he wrote that France's present distress stemmed from betrayal from both the Left and Right. The truth, however, "is that neither of these elements would have enjoyed their opportunity if the ground had not been laid by stolid indifference to religion, social justice and spiritual values among the economically solid and politically entrenched groups who formed a good part of France's bourgeoisie."[5] The defeat of France and its humiliating occupation for over four years by Germany, however, did have, to LaFarge at least, a positive effect on the French Church. By late 1944,with an uncharacteristic display of smugness and self-satisfaction, he could write that the Church in France was stronger than it had been in two hundred fifty years.[6]

With the fall of France in June 1940, and the ensuing Air Battle of Britain that began soon afterward, LaFarge had to agree that total American neutrality was no longer feasible. We had to help Britain, while at the same time arming ourselves to prepare for a possible total German victory in Europe. We might have to fight to save our democracy. But he wondered if American democracy was one based wholly on man himself without God. If it were, then it was not a genuine democracy.

"You are ready to die for democracy," he wrote in early 1941. "Are you equally ready to die for the full and adequate rights of the individual human person, in the light of what revealed religion teaches concerning the worth of the human soul." If the answer is no, then it "is obvious that their attitude is far closer to the anarchists, the leftists, and the dictators themselves than they fondly imagine."[7]

Germany's invasion of Russia in June 1941 presented a major problem for LaFarge. During the Spanish Civil War he had repeatedly criticized Soviet aid to the Republicans, and rejoiced when Franco finally prevailed over them. Even after Franco's victory he continued to attack Russia for its godlessness. "Russia's political existence," he wrote in December 1939, "must be cut off at *the source,* which is world secularism, from which the Soviet Union draws its lifeblood. It is not cut off at the source until the leading civilized nations agree to recognize the worship of God as necessary for the well-being and for the very existence of the modern state."[8]

In March 1941, the American Congress approved the Lend-Lease Act. Unlike World War I, when the United States sold aid to its allies on credit, resulting in bitter recriminations over non-payment of these debts after the war, the Lend-Lease Act was more sensible and generous in its terms. It permitted President Roosevelt to "sell, transfer title to, exchange, lease, lend or otherwise dispose of" any articles of military value to any countries whose defense he deemed vital to the protection of the United States. At that point the act was designed almost solely to aid Great Britain, then the only credible adversary of Germany. As of March 1941, it seemed more than possible that Britain might not be able to hold on much longer. If she surrendered to Germany, and Hitler acquired the British fleet as part of a peace treaty, the Western Hemisphere might be next on his agenda. Three months later, however, on June 22, 1941, Germany invaded the Soviet Union. Stalin's appeal to the United States for aid was granted, and Russia was soon added to the list of Lend-Lease recipients.

LaFarge's dilemma was profound. He scattershot his feelings in the September 20, 1941, issue of *America.* It was a rambling, almost hysterical reaction to American military aid to the Soviet Union. He wondered if this was not making a "covenant with Hell." Should not, he asked, all Catholics become conscientious objectors as long as the United States aids Russia?

To help answer these questions he drew upon Pius XI's encyclical on atheistic Communism, "*Divini Redemptoris.*" In that encyclical the pope had written "Communism is intrinsically wrong, and no one who would aid Christian civilization may collaborate with it in any undertaking whatsoever." Neither Pius XI (who died in 1939 and was succeeded by Piux XII), nor LaFarge, however, had foreseen that the Soviet Union might someday be a bulwark against Nazi Germany's conquest of a good portion of the Christian world, bringing an end to religious freedom in those countries.

Pius XII, after the German attack, hedged on the problem of support for Russia against Germany, as did LaFarge. After articulating his rage against atheistic Communism, he went on to point out in the same article that Pius XII did not condemn all collaboration with the Soviets. The pope, in fact, had decided not to take an official position on the issue. "From this," LaFarge wrote, "we need not rashly infer the pope was indifferent to the extreme gravity that the Russian war problem presents to the conscience of American Catholics. But we may suspect that he relies upon us to use our own wisdom and prudence."

LaFarge agreed that denying aid to Russia would help Germany, at the moment the greater threat to the United States. If aid is to be given Russia, however, it must somehow be tied in with religious freedom in that country. "Last but not least," he wrote, "no stone should be left unturned by our Department of State to keep insisting that whatever aid is granted carries with it an understanding that full unequivocal guarantees that religious freedom shall be given by the Soviets."[9] This did not, however, become an issue between Russia and the United States. The aid that was given was for the purpose of defeating Hitler—not assuring religious freedom for the Russian people.

LaFarge was furious when Maxim Litvinov was appointed Soviet ambassador to the United States in November 1941. Litvinov had been Soviet commissar for foreign affairs from July 1930 to May 3, 1939, when Vyacheslav Molotov replaced him. Being Jewish, Litvinov was seen by Stalin as a possible obstacle to a Soviet rapprochement with Germany. Two of Litvinov's major achievements while heading the Soviet foreign office were winning American diplomatic recognition of his country in 1933, and bringing Russia into the League of Nations in 1934. Once Hitler invaded Russia, Stalin brought Litvinov back into favor, shipping him off to Washington as ambassador. LaFarge angrily pointed out that to win American recognition in 1933 from President Roosevelt, Litvinov had promised to work for religious freedom in Russia, then later mocked that promise. LaFarge predicted that all we could expect from Litvinov was further treachery and deceit.[10]

When Japan attacked Pearl Harbor on December 7, 1941, plunging the United States into the war, there could no longer be any question of

American priorities. America had to win the war. While it was painful to
LaFarge to accept Russia as an ally of the United States, even he realized how important this was to accomplishing the goal of victory. Es-
tablishing a second front in southern or western Europe would be greatly
facilitated by tying up Hitler's divisions on the eastern front.

On July 12, 1942, Father Talbot asked LaFarge to take on the newly
created post of executive editor of *America,* making him number two
man on the publication. A little over two years later, in October 1944,
Talbot stepped down from the top spot and asked LaFarge to replace him
as editor in chief. LaFarge reflected on his appointment in *The Manner
Is Ordinary.*

> I was therefore called upon to direct a national religious weekly
> magazine at an unusually difficult time, the climax of World War
> II. The problems of any war are appalling, but none were ever as
> vexatious as that catastrophic time. For the first time in history, our
> country was engaged in war against an armed ideology quite as
> much as against a nation in arms. In fighting for our country the sit-
> uation was enormously complicated by the fact that we were allied
> with a great and powerful nation whose ideas, aims, and ultimately
> policies we were obliged in conscience to combat to the very end.
> Communism was not simply an excess, or a distortion of the truth;
> it was, in the words of Pope Pius XI, intrinsically wrong.[11]

But if Communism was "intrinsically wrong," so too was Fascism.
"The Nazi ideology was inflamed with hatred of Christ the God-Man and
His Church," he wrote, "as I had seen on my visit to Germany in 1938."
Hatred of Christianity forged a common bond between Hitler and Stalin,
making possible the Nazi-Soviet Pact in August 1939. He reminded his
readers that he had predicted that pact nearly a year before it was signed.
"On November 5, 1938, I had already written that Nazism might salvage
for its own purposes the irreligious tyranny of Communism—in short,
that Brown and Red Bolshevism might come to terms more easily and
more readily than we dared suspect."[12]

When Mussolini was overthrown on July 25, 1943, LaFarge again af-
firmed the interchangeability of Communism and Fascism, despite their
ostensible hatred of each other. To Communists, all anti-Communists are
Fascists. He wondered, now that Mussolini was gone, would there be a
Communist revolution in Italy. So far it had not happened, but it could.
Fascism can lead to Communism.

"If I were planning now for another Mussolini," he wrote in *America* on
August 21, 1943, "I could think of no other surer recipe than the prepara-

tion of a genuine Communist revolution. . . . Fascism and Communism generate each other, since they arise ultimately from a common source: the spiritually and socially uprooted individual struggling with the torment of economic exploitation and the might of a completely secular state."[13]

Again, as he repeated so many times in his writings, religion was a necessary adjunct to any successful, just society. Lest his readers misunderstand him, however, he made it clear that he was not calling for a Catholic totalitarian state in Italy. That would be grist for the mill of Communist propaganda. What Italy needed was some form of democracy. What that form would be should be left up to the Italian people. Fascism however, had to be expunged and never allowed to return.[14]

As the war in Europe was coming to an end in the spring of 1945, and Russian armies were overrunning Eastern Europe, LaFarge was distressed, while at the same time most undecided what to do about the situation. "Are we faced with the dilemma," he wrote on June 9, "either to appease Russia—moving, or being driven, from concession to concession—or else resort to war?" It was a terrible choice, but LaFarge had no answer.[15]

A possible way out of the dilemma offered itself on August 6, 1945, when the United States dropped an atomic bomb on the city of Hiroshima in Japan. Three days later a similar device was dropped on Nagasaki. An estimated seventy thousand people died in each attack. It was immediately apparent that the United States was the sole owner of these terrible weapons. Might this fact be used to threaten the Soviets, and by the threat force her to retreat from Eastern Europe? Certainly the thought crossed many people's minds. But it did not cross the mind of Father John LaFarge, who was appalled that the weapon had been invented, and even more appalled that it had been used. "The atom bomb," he wrote years later, "was a messenger of fear. I immediately asked myself, what can that fear accomplish? How far can it arouse the public to the deepest realization of our present danger."[16]

An editorial in *America* on August 18, 1945, probably written by LaFarge, called it a weapon that could destroy mankind. "It is extremely deplorable that this marvelous discovery has come at a period in the world's history when nations are least capable of using it constructively." The editorial went on to predict that soon other nations would also have the weapon. It could not be kept secret for long.[17] It was not— by 1949 the Soviet Union exploded its first nuclear device.

LaFarge followed up the editorial with an article calling for international control of atomic energy. "Gradually but steadily," he wrote on November 17, "there is dawning on the public mind the full horror of the atomic destruction which has been released. It is hard to say which is the more disquieting, the manifestation of power or the letting loose of an incalculable degree of radio-active poison, the most subtle destructive agency the world has ever known."

There was no defense against the weapon, he added. An international agency had to be created that would supersede national sovereignties and take custody of the bomb and all atomic energy. It had to be assumed that, out of fear of mutual annihilation, all nations would agree to this.[18]

LaFarge's anxiety over the bomb was increased by a conversation with his nephew Oliver Claxton, his sister Emily's son, who as a reporter witnessed the atomic bomb tests on Bikini Island in the Pacific in the summer of 1946. On July 1, a device with about the same force as the one dropped on Nagasaki was detonated over a fleet of seventy-five unmanned Japanese and obsolete American ships anchored in Bikini's lagoon. It did extensive damage to the fleet, and released high amounts of lethal radiation into the atmosphere. A second bomb was dropped on July 25 with similar results. LaFarge recounted his conversation with Claxton in his autobiography.

> After his return he told me that he himself was shaken and appalled beyond anything he could express by the horror that the event inspired in him. At the same time he was disgusted with the incompetents whom the United States Navy sent out to report on the affair; disgusted, too, at the levity with which they tried to make capital out of the fact that the animals poisoned by irradiation lasted a couple of weeks longer than they were expected to. Again it was an example of the sterility of mere terror.[19]

Ever since coming to *America* in 1926, LaFarge was concerned with world peace. In 1927 he helped to found the Catholic Association for International Peace. Now, as much as any other event or circumstance, the atomic bomb convinced him of the absolute necessity of a world organization. Even before the bomb's existence was revealed, however, he was urging international collaboration to keep peace in the postwar world. On January 2, 1945, he wrote to Msgr. Howard J. Carroll, general secretary of the National Catholic Welfare Conference, mentioning that *America* had been "carrying on a little campaign against the legislation providing for universal military service in peacetime. It is being said, publicly, that the President in his address to Congress on January 6 will ask for legislation in its behalf in spite of the Bishop's recommendations against taking action before the war ends."

He was concerned that a peacetime draft would reduce the public's confidence in a world organization.

> Advocating a program based on the frank admission at such an early date that our hopes for lasting peace are illusory may bring on a repetition of the cynicism of the twenties. Enemies of international collaboration will be quick to point out with scorn that as the Atlantic Charter is being explained away, so also the Four Freedoms are now going by the boards, one by one. They will remind us that on this same occasion, after his election four years ago, on January 6, 1941, Mr. Roosevelt said: "In the future days, which we seek to make secure, we look forward to a world founded upon four essential human freedoms. . . . The Fourth is Freedom from Fear which, translated into world terms, means a worldwide reduction of armaments to such a point and in such a thorough fashion that no nation will be in a position to commit an act of aggression against any neighbor—anywhere in the world.[20]

At least partial disarmament, the end of peacetime drafts, and a vigorous international organization, therefore, were all part of LaFarge's prescription for world peace. From the perspective of a half-century later his thinking was naive. Still, in 1945 and 1946, before the Cold War and the massive buildup of armaments—especially nuclear warheads—started, it was possible to imagine a new world order, chagrined at the horrors of World War II, listening to reason. It was even appropriate to add morality to the equation, to buttress the desperate needs and fears of mankind. Sometime in 1946 (the exact date is not specified) LaFarge issued a statement on the atomic bomb and the newly created United Nations. It was a thoughtful blending of moral law and international self-interest.

> In the first place, the worldwide terror caused by the Atom Bomb has brought us face to face with the fact that only one frail defense lies between us and absolute destruction, not of our nation or of our cities alone but quite possibly of the human race itself. This defense is the moral law and man's adherence to the same. All the scientific ingenuity, all the military strategy, all the political wisdom in the world cannot protect us against this evil unless our international good will is based on moral convictions with respect for the duties and rights that stem from the Creator and the human race itself.
>
> But the consciousness of our lack of any other defense against destruction has made us correspondingly aware of the shortcomings

of the instruments which we are now in the process of creating in the cause of peace. This has made us doubly critical, but constructively critical, of the truly remarkable achievements of the United Nations Organization. It makes an intensely alive and immediate issue of what for a great part of mankind has rested largely in the field of idealism and theory, namely, our need to implement as best we may the moral law as existing between nations. As Messrs. Atlee and Anthony Eden have both so clearly seen, it is impossible to cling to the idea of unlimited national sovereignty and hope to escape an armament race with its ensuing horrors for all concerned. I see only one possible escape from the impasse in which we are now caught, namely, to abolish the Veto proviso in the United Nations Organization; to place the whole question of the control of atomic energy, not merely destructive but benignant as well, in the hands of an international commission under the General Assembly of the UNO; and a policy of general disarmament by which we shall pool our resources in an international police force with the power of inspection and control of individual transgressions.[21]

LaFarge never completely lost hope in the United Nations, but as the Cold War intensified after 1946, and his perceived fear of Communism at home as well as abroad increased, he came to realize that the United States, to preserve its freedom, had to rely more on itself than on any international organization. The Communists were doing their best to obstruct the United Nations. Through its branches and committees, however, it had shown "extraordinary power of resistance to even the most violently disruptive tactics on the part of the Soviet delegations and the Soviet satellites. . . ."[22]

After 1948 neither LaFarge nor *America* had much to say about the United Nations. The organization is not even mentioned in *The Manner Is Ordinary,* published in 1954. In 1950 he wrote to Norman Cousins, editor of *The Saturday Review of Literature,* about the necessity of reconstructing the United Nations. Perhaps, he thought, national memberships might be replaced by some sort of individual people's organization, representing mankind rather than their own countries. "I am in favor," he wrote Cousins on August 15, 1950, "of a revised and strengthened United Nations. Moreover, I earnestly look forward to the day when we shall have, as you say, such a Congress of the peoples, with individual membership and individual representation. It is obviously the goal to work for, the goal towards which the world is inevitably tending, once the unspeakable confusion is out of the way that the Communist *betrayal* of these ideas has caused."

If a new start is to be made, however, "there must be a clear and definitive resolution of the question that Communism's world assault has posed: a definite recognition by the free peoples of the world, and by the United Nations as their representative, of the Creator and His place in the life of all peoples and all nations." Once again LaFarge's call for a God-inspired world brought him to the brink of unreality. His own religious fervor blinded him to the historical fact that religion, rather uniting great numbers of people in a common cause for peace, has consistently divided people and turned them against each other.[23]

In the meantime, LaFarge acknowledged, the United States could not supinely lay down its arms or dilute its military preparedness. He made no objection when President Truman called for a revival of military conscription in 1948. The spread of world Communism made it imperative that we remain strong.

Not only Communism abroad, however, but Communism at home as well. When the Vatican declared Communism to be sinful, LaFarge had all the moral authority he needed to support anti-Communist actions in the United States. On June 30, 1949, the Vatican issued a four-part decree against Communism, which *America* enthusiastically endorsed in an editorial. The four points were:

1) It is unlawful to "enlist in or show favor to the Communist Party."
2) It is unlawful to "publish, read, or disseminate books, newspapers, periodicals or leaflets in support of the Communist doctrine and practice, or write in them any articles."
3) Any Catholics doing either or both of the above two are to be denied the sacraments.
4) Catholics who profess Communism will be excommunicated.

America hoped that this decree would have a salutary effect on countries such as Italy, discouraging Catholics there from joining the Communist Party.[24]

When eleven American Communists were found guilty of violating the Smith Act (a law passed by Congress in 1940 making it a crime to teach or advocate the violent overthrow of the government) on October 15, 1949, *America* applauded the decision. If the convictions were upheld by the Supreme Court it would be a blow against Communism. "The peril to which democracies have exposed themselves through an excess of freedom, will then be at an end."[25]

Despite the argument that the Smith Act violated the free speech provisions of the First Amendment to the Constitution, the Supreme Court did uphold the convictions in *Dennis v. United States* in 1951. This came at the height of the anti-Communist mood that hit the country in the early years of the Cold War. Six years later, during somewhat calmer times, the Supreme Court, in *Yates v. United States,* held that merely advocating the violent overthrow of the government as an abstract doctrine — without incitement to action — was not a violation of the Smith Act.

America also endorsed the New York State Feinberg law, passed on March 30, 1949,which directed the State Board of Regents "to purge the public school system of teachers and other employees who are Communists or fellow-travelers." In this same editorial *America* also applauded the University of California for demanding a loyalty oath of its teachers.[26]

Despite its consistent and unremitting opposition to Communism, *America* was surprisingly unwilling to support Senator Joseph McCarthy's campaign to root Communists out of the government. The Republican senator from Wisconsin first came to national attention with his infamous "Communists in the State Department" speech made before the Women's Republican Club of West Virginia on February 9, 1950. Waving some sheets of paper in his hand, he astonished the audience by claiming that the papers contained the names of 205 State Department employees known by the secretary of state to be card-carrying Communists. Although he never named any of these Communists, McCarthy received enormous publicity and overnight fame by tapping into the public's anti-Communism hysteria.

Most of his fellow Republicans (although not all) supported McCarthy in what became a notorious witch hunt. Looking ahead to the elections of 1952, they welcomed McCarthy's charges, since they were primarily directed at Democrats. Even Dwight Eisenhower, while personally detesting McCarthy, accepted his help while campaigning for the presidency in 1952, and in turn endorsed the senator's successful bid for re-election.

At first LaFarge and *America* cautiously supported McCarthy, although they had some qualms about his tactics. In April 1950, McCarthy insisted that the Federal Bureau of Investigation open up its files to him. The bureau refused. In an editorial, *America* supported the bureau, but at the same time showed sympathy for McCarthy. "The Senator from Wisconsin has tried to prove too much. But if he can produce well-informed witnesses to prove *something,* we contend, against much of the public press, that he should have his innings."[27]

Within a month, however, *America* was having second thoughts about McCarthy. In an editorial, "Is the Red peril a distraction?" it affirmed that

Communism in this country must be destroyed. But a wholly negative campaign, such as the one being waged by McCarthy, was not the way to do it. "The great charter of the Church's warfare against atheistic Communism, the encyclical *Divini Redemptoris* of Pius XI, is explicit and detailed in its insistence on a fundamental and constructive program of social renovation as an antidote to Marxism. We ought to be very careful, therefore, not to identify ourselves too closely with anti-Communists like Senator McCarthy, who has never identified himself with the Catholic social movement."[28]

While backing away from McCarthy, *America* still enthusiastically supported official efforts to weed out Communists in government and in the schools. Under President Harry Truman the Loyalty Review Board was set up in 1947 by executive order. Commenting on the board's activities through 1951, *America* noted with approval that since its establishment it had questioned the loyalty of 13,842 government employees, "getting reports on them from the FBI and other investigating agencies. Of these, 2,877 have resigned on learning that their loyalty was being looked into. A total of 294 have actually been discharged on loyalty grounds." *America* clearly believed that the loyalty board was doing good, effective work. It gave no thought to the possibility that some of those who resigned might not have had anything to hide, but had quit on principle.[29]

One month later, in another editorial, *America* deplored a recent decision by the Third District Court of Appeals in California, which ordered the University of California to reinstate eighteen teachers who had been dismissed for refusing to take an anti-Communist oath. This, in effect, repealed California's loyalty oath law.[30]

In 1950 *America* had distanced itself from McCarthy because he failed to identify himself with Catholic social action. By late 1952 it was condemning him for his reckless smear tactics. An article by Rev. Robert C. Hartnett, S.J., who had succeeded LaFarge as editor in chief in 1948, attacked McCarthy for charging that Adlai Stevenson, the Democratic presidential candidate in 1952, had been endorsed by the *Daily Worker,* a New York Communist newspaper. This was not true, wrote Hartnett. Stevenson was not even mentioned in the issue referred to by McCarthy. "If anyone wonders why *America* has been very cool to what are euphemistically called Senator McCarthy's 'methods,' perhaps this cheap stunt will explain why." *America* might not have finished its campaign against Communism, but it was finished with McCarthy.[31]

LaFarge was in accord with his Jesuit colleagues on the subject of McCarthy. In response to a letter sent him in April 1952 from a subscriber, he wrote that while the senator had been abused by the "evils which he denounces," he used unacceptable methods. There were other forces at work to root out those evils. Granting that McCarthy's goal in fighting Communism was laudable, "a good many people find it difficult to justify the means he used." He explained *America's* position on McCarthy and Communism.

> AMERICA has from the beginning been very careful to use a balanced judgment and, since we have been pioneers ourselves from many years ago in exposing Communist evils, we are naturally inclined to give the benefit of the doubt wherever possible. I understand that in the near future there will be some further discussion of Senator McCarthy in our pages. At present he has certainly incurred the displeasure of a great many persons in Congress who are not in the least bit sympathetic to anything communistic.[32]

By 1954 much of the country had also turned against McCarthy. While to this day the Wisconsin senator still has his admirers, his attack on the United States Army, accusing it, among other things, of protecting and promoting a known Communist dentist from captain to major, then honorably discharging him, backfired against him. The Army counterattacked by showing that McCarthy and his aide Roy Cohn had tried to blackmail the Army into giving a commission and special treatment to a draftee, G. David Schine, a close friend of Cohn. It was probably not so much the substance of the Army-McCarthy arguments that turned many Americans off to McCarthy, as what they revealed about McCarthy himself. Since the hearings were televised, millions of Americans could see, as well as read about, McCarthy in action. He came across as a ruthless, boorish, insensitive prosecutor.

Shortly after the Army-McCarthy hearings, held in the spring of 1954, the Senate appointed a committee to investigate the Wisconsin senator. It recommended censuring him for contempt of the Senate. Technically, the charge was that he had refused to appear before a Senate committee dealing with election irregularities in 1952. In reality, he had become an embarrassment to that body. All Democrats, joined by twenty-two Republicans, voted for censure. Another twenty-two Republicans, nearly all from the West and Middle West, voted against it. Since the voters in Wisconsin had sent him back for another six-year term in 1952, McCarthy was still secure in his Senate seat. He died, however, in May 1957 of a liver ailment worsened by acute alcoholism, a virtual outcast among his colleagues.

Although Cold War fever abated somewhat in the mid-and-late fifties, it still remained a major cause of international tension and instability for decades to come. The United States was the leader of the western democracies against the Soviet-led Eastern Bloc. LaFarge urged the West not to let down its guard. He expressed his deeply felt concern in *America* on November 2, 1957.

> . . . the spread and permanence of the Soviet regime have proved beyond doubt its extraordinary toughness as well as its paradoxical flexibility. It can always reverse itself. It can adapt itself to new circumstances. It can drop for the time being ardently sought goals. It can mask itself in numberless attractive disguises, and there are no limits to its intrigues and infiltrations; it calls for equally increasing vigilance on our part.[33]

LaFarge's hatred of Communism had affected his decision, and that of *America* and most of the American Catholic press and hierarchy, to support Franco in the Spanish Civil War. It continued to affect it after Franco's victory in 1939, despite the knowledge that his regime often resorted to brutality against its opponents. Near the end of 1944 rumors were circulating that Franco had either resigned, or was about to be overthrown. If it were true, LaFarge wondered, who or what would take his place? He acknowledged that both Right and Left had committed atrocities in Spain. He condemned these atrocities, and insisted that Spain adopt a democratic form of government. He did not, however, criticize Franco directly. He especially deplored the fact that Catholics were assaulting Catholics in that country.

> Even if the balance of atrocity may be found to tip the scales far deeper on the side of the Reds than that of the Nationalist purges, there is a peculiar grievousness, for a Catholic conscience anywhere in the world, at the sight of fellow Catholics using any form of violence or cruelty in the name of Our Blessed Lord Himself.[34]

During World War II the Spanish Republicans set up a government in exile in Mexico. Shortly after the war ended, a suggestion was made that the United States give diplomatic recognition to this government. At the Potsdam Conference on August 2, 1945, Great Britain and the United States, at Stalin's insistence, agreed to blackball any Spanish application for admission to the United Nations. Recognizing the government-in-exile was probably not seriously considered by this country, but *America* quickly went on the offensive, reminding its readers that not a single member of that government was Catholic. It consisted of a group of men who had dedicated their lives "to the most violent attacks upon the very foundations of religion."[35]

Another argument used by LaFarge was that to withdraw support from the Franco regime might lead to a resumption of the civil war. The argument had some merit. Brutal and tyrannical as he was, Franco did represent stability in a nation that had gone through three years of turmoil and ferocious bloodletting. On December 1, 1945, LaFarge published a review of a recent book by Carlton Hayes, American wartime ambassador to Spain, titled *Wartime Mission in Spain*. According to LaFarge, Hayes made a forceful case against any foreign intervention in Spain to change the government. Hayes was "not holding a brief for the Franco government," LaFarge insisted. What the ambassador was hoping to see was an "evolution" in Spain. "Any type of interference in Spain . . . inevitably threatens to result in Civil War and its attendant horrors."[36]

LaFarge did not claim that the Franco government was not violating human rights. He deplored these violations, but saw no way that the United States could stop them. In its "Comments" section on March 2, 1946, *America* criticized attacks by members of Franco's Falangist Party on foreigners in Spain who were perceived as opposing Franco. "These attacks help to form the impression abroad of Falange disregard for the basic right of free speech."[37]

Acknowledging Falangist excesses, however, was not sufficient reason for taking action against Spain. When a United Nations subcommittee urged international severance of all relations with Spain in June 1946, *America* quickly opposed the suggestion. "That Spain is not a democracy as the United States is, and that civil liberties there are far below the standard we enjoy, is a simple fact; that Spain is a fascist nation . . . is simply not true." The editors correctly pointed out that there were much greater human rights abuses in other countries, such as the Soviet Union.[38]

When at the end of the year, the UN General Assembly voted to ask for the "recall from Madrid of the heads of diplomatic missions now there," *America* pointed out the hypocrisy of such a step.

> But the argument that the Franco Government is fascist or a threat to peace is not half so relevant as the fact that a great to-do is made about charges of tyranny in one small portion of the world while nothing dares be said about tyranny on a wholesale scale in Eastern Europe.[39]

While denying that Franco's regime was fascist, it was admitted that it was a one-party-rule dictatorship, a fact which did bother the editors at *America*. LaFarge, however, does not appear to have wavered, in public at least, in his personal support of Franco. His last *America* article on Spain was published in the April 14, 1951 issue, shortly after the United States restored its full embassy in Spain, which had been reduced in status. The American ambassador to Spain, in response to a UN resolution in 1946, had been withdrawn. Along with sending back an ambassador in 1951, the United States granted a large loan to Spain. LaFarge was delighted with both actions. "The mending of U.S.-Spanish relations, it is clear, will have a considerable influence on the relations of Spain with other Western European countries."[40]

Two months before publication of LaFarge's article, in anticipation of the return of an American ambassador to Spain, *America* proposed that Spain be invited to join the North Atlantic Treaty Organization, since the Spanish regime was "irrevocably committed to the anti-Communist cause."[41] This was, of course, premature. Spain would eventually join NATO, but not until 1982, years after Franco's death and the establishment of democracy in Spain.

Later on in 1951, however, *America* did lose patience with Franco personally, criticizing him for failing to introduce social and political reforms. *America* could resist international hostility to him, but it could not ignore its own Church's leaders in Spain. In the summer of 1951 there was considerable unrest among the working classes in Spain, actually leading to almost unheard of strikes in several cities. A quarter of a million Basques walked off their jobs, demanding a 50 percent pay raise. The Spanish clergy gave them moral support, saying they were justified in using this method to seek redress of their grievances. In a public statement the Spanish bishops reminded the government of its responsibilities to the people. They also referred "to the touchy question of corruption in the Franco government." An editorial in *America* on July 14, quoted from the bishops' statement.

> In addition to encouraging clerical and lay leaders to work for social reconstruction, the episcopal statement should be a sufficiently clear indication to the Franco Government, and to its uncritical supporters abroad, that something more than anti-Communism is expected of an avowedly Christian regime.[42]

Whether or not LaFarge agreed with the sentiments expressed in this editorial is not known. For *America,* however, it represented the harshest criticism of Franco since he first stepped on Spanish soil in July 1936, precipitating the Spanish Civil War. In another editorial in the middle of

December 1951, *America* reported that Cardinal Segura, archbishop of Seville, was severely critical of the government for its failure to help starving workers. The workers, in despair, had simply stepped out of politics. There was nowhere for them to turn for aid.[43]

Franco's stock, however, rose dramatically in the early 1950s. A long-term drought that had severely curtailed agricultural productivity came to an end. Heavy rains started falling, filling the reservoirs and allowing for substantial irrigation. Food, which had been rationed, became plentiful and cheaper. Rationing was abolished.

Spain and the Vatican signed a Concordat on August 27, 1953. It confirmed special privileges for the Church. In exchange for these privileges, however, the Vatican agreed to accept Franco's right to appoint Spanish bishops and to have veto power over lesser Church offices.

Franco's greatest coup in removing his pariah status, and bringing Spain into semi-partnership with the West, came on September 26, 1953, when the United States and Spain signed agreements that would allow America to build four air bases and one naval station in Spain. These bases would at all times remain under Spanish command, and the Spanish flag would fly over them. The United States would pay for their construction and maintenance, and would grant Spain eighty-five million dollars for industrial development and the purchase of needed food. The Cold War had finally driven Spain and the United States into each other's arms.

With Spain on its way into favor in the West, hostile American criticism of Spain greatly declined. Franco might still be a dictator, but now he was America's dictator. Spain had all but become a non-controversial issue in the United States.

The World War II years and those immediately following them were exceptionally active ones for LaFarge. He served as editor in chief of *America* until 1948. After stepping down from that position he returned to his rank of associate editor, where he remained until his death. He continued to write extensively for his magazine, and also contributed pieces to the *Interracial Review, Commonweal,* and other publications. He published three books in the early 1950s, including his outstanding autobiography, and two volumes on race relations. And in 1947, and again in 1951, he made tours of Europe, enabling him to see at firsthand the changes wrought on that continent by the war and the Cold War that followed.

Chapter 13

Europe Again, 1947 and 1951

LaFarge's return to Europe in the spring of 1947 coincided with the start of a major intensification of the Cold War. The euphoria at the ending of World War II did not last long. The marriage of the Soviet Union and the United States had never been more than one of convenience. The hardening of postwar attitudes was forecast as early as March 5, 1946, when Winston Churchill, wartime prime minister of Great Britain, delivered his "Iron Curtain" speech at Westminster College in Fulton, Missouri. Replaced by Clement Atlee a few months after Germany's surrender, he was busy writing his war memoirs. He was not too busy, however, to address the students and faculty at a small midwestern American college.

With President Harry Truman at his side, Churchill denounced the Soviet Union for its aggression in Eastern Europe, and called for a strengthening of will in the United States and Great Britain. He also called for a resumption of the wartime alliance between the two countries to stem the Communist tide. "From the Baltic to the Adriatic," he said, "an iron curtain has descended across the continent." Rejecting appeasement of Russia, he maintained that "there is nothing they so much admire as strength."

Initially, Churchill's speech was not received with much enthusiasm by many Americans. Some called it outright saber rattling. As of March 1946, Americas were more concerned with inflation, demobilization of the huge military raised to fight the war, and the problems of converting factories from war production to peacetime production, from building tanks and planes to making cars and refrigerators. Fear of the Communist menace took second place to concerns about the economy. By early 1947, however, due in part to Russian intransigence in Eastern Europe, but also in part to the Truman administration's insistence that Communism threatened the very survival of the free world, the American public increasingly worried about that threat. Truman, in a speech delivered on March 12, 1947, called upon the United States to "help free people to maintain their free institutions." Quickly dubbed the "Truman Doctrine," it launched the nation into decades of economic and military assistance to countries perceived as threatened by a Communist takeover.

Economic aid came first, under the form of the Organization for European Economic Cooperation, better known as the Marshall Plan. This was intended to bolster the economies of Western Europe so their people would not respond to the call of Communism. In the late 1940s it seemed at least possible that French and Italian voters might put Communist majorities into power, taking over those countries by ballots rather than bullets. Most of the countries of Western Europe had been devastated by war, their factories demolished by air raids, their infrastructures torn apart. What was needed were immediate infusions of American capital to restore their shattered economies, create prosperity, and stop Communism in its tracks.

The necessity of Marshall Plan aid was generally accepted by the administration and a bipartisan Congress by the spring of 1947. One question arose immediately, however, and it was an important one—should aid be offered not only to Western Europe but to Eastern Europe as well, and even possibly the Soviet Union? George Kennan, a principal State Department adviser, and author of the "containment policy" toward the Soviet Union, argued that the United States would have to invite them to participate, otherwise it would lend support to the Soviet charge that the United States was trying to isolate that country, which had suffered so terribly from the Nazi invasion.

At the same time, however, it should be made clear that the United States, not the United Nations, was the donor of the aid, and that it expected to supervise its expenditure. This meant that the United States would impose conditions for the aid, and would have to place monitors in the countries receiving it. Kennan and other State Department officials predicted, correctly as it turned out, that the Russians would refuse to participate in the Marshall Plan rather than accept what would amount to American intrusion on their sovereignty.

On June 26, 1947, Soviet Foreign Minister Molotov, along with eighty-nine advisers from the Soviet Union and a number of Eastern Bloc Communist nations, arrived in Paris to meet with French, British and American delegates to discuss the Marshall Plan. As expected, three days later Molotov stormed out of the meeting, protesting that the United States was seeking to dominate all of Europe. Despite their desperate need for help, the Soviets and their Eastern European satellites refused to take part in the Marshall Plan. By coincidence, Father John LaFarge was in Paris on the day Molotov arrived, and was still there on the day he left.

LaFarge went to Europe in 1947 as a Catholic journalist reporting to a Catholic publication. It meant that he had press credentials and could attend briefings for accredited reporters. He believed that Catholic journalists had a special mission. One year earlier he had received a hand-written letter from Pope Pius XII on the mission of the Catholic press. In his letter the pope praised *America* for "analyzing in a careful and scholarly manner the complex issues of the day, and pointing to the solutions offered for them by the principles of Christian philosophy."

One of these principles was racial justice. Another was "economic self-ishness," with its "disastrous effects on family life." It was the mission of the Catholic press, he reminded LaFarge, to bring "Our teachings into the home, into the circles of labor and management and to the knowledge of those who write and execute the laws of the land, and we are pleased to observe that your Review has been attaining no little success in this noble apostolic mission."[1] LaFarge was naturally pleased with this letter. It confirmed his conviction that *America,* and the Catholic press in general, must take moral stands on the major issues of the day.

For LaFarge, the year 1947 was a mixed bag of good things and bad things. He summed up what the year had meant to him in *The Manner Is Ordinary.*

> The year 1947 was one of the most interesting as well as one of the most difficult of my life. It began with the discovery that I would need a second minor operation. After I left the hospital, I felt vigorous enough to avail myself of an opportunity generously offered me by Superiors, with the aid of kind benefactors, an experience which would be very valuable for an editor. This was to make a postwar trip to Europe. Again I would learn at first hand of conditions abroad. I would resume contacts with my intellectual, spiritual friends and colleagues and would possibly be able to present in person to the Holy Father my thanks for his gracious letter.[2]

While in Europe LaFarge hoped to visit the American occupation zone of Germany. It had been agreed by the Big Three (United States, Great Britain and the Soviet Union) near the end of the war, that Germany would be temporarily divided into four zones of occupation. In addition to the Big Three, France would also receive an occupation zone. The same was decided for Berlin. Because of the Cold War these temporary zones continued until 1989, when East and West Germany were reunited.

Before leaving for Europe, LaFarge had received permission from the War Department to stay up to fourteen days in the American area. He received this permission in a letter from the Public Information Division of the War Department on April 28, 1947. The department recognized him as an accredited correspondent for *America,* and authorized him to enter the zone on or about June 7.[3]

He would spend six weeks in Europe on this tour. For a sixty-seven-year-old man not long out of the hospital, it was a demanding, at times exhausting, six weeks. He flew from New York on May 13, stopping briefly in Paris, then on to Rome, reaching the Eternal City on May 16. He found conditions in both cities depressing. "I found Europe without milk and almost without meat, without beer, without wine, without butter, and without bread except for a wretched sandy substitute. In Paris the elevators were out of order, so that you walked up four, five, or six lengthy flights of stairs."[4]

The high point of his visit to Rome was a private audience with Pius XII. He had met him before, in 1938 when Pius XI asked him to write the encyclical. At that time, however, Pius XII was only Cardinal Pacelli, the papal secretary of state. Now he was pope, and the atmosphere, for LaFarge at least, was very different from the time he had fleetingly passed Pacelli in the hallway on his way to the papal chambers.

He found the pope easy to talk to. He thanked him for the kind letter he had sent him the year before on the role of the Catholic press. During their conversation the bell rang at 12:15 to announce the anthem to the Blessed Virgin. The two men knelt next to each other and said the anthem together, Pius reciting the prayers with LaFarge answering them. As usual, during the times he was in the presence of a pope, LaFarge had a special feeling. "To me," he wrote, "it was inexpressibly touching to be privileged to recite them there alone with the Vicar of Christ Himself." Nothing important happened at this meeting, but to LaFarge it was akin to a spiritual renewal. "Having seen and spoken to four popes, beginning with Pope Leo XIII, as well as to a future pope, the late Benedict XV, I felt that they had been generous with their blessings on a life desperately in need of them."[5]

He flew back to Paris on May 31. Despite having obtained permission to visit American-occupied Germany before leaving New York, he found he still had some more formalities to go through in Paris. Eventually everything was straightened out, but then he was almost torpedoed by a French railway strike. He got around that problem, however, by securing a flight to Strasbourg on an American army plane. The plane had uncomfortable bucket seats. To add to the discomfort, he became really apprehensive, when he noticed that the plane door next to him did not look secure. The crew managed to close it with difficulty. He was relieved to land safely at Strasbourg two hours later, where he was met by his old friend Father Minéry, who had once visited LaFarge at Campion House in New York.[6]

After returning to New York, LaFarge described the German part of his tour in *America*. His saddest experience was probably his visit to Coblenz, where he had stayed for a few days in May 1938 with one of his Innsbruck classmates, Dr. Heinrich Chardon, pastor of the Church of Our Lady. Then, because of the Nazis, LaFarge had had to say mass in the chapel in secret. Now, in 1947, he could say mass openly—but there was very little left of the church to say it in.

There were great changes because of the war. He first took the train from Mainz to Coblenz, riding along the banks of the Rhine River. It was a pleasant ride. He had a compartment all to himself. It was a beautiful June afternoon, and the scenery was quite lovely. Most of the countryside had been untouched by the bombing, even though the allied planes were, at the same time, pulverizing the cities. When he got to Coblenz he found the magnificent old church, which he had visited nine years before, mostly in ruins. His old friend Dr. Chardon was living in the sacristan's quarters, since the rectory had been bombed out. His curate lived in the one room of the church which had not been shattered, the circular basement under the tower. Mass was held in what was still standing of the church, "though the boarded-off choir is open to the air; and the stained-glass windows were destroyed."[7]

He was pleased to see that the cross was once again a major symbol in Germany. It stood where the swastika had once been flaunted. The cross of glory, however, stood in the shadow of the cross of suffering. And the suffering was great. Germany had been beaten down. She felt isolated. Restrictions on emigration, LaFarge wrote, had to be lifted. Germans had to feel they could get out, at least for a while. Otherwise, he warned, "the philosophy of Communism will make its skillful way among them."[8]

All the parts of Europe he visited in 1947, with a few bright exceptions, distressed him. Germany was the hardest hit, but devastation was everywhere. He wondered at his own country, which had caused so much of the damage, and yet was now trying hard to help repair that damage; even in Germany, where so many horrors had been committed by the leaders of the Third Reich and their willing subordinates. He wrote of his feelings about this in *The Manner Is Ordinary*.

I could not shake off the sense of paradox that pervaded every aspect of American travel in postwar Europe and was acute in Germany. On all sides there was evidence of the destruction that we had caused, and yet we were there now to take stock of all we could do to bring life and order and peace to these ruins. And all the time great, glowering Russia breathed down our necks.[9]

He returned to Paris on June 20. While there he met privately with the archbishop of Paris, Cardinal Suhard. Suhard told him that there were five million Catholics under his jurisdiction, most of whom were "completely inaccessible to the ministrations and even to the approach of the Church." He told LaFarge about the French worker priests, "who while keeping their priestly character and fulfilling the essential liturgical obligations of the priesthood work during the daytime as ordinary factory hands."[10]

Suhard spoke very pessimistically about the Church in France. "The truth is," he said, "we have a vast completely paganized population for whom not only Catholicism but religion itself is completely dead. All they know of it are a few half-civic observances." LaFarge agreed that the faith was in trouble, not only in France but in all of Europe.

The situation which existed in such tragic acuteness in France did appear after all in greater or lesser degree in other parts of Catholic Europe. In Belgium Canon Cardijn and his Young Christian Workers were valiantly working to close the social gap. In Catholic Bavaria, rich in ancient Catholic traditions and practices, young people abandoned their habit of religious practice when transferred to the city, unless they received special care.[11]

This was a far cry from LaFarge's enthusiasm about the French Church in 1944. What had gone wrong, he believed, were Communist inroads in Western Europe after 1945, along with the despair and misery accompanying economic destitution. The Marshall Plan could be a godsend—it could deal with the root cause of the troubles by stimulating economic recovery, while turning Western Europeans away from atheistic Communism. He was just as anxious as the American policy planners that the Soviets reject the plan for themselves. He could not know what Molotov and his opposite numbers from the West were saying to each other during the conference that was then going on, but he correctly sensed that momentous decisions were in the making. During his last few days in Paris he was actually able to see Molotov pacing back and forth in the Russian Embassy garden from the window in the house of a friend who lived next door to the embassy.

> My last days in Paris were those when the Big Three, Messrs. Bevin, Bidault, and Molotov were discussing the administration of the Marshall Plan. The plan put the last-mentioned gentleman in a tough spot, for the objections he raised to the other two Foreign Ministers showed how conscious he was of the blow the Plan would deal to Soviet prestige in Europe. Julian Green and his sister Ann invited me to lunch at their apartment in the Rue de Sevres. From the room of their apartment the window looked out on the leafy garden of the Russian Embassy where all looked peaceful while a shirt-sleeved gentlemen was somberly pacing to and fro. "That," said Mr. Green, "is Mr. Molotov." He was doubtlessly pondering over his reply to Bevin and Bidault.[12]

Green was a French-American novelist and short story writer born in Paris to American parents in 1900. He studied both in Paris and the United States, but ultimately opted to make France his home and to do most of his writing in French. He retained his American citizenship, however, and served in the United States Army during World War II. Born and raised a Catholic, Green broke with the Church as a young man, but returned strongly to the faith in 1939. LaFarge was drawn to the younger man intellectually and socially.

In a letter to Green written on December 9, 1947, he humorously referred to the afternoon when they looked down on Molotov pacing the Russian Embassy garden. He had, he wrote his friend, suffered through another operation in October, where the surgeon took him "apart." But the operation was successful and he was quite recovered. While recuperating in the hospital for three weeks he was able to read some fiction, a luxury he rarely enjoyed. Among other works he read Green's short story "Si J'Etais Vous."

> It meant so much the more to me since the scenes of it were laid in a neighborhood which had become so familiar to me during my stay in France this summer and a few years ago. Once or twice a bit light in the head I became a bit confused and wondered whether I was really myself or Julian Green, or possibly Mr. Molotov, but I managed to disentangle the threads, for I still feel sort of vague regret that you did not or could not take more direct action with regard to the gentleman who walked in the garden below you on those summer evenings in his shirt sleeves, I still think that some sort of

a pot-shot would have made such marvelous history. I think we all missed our chance. We would have all been martyrs to the great god of publicity, and for the modern mind what greater publicity can this be.[13]

. As a journalist, LaFarge had been allowed to attend the press conference on the Marshall Plan at the French Foreign Office in the Quai d'Orsay on July 1, the day before he flew back to New York. It was evident by then that Molotov and his Eastern European colleagues had turned down the plan. There is some reason to believe that Molotov was disappointed in having to take that step; but of course he had to obey Stalin, his master in the Kremlin. The countries in Eastern Europe also had to turn down the plan, since they were occupied by the Red Army. Two days before the press conference Molotov had made a great show of anger as he stormed out of the meeting with the foreign ministers, accusing the United States of trying to dominate all of Europe.

LaFarge strongly approved the Marshall Plan, but feared that it might have come too late to save Italy and France from Communism. Shortly after returning to New York he wrote in *America:*

> In Italy, especially, the situation is peculiarly terrifying. Alone of all the groups and parties, the Communists emerged from the Resistance movement fully organized, amply financed, with trained men and a definite program. . . .
>
> In France the Communists are clamoring for a return to the Government, even threaten to seize power, and brandish the threat of what they can do through their control of the CGT (General Confederation of Labor). . . .
>
> In addition, western Europe is paralyzed by the fear of war, for the vision of its horrors is immediate and devastating.[14]

The Marshall plan turned out to be one of America's most successful foreign policy initiatives in its history. Before it came to an end, seventeen countries, including Germany, had received some seventeen billion dollars in economic assistance. By 1950 the countries of Western Europe were exceeding their prewar production by 25 percent. And with each economic advance the threat of Communist takeovers receded. The Communist parties of France and Italy remained strong, but offered nowhere near the challenge they had right after the war.

Fear of Soviet military power lay behind a second major American initiative—the founding of the North American Treaty Organization in 1949, the first peacetime military alliance in American history. On April 4, 1949, that treaty was signed in Washington, D.C., by delegates from Great Britain, France, Belgium, the Netherlands, Portugal, Italy, Denmark, Iceland, Norway, Canada and the United States. Article six of the treaty reads, "an armed attack on one or more of the Parties is deemed to include an armed attack on the territory of any of the parties in Europe or North America. . . ."

While specific military response to such an armed attack was not spelled out, and serious cracks in the alliance would occur in the years ahead, on the surface it expressed determination among the NATO powers to unite against any military assault coming from the Communist side of Europe, specifically the Soviet Union and its reluctant Eastern European allies. Eventually, Greece, Turkey and Spain would also join NATO.

LaFarge returned to Europe again in 1951. He had been scheduled to go the previous summer, but his health once again presented a problem and he had to postpone the journey. The trip was to be sponsored and financed by the Department of State, which hired him as a consultant for seven weeks in Germany, where he was to visit various theological schools. He was to concern himself "chiefly with their social studies programs, and present the fruits of my observations to the United States Occupation Government in order that the latter might better understand some of the really fine work in that line that was being done in Germany by the religious groups." His mandate did not restrict him to just Catholic schools.[15]

Dr. George S. Shuster, president of Hunter College in New York, arranged the trip. Shuster was at that time acting high commissioner for the United States in Bavaria. LaFarge's fluency in German led Shuster to conclude that he would be a good man for the job. He was scheduled to arrive in Germany on July 19, 1950. He asked for a postponement however, at practically the last minute, explaining to Dr. LeRoy E. Colby of the State Department that he was not physically able to go.

> I am very much distressed to say that I fear I will not be able to utilize the opportunity for participation in the six weeks visit to Germany July 19 to September 1. About three weeks ago I had a slight attack of arthritis which caused me quite a little inconvenience. Happily it has been cleared up and I am feeling again quite normal,

but I still feel the effects of the illness and the need of taking a moderate period of quiet and rest in order to get back to normal. While I should not expect any great inconvenience from the trip, it would, nevertheless, be unwise to go abroad in a somewhat depleted condition and subject myself to a certain amount of unusual strain.[16]

Near the end of August he wrote another letter to the State Department asking if he could make the trip the following spring.[17] The reply from the department is not on file, but it was obviously favorable. On February 21, 1951, he wrote that he was ready to go, informing his contact in Washington that he had obtained his passport. Since his old one had expired he needed a new one. He hoped the government would refund the ten dollar filing fee which he had laid out. He also requested permission to revise his return itinerary slightly so that he could make stops in Paris and London. This would be at his own expense. "I do not wish to do anything," he wrote, "that would get me into conflict with the reservations provided for me by the normal operation of the schedule. My desire is simply to get a week in Paris by hook or crook if that can somehow be fitted into the picture."[18]

Much had happened in Germany since LaFarge had been there in 1947. Aiming to merge their three occupation zones into a single, united West German nation, Britain, France and the United States introduced into West Berlin a new, all-West German currency on June 23, 1948. Stalin objected strenuously, asserting that since the West had abandoned the idea of complete German reunification, there was no reason for it to remain in Berlin. He ordered the Western Allies to withdraw their forces from the city immediately. On the following day a Soviet blockade of all overland traffic into the city began.

This presented a major dilemma for the three occupying powers, but mainly for the United States, since it would have to bear the brunt if any military action was decided upon. General Lucius Clay, the American occupation commander in Germany, wanted to shoot his way through the blockade. What would have happened had this been tried, of course, will never be known. The Soviets did not yet have the atomic bomb, still an American monopoly, so they might have backed down. Truman, however, while determined to stay in Berlin, did not want to risk war by such a direct challenge. Instead, for nearly a year, the West carried out the famous "Berlin Airlift," round-the-clock flights of cargo planes into West Berlin. At its peak some thirteen thousand tons of food, fuel, medicine, and other supplies were being flown in every day. It was Stalin, overwhelmed by this peacetime display of air power, who lifted the blockade; and it was a humiliation for him and the Soviet Union. One historian of the Cold War wrote of the airlift, "Only three years after its war against the German armies that had devastated its lands, the Soviet Union watched helplessly as the bulk of the German nation was revived and integrated into an anti-Soviet bloc."[19] So it was a very different Germany from the one he saw flat on its back in 1947 that LaFarge would visit this time.

His trip was a grand success, giving him material for several articles when he returned home. He spent a busy and fruitful six weeks in Germany, four of them in Munich visiting a number of theological schools (including some Lutheran ones) talking to students and faculty. He found that the students were uniformly interested in the racial situation in the United States.[20] He later wrote in the *Interracial Review* that American racism gave the Soviets a major propaganda weapon. They had "worked a deadly effect all over Europe in representing the United States as a land of race hatred and actual social conflict . . ."[21]

Living conditions in West Germany, although still poor by American standards, were much improved over what he had seen in 1947. At Frankfurt he stayed at the plush Hotel Carlton. The rubble had been removed from most of the city, and a vigorous rebuilding program was in high gear. "The Bahnhof," he wrote, "scene of desolation in 1947, was now for the most part repaired and as cheerful and lively as any railroad station in the United States. Ruins were giving way to new apartments; the city hummed with activity. I learned later that in the year 1950 seventy thousand more housing units were put up in Germany than in the entire United States during that period."[22]

He also visited Cologne, Regensburg, Freiburg, and even managed to swing briefly into Austria for a sentimental return to Innsbruck. He found, to his distress, that Austria, unlike Germany, was still clinging to remnants of Nazism, especially in the way of a number of Reich-German laws still being enforced. One example that especially angered him concerned the Jesuit college seminary at Innsbruck, and the non-Jesuit seminary the Canisianum. The Nazis had unceremoniously ousted the Jesuits from their buildings, giving them half an hour to clear out. Since Germany's defeat the Austrian State Police had taken over the college, and the State Finance Administration the Canisianum. Legally the Jesuits still owned the property, but had been prevented from reoccupying the seminary. To make matters worse, much of the facility was damaged, in parts even gutted. As for the Canisianum, when LaFarge went there in

May he was horrified to see the one hundred thousand volumes of its library scattered in the dusty corridors. There was one bright spot—he was "thrilled with joy to see the little 'Prince's Chapel' entirely restored." This was where he had celebrated his first holy mass in 1905.[23]

The high point of his tour were the six days he spent in West Berlin. He wrote a long letter to his sister Margaret from Berlin on May 10, 1951.

> On Monday I said good-bye to Munich, after four weeks there, and flew in an army plane to Heidelberg, where I gave a talk that night to the Serra Club, mostly military, both officers and enlisted men. I had never seen Heidelberg, and it was as lovely as I had always imagined and then some, comparatively little damaged by the war.
>
> The next day, after Mass at the American church here, I was driven to Frankfurt, where I had a good rest overnight. The next morning I left by plane 8 A.M. from the Frankfurt military airport, again per army plane, and reached Berlin at 10:45 A.M.

He was "so glad" he had come to Berlin, the one place in the world an American tourist could not visit. He felt very cut off from that world while there. His brief, escorted visit to the Soviet sector included seeing the "crushingly impressive Soviet War Memorial," which gave him "an idea, as nothing else has, of the terrific Russian propaganda."

> The Russian Sector of Berlin is in strong contrast with the Western Sector, and except for the Soviet owned government store, with its outrageous high prices, desolate and pitiable looking, with the people looking fearful and unhappy. You feel as if you had stepped into another world, once you cross the Sector line. I spent part of the day with the Jesuits who live in the Russian Sector, and learned of their difficulties, and talked with a priest who gives missions all over the East Zone of Germany. The pressure on the German youth in those parts is subtle and continual. But so far nothing is done to prevent the work of the Church, or to stop preaching, as long as prudence is observed.

In the Western Sector the Jesuits had a "wonderful boys' school—over seven hundred fifty pupils—in many ways the best Catholic boys' school in Germany." He thought that "Berlin must have been a wonderful place in the old days." Everyone had heard of the famous Nazi spots, the Chancellery, the Reichstag, and the ruined Kaiser Wilhelm Memorial, "but it is a thrill actually to see them. As I have a car at my disposal in every place I visit, I have little trouble getting around."[24]

After seven weeks in Germany he took an unanticipated side trip to Rome, where he was invited to attend the beatification of Pope Pius X on June 3, 1951. He flew from Frankfurt to Rome on June 1, on a KLM plane via Stuttgart and Munich. There was a brief ceremony at St. Peter's. The pope's body had been taken from its tomb and placed in a crystal casket, clothed in vestments with a silver mask on his face. LaFarge was struck by the fact that these were "the remains of a man from whom I had received Holy Communism some forty-six years before, and that he had gazed into my eyes."[25]

From Rome he flew to Paris, where he had a brief reunion with some of the French LaFarges. Then, after a European tour that had lasted two weeks longer than planned, he flew back to New York from Paris. He did not make it to London, but unexpectedly made a brief landing in Iceland.

> I had never expected to see Iceland; least of all did I associate it in any way with this (as it were) summer afternoon trip between an editor's desk in Paris and an editor's desk in New York. After all, life is really worthwhile if in your autumn you can see realities which in the springtime would have surpassed all your dreams.[26]

Some months after his return, he received a letter from J. Manuel Espinosa, chief of the Leaders and Specialists Branch, Division of Exchange of Persons, of the United States Department of State.

> I wish to express to you the Department's appreciation for your study of social teaching and practice in German theological schools. Your report has been read with interest within this Division, and has been circulated to officers concerned with this project, not only within other areas of the Department, but also within other Government agencies.[27]

One postscript to his German tour concerned his old friend Father Chardon. When he had visited Chardon in Coblenz in 1947, the old priest was still active, despite the loss of a foot during the war. By 1951, however, he was so crippled that he had been given light duty at the diocesan seminary in Trier, called the Rudolfinum. He had only a meager salary, just enough to live on.

Two weeks after LaFarge returned to New York, he learned that Chardon had a chance to visit Frankfurt and Switzerland, thanks to a friend who would drive him to those places. He wrote of this to LaFarge on July 18, telling him about the trip, but revealing that he would "need a little financial help in order to carry it out." LaFarge immediately wrote to the bishop of Paterson, New Jersey, on Chardon's behalf, wondering "if it would be possible to get a few stipends from the Diocese of Paterson?" It is not known exactly how the bishop responded, but it would have been surprising had he turned LaFarge down, since he could be very persuasive in these matters.[28]

Chapter 14

The Faith of John LaFarge

Based on what he said and wrote about himself, and on what others said and wrote about him, it is clear that Father John LaFarge was an intensely religious man, a true believer in the Roman Catholic religion. Nothing has been discovered to suggest that he ever doubted his faith. There was also a streak of mysticism in him, if that word is defined as a belief in personal communion with forces beyond intellectual explanation. While working in the Maryland missions he described several personal mystical experiences. There were times when he just knew that there were things happening that only he could see or feel and comprehend, that were coming to him from God.

In 1918, for example, he wrote to his sister-in-law Mabel about a Mr. Fabbiri who had built a small wooden chapel, which then burned to the ground. It made him think of his own little wooden chapel in the woods at St. Inigoe's. He asked himself, "Just what would you do now, if you got there, and found your little chapel burnt to the ground, without anyone's knowing it?" The thought at first appalled him, but the answer came to him suddenly. "The chapel cannot burn down," he wrote Mabel. "The wood may burn, and all the objects that are therein; but the chapel is an embodiment of an idea in the mind of God, which He has put by His Grace into my mind, and the ideas of God are infinitely fruitful, and are like the roots of a tree, which if you cut it down once, only grow up stronger and more beautifully a second time."[1]

While touched with mysticism, LaFarge was not an aloof contemplative concerned only with spiritual experiences, ignoring the real world. He was very much in that real world. At the same time, however, he could become quite angry with people who considered spirituality a waste of time. He wrote of one such person to Mabel in early December 1918.

I am not in very good humor, I fear, just now, because I have been talking to the sort of person who sets me a little on edge: a good Catholic lady, who insists that Catholics do altogether too much praying, that we are altogether too medieval, that there is too much attention paid now-a-days to the spiritual, and not enough to the corporal. Whereas the exact opposite is flagrantly true: we are altogether too much for the outside and the visible. Of course spirituality, no matter how delicate and thoughtful, is all humbug, if it does not inspire us to practical charity, and very real self-sacrifice for our neighbor, but on the other hand, I find that those who pray best are those who work best. It is easy to ask why the sisters pray so much, until you find that the sisters will do things that no one else will do.[2]

In this same letter to his sister-in-law he wrote that he had been reading *The Education of Henry Adams,* which had recently been issued in its first public edition. (The first printing, in 1907, had been private). On the whole he liked the book and thought it a work of genius. He wondered, however, "after all his thoughts and penetration, he could have wandered off into such strange vagaries as mark the quasi-philosophical pages at the end, where he outlines his theory of history."[3]

Mabel was Adams' wife's niece. LaFarge had met Adams only once, in the winter of 1913, shortly after Adams had suffered a stroke. LaFarge had thought of visiting him shortly before his father's death, in his search for people who had known the artist in his younger years, but for reasons already given he had decided against it.

"On a visit to Washington in the winter of 1913," LaFarge wrote, "the idea occurred to me to call upon Father's old companion, Henry Adams." According to his account the meeting went well. Although not a Catholic, Adams was interested in medieval church liturgy and music. He had recently received some medieval liturgical books and was having his secretary, Miss Aileen Tone, trying "to find some explanation of the plain-chant notation which they contained." When LaFarge arrived Miss Tone asked him to help her decipher them, and the two of them spent a pleasant hour at Adams's piano as he explained the basic idea of the chant and its notation.

When he finally got to see Adams, who welcomed him warmly, he thought the older man inwardly troubled about his faith. Adams, for all his genius and sophistication, seemed to LaFarge a closet Catholic, yearning for the ritual and symbolism of the Church, but intellectually unable to embrace it as his own. A few months after LaFarge's ordination in 1905, Adams wrote to Mabel from Paris, "Perhaps John will kindly stick me into his Mass. I need it more than you. I've not the least objection to being prayed for. For that matter I have no objection to be taken to all the churches there are."

LaFarge had not known about this letter when he called upon Adams in 1913, so he did not press him on the matter of religion. "One thing none could venture with Henry Adams," he wrote, "not even his nearest and dearest: that was to put to him any questions. I might have learned more if at the time I had known better the intimate, spiritual side of his nature that he partly disclosed to Mabel."[4]

It is likely that Adams's letter to Mabel was partly facetious, not meant to be taken seriously. LaFarge, however, did take it seriously. Had he raised the subject of religion with Adams, he might well have been soundly rebuffed. Adams was tolerant of religion, and admired the Church for its beauty, but decidedly not for its religious teachings. He had no yearnings, secret or otherwise, to be a Catholic. One of his biographers, Ernest Samuels, has made this clear.

Describing friends who visited Adams after his stroke, Samuels wrote:

> A less trying visitor was Father Sigourney Fay, a professor at Catholic University, who, like Father John LaFarge, the son of the artist, came in for the little recitals, for Aileen Tone was "having a *succès fou* with her twelfth century songs." Father Fay was no bore . . . but he "has an idea that I want conversion, for he directs his talk much to me, and instructs me. Bless the genial sinner! He had best look out that I don't convert him, for his rotten old church is really too childish for a hell like this year of grace."[5]

The "year of grace" referred to by Adams was 1915. Samuels was incorrect in writing that LaFarge came in for the recitals. LaFarge visited Adams only that one time in 1913. "I was hopeful," he wrote in *The Manner Is Ordinary,* "that I could pay another visit and enjoy further conversation, but traveling from Leonardtown to Washington was not easy, and I did not see him again."[6]

As far as LaFarge's role in the Church is concerned, he was very much a team player. He respected and subordinated himself to the Church hierarchy, especially the pope. While he might occasionally have been disappointed with his superiors, he never openly opposed them. Even in the case of the racism encyclical, whose rejection must have pained him, he made no known display of anger or disappointment.

As already noted, keeping his relatives in the faith was very important to him. He did not want to lose any of them, and they in turn did not want to disappoint him. Although a fair number did drop out of the Church, they were usually circumspect and tried to spare him the truth. While it was not pleasant for him to see some of his relatives marry non-Catholics, he always accepted it with good grace, sometimes conducting the ceremony himself, and then subtly began the process of persuading the non-Catholics to seek conversion.

In general he strongly opposed the practice of mixed marriages between Catholics and non-Catholics. In April 1932, he published an article on the subject in *America*. A marriage, he wrote, is a spiritual union, where the spouses seek to maintain spiritual unity and cooperation between them. "Differences in religion, however, place obstacles to such spiritual cooperation." Where there is danger that the Catholic partner, or the children, might lose their faith, the Church prohibits such a mixed marriage. This is called "danger of perversion." Where the element of "perversion is not necessarily present, but the religious disharmony persists, the mixed marriage is seen as a lessening or weakening of the ideal in greater or lesser degree according to varying circumstances." In his own personal observation, and those of other priests he had spoken to on the subject, he concluded that it was a rare mixed marriage that succeeded.[7]

In 1932 he performed the marriage ceremony of his nephew Tom to Marie Iselin, an Episcopalian. He wrote about Marie to his sister Margaret. "Marie seems a fine girl; sensible and modest; and well suited to Tom. All the family like her immensely. She was most satisfactory on the religious question. Both she and her mother wished absolutely for her to sign the promises for educating the children in the Catholic Church."[8] He was apparently satisfied that with Marie there was no "danger of perversion."

Marie and Tom, the nephew who was drowned off Newfoundland during the war, had two daughters, Phyllis and Sheila. In the summer of 1943, LaFarge gave these girls their First Holy Communion at St. Gabriel's Church in New Rochelle, New York. Perhaps because they lost their father when they were so young, LaFarge took a special, continuing interest in them. The girls were precocious, questioning and deeply thoughtful. When Phyllis was in her senior year in high school, and was preparing to go away to college, he wrote her about the need for contemplation in her life.

> I am entirely in sympathy with your desire to think things out for yourself. In point of fact, what else is there to do? One of the great maxims of Saint Ignatius, which he uses in his Spiritual Exercises, says that nothing really deeply affects us as much as that which we

have "discovered" for ourselves. That is the reason why we absolutely need some contemplation in our lives; and by contemplation I don't mean just some day-dreaming, but some time for recollected, prayerful thought from time to time in our busy careers.[9]

Phyllis was heading for Radcliffe, a secular college, which probably
disturbed LaFarge, knowing his feelings about Catholics going to non-
Catholic schools. To buttress Phyllis in her faith, he attached to this letter nine "*Notes for a Collegian.* Christmas, 1950," a kind of daily check-
list of thoughts and practices concerning God.

On the occasion of Phyllis's marriage to Chester Johnson in 1958, she,
her mother, and LaFarge had a sharp disagreement as to where the wedding should take place. The family had recently moved from one part of
Manhattan to another, putting them into a different parish. Their previous parish was St. Thomas More, and that is where Phyllis and Marie
wanted her to marry Chester. At that time, however, the Church was
more insistent that the ceremony be performed in the bride's parish,
which for Phyllis was no longer St. Thomas More.

Phyllis asked LaFarge to obtain permission for her to marry in her old
parish. He said that he could not do this, which angered Phyllis and her
mother, one of the few recorded instances when LaFarge was openly
criticized by a family member. Marie said some sharp words to him,
which, however, she quickly regretted, and sent him an apologetic letter
a few days later.

> I am sorry to say that I lost my temper over it all which I should not
> have—which I feel that I must confess to you—I am afraid that I
> upset Phyllis but I was upset because she was—also just between
> you and me—I worry over Phyllis and her religion which I don't
> want her to lose. . . . I have been praying that Chester become a R.C.
> and I think with the proper handling he may as he is looking for
> something and I had so hoped that if we could have the wedding in
> the *small* St. Thomas More we could show him how easy and nice
> religion can be.[10]

The writer sent this letter to Phyllis, who had never seen it before. She
said it perplexed her, since her mother, who was never converted to
Catholicism, had never seemed concerned about hers or Sheila's faith
before. At her own marriage, however, Marie had made the promises
about raising her children Roman Catholic. Phyllis now feels that her
mother intended to keep those promises.[11]

Neither Phyllis nor Sheila, however, remained in the Church. Phyllis simply drifted away. Sheila, more spiritual than her sister, also abandoned Catholicism. But she did not abandon religion. After LaFarge's death in 1963 she became a Buddhist, eventually entering the Buddhist priesthood. If LaFarge were still alive at the time he might not have been surprised. Sheila remembers that her uncle, in discussing religion with her, once remarked that she sounded more like a Buddhist than a Catholic.[12]

He was more successful with some other LaFarge spouses. His brother Bancel's wife, Mabel, was also a convert. LaFarge probably had little or nothing to do with her conversion, since he was just a freshman at Harvard when it took place. Mabel became a devout Catholic, more so than her husband. Edward, one of Bancel's and Mabel's sons, married Anne, a non-Catholic. As did Marie Iselin, she also promised to raise her children Catholic. Married in 1935, then bearing seven children, she did not accept conversion until twenty years later. In the meantime, however, she attended mass with her husband. She told the writer that the only pressure LaFarge tried to exert on her was a mild suggestion, in a letter to Edward, that he bring up the subject with her, and coax her along a bit. Edward, however, made no mention of the letter until her conversion.[13]

LaFarge was involved with her conversion ceremony, and wrote about it to his cousin Schuyler Brown, who was just beginning his studies for the priesthood in the Jesuit order.

> Saturday, June 11, I received into the Church at the Cathedral in Providence, Anne Woolsey, Eddie LaFarge's wife, who had been taking instructions from Father Kirkman, of the Cathedral staff. Of her eight children, seven were present at the event, and also at the Mass which I celebrated the following morning at the Elmhurst Sacred Heart Convent, where she received her first Holy Communion. The same afternoon, June 12, she was confirmed in the Providence Cathedral by Bishop McVinney, along with 448 other adults, mostly converts. It was a very beautiful and impressive affair.[14]

LaFarge counted Anne an extra child. All seven of the children she did have attended the ceremony.

LaFarge was always pleased when someone in the family married a Catholic. His nephew Henry, another of Bancel's sons, married Mary Lathrop Allen, a graduate of Manhattanville, a Catholic women's college. Knowing she was a practicing Catholic, he could write to her as someone well grounded in the faith. He gave her some perceptive and candid advice before the ceremony.

First, about the ceremony itself, including the nuptial Mass and Communion. Do not try to have any particular pious or holy feelings at any part in the proceedings that morning. Make your offerings and say your prayers on some previous occasion, e.g., at the Sunday before. But on the day itself you have just one single job to do, and that is to go through the event with the least fatigue and simply to carry things out as *purely as a ceremony,* not in *any* way as a spiritual experience. Do not make *any* effort to be devout, pious, recollected, or what not; but merely be a nice, decorous bride and groom, presenting a proper appearance to the photographers, if any.[15]

He also took the occasion of her wedding to fill her in on the LaFarge family, a subject that periodically intrigued him.

I don't know what the arrangements are, but I presume you will be meeting shortly most of the various LaFarges. Don't take them quite as seriously as they are, perhaps, all of us, inclined to take themselves. They are not bad on acquaintance, and are more human than they appear. At any rate, really the best of them, for the most part, in each generation, seem to have been their various in-laws. Just why that has been, you and Henry can probably figure out; and it is pleasant to know that there will be no exception to the rule in your case.[16]

In addition to Phyllis and Sheila, LaFarge took a special interest in another of his brother Bancel's grandchildren—Ben LaFarge, presently a member of the English department at Bard College in Annandale-on-Hudson, New York. LaFarge found his grandnephew precocious and inquiring, the same traits that drew him to Phyllis and Sheila. And since all three of them were children of non-Catholic mothers, he worried about their faith. In looking back on his youth, Ben told the author he never really had any belief in the Catholic Church, nor in any religion. He considers himself to have always been an atheist. He did not want, however, to hurt his uncle's feelings, and LaFarge continued to talk and write to him about religion until Ben was well into his twenties.

In March 1950, when Ben was a senior in a Pennsylvania prep school, LaFarge was worried that he might come under the influence of a cousin who had recently been proselytized by Father Leonard Feeney of Boston. A Jesuit priest, Feeney had been a colleague of LaFarge's at *America* for a few years. In the 1940s, however, Feeney became an embarrassment to his order and his Church by his extreme theological pronouncements, including the preaching of the doctrine that there was no salvation outside the Catholic Church. Excommunicated by the pope and dropped from the ranks of the Jesuits, Feeney eventually recanted and was reconciled to the Church.

During the years of Feeney's apostasy, he and LaFarge were anathema to each other. Hearing that a Feeney disciple had visited Ben at school, LaFarge wrote him that he should be very wary of the Boston priest and his absolutist teachings. The T.M. referred to in the letter was Temple Morgan, Ben's first cousin on his mother's side.

> I understand that you were evangelized by your zealous cousin, T.M. I have no idea what effect he had on you, if any, nor is it my concern, but I did feel some disturbance on hearing of it, because I should wish to dissociate myself from the notion that any man can undertake to force another man's belief. Nor do I hold that if you find those who do not agree with you, it is right to conclude, as the eccentric group he has identified himself with concludes, that therefore you are in bad faith and should be turned over to the secular arm.[17]

LaFarge added that his "fear of such a misconception on your part is probably idle, and your own good sense has doubtless been your guide."[18] Ben did have a bad experience at Feeney's hands the following fall, after he had begun his freshman year at Harvard. Temple invited him to attend a Feeney lecture in a hall not far from Harvard. He introduced Ben to the former Jesuit, which from Ben's side was a big mistake. Learning that he was a nephew of Father LaFarge, Feeney pointed Ben out to the audience and proceeded to savagely attack his uncle, to Ben's great humiliation. He told the author that he was "reduced to tears."[19]

LaFarge's epistolary homilies to Ben continued through his nephew's college years, and during a hitch in the army after graduation. As early as his senior year in high school, however, Ben was trying to send up some trial balloons to his uncle, hinting that he may have had some doubts about God. In the beginning LaFarge responded to these doubts as if they were quite natural. Ben was still a very young man, and was searching for the answers to the big questions. "I can see your idea," he wrote Ben, "that you could forget God—in whom you fundamentally believe, for a time, with the idea that you could eventually come back to Him, or become preoccupied with Him." God had a way of welcoming back even those who had been away for a long time. "Yet there is a difficulty about that plan. Since God is the total source of our being, and of our existence itself—not just at the beginning, but all the time, by His continual support—it doesn't seem quite logical not to revert from time to time to the

Source. . . ." Why, LaFarge wondered, "should we just give the scraps of our life to God, and not at least some parts of the best of it?"[20]

As late as January 1955, when Ben was in the army, LaFarge asked him to pray for some relatives who were having some serious marital problems. "Such prayers are heard," he wrote with some poignancy, "so many prayers are heard; all kinds of prayers are heard: yet it's not the 'hearing' but the dialog itself that counts."[21] There seemed almost a note of despair in this letter that his nephew was slipping away from God, or perhaps had already slipped, and he was trying to throw him a lifeline to haul himself back to the faith.

By the time Ben was in his mid-twenties, however, LaFarge finally accepted that he was beyond the pale, at least for the time being. In keeping with his practice of staying close to family members, even those who had strayed from the true faith, LaFarge continued his relationship with Ben. It was his firm belief, of course, since this is what his Church taught, that no one ever irretrievably lost his chance for salvation while he still lived. One could save himself even in the last moments of life if he made his peace with God. He no doubt counted on this as a possibility with all his fallen-away kin. Only someone with LaFarge's steadfast convictions about the existence of a merciful God, and an afterlife for those who believed in Him and were truly sorry for their sins, could persist in trying, subtly or otherwise, to "work on them." Ben was no exception.

His relationship with Ben continued to be amiable and pleasant. They enjoyed each other's company. If LaFarge were disappointed in his nephew he did not show it. When Ben married a Jewish woman, Susan Seidner, LaFarge would sometimes dine with them at their apartment. For awhile these appear to have been annual events. Following these visits he would write short notes thanking them for their hospitality. Appropriately these notes were always addressed to Susan. LaFarge could adapt to his family's religious vagaries. He wanted them to remain Catholic, but if they strayed he still stuck with them.

The only other LaFarge to become a priest was Schuyler Brown, a second cousin once removed on his mother's side of the family. Father Brown gave copies to the author of letters he had received from LaFarge during the years he was studying for the priesthood, some mailed to the Jesuit seminary at Woodstock, where LaFarge himself had been a student many years before. Although they were cousins, Brown was much younger than LaFarge.

Brown was born an Episcopalian, but by the time he reached high school he had accepted conversion to Roman Catholicism. LaFarge did not influence him to become a priest—he decided that on his own. He was influenced by him, however, to become a Jesuit, partly through his reading of LaFarge's *The Jesuits in Modern Times,* published in 1927. It was LaFarge's first published book.[22]

In one of the early letters, dated December 17, 1955, LaFarge wrote about specialization as a priest. Brown apparently had asked his advice on the areas of study he should concentrate on in preparing for the priesthood. Should he emphasize scholarship, he wondered, since that was his principal interest.

LaFarge gave him mixed advice. On the one hand he thought his cousin should perfect himself in the academic field, "using all means the Society provides for you, until such time that you can meet those scholars—within and without the Church—on a footing of real equality."

On the other hand specialization could be a sort of "prison," that sometimes cut one off "from the apostolic works that your vocation drives you to." The scholar, he wrote, "if he has the true spirit of St. Ignatius, will always feel a tension, sometimes an almost intolerable one, between the smallness of the vineyard plot that he can actually cultivate and the great field that seems to lie white for the harvest." But he will also find that his prison has "many more apostolic windows than he imagines."

LaFarge revealed something about himself in this letter when he predicted ". . . apart from this deeper aspect of the matter, there is the circumstance that with your past experience, and your connections, you will find souls simply coming to you, as it were forcing themselves upon you for individual guidance and direction, in your later life. You will deal with them much more securely, even more efficiently *in the long run,* if you have established yourself in your permanent status as a scholar."[23]

LaFarge preached the sermon at Father Brown's First Solemn Mass at St. Ignatius Loyola Church on Eighty-fourth Street and Park Avenue in New York on June 23, 1963. He was eighty-three years old—just six months away from his death the following November. It was a well-constructed, highly literate sermon, which is what one would have expected of him. He wove together an explanation of the mass, along with a commentary on the world as he saw it that day. He realized that some of those attending the mass were not Catholic, and that even some of the Catholics were not sure what was going on. Brown remembers that the loudspeaker system was acting up, and that much of the sermon was heard only by the people sitting near the front of the church.[24]

As LaFarge explained, the essence of the mass was the Eucharist. "It may," he said, "be summed up as the sacred words of consecration spoken by the priest over bread and wine that was previously set aside and offered for that purpose, and changing it into the body and blood of the Saviour." Prayers and other rituals were worked in and woven through the whole ceremony. The final words spoken by the celebrant were *In unitate Spiritus Sancti*—in the unity of the Holy Spirit."

Near the end of the sermon LaFarge took advantage of his control of the pulpit to expound on some of his concerns of the day, concerns that might seem to mock any priestly call for unity.

> No matter how discouraging is the present human picture, no matter how much the world is tormented by outbursts of hate and enmity, the Church's prayer for unity is never silenced. Even the hidden Church, or Church of silence, in the countries oppressed by the Iron Curtain, still offers this constant plea. Sometimes the word "unity" seems a mockery, in view of the hatred and conflict now existing in the world. How can we talk of unity and peace when the entire body of humanity is divided into armed camps, when total destruction is right around the corner? When we see a Communist-tormented Cuba next door? Yet day after day, all over the world, from innumerable altars, the prayer for unity and peace, inspired by the Holy Spirit of God, ascends to the Father in Heaven, through the sacrifice of His Son.[25]

Schuyler Brown remained a Jesuit priest until 1982, when he left both the Jesuits and the Roman Catholic Church to move to Canada and return to the Episcopalian faith of his childhood. He is now an Episcopal priest and scholar, specializing in the scripture. He is also a married man. He did not meet his wife, however, until after he left the Church. (The author discovered this footnote when he lunched with Schuyler Brown at the New York Harvard Club in 1990.)

Probably because of his father's extensive work in stained glass windows and church murals, LaFarge had a special interest in liturgical art. He claimed not to know much about the subject, since he was far from being an artist himself, but he did have a good sense of what was creative and beautiful, and what was trite, uninspired, and obviously mass-produced for public consumption. In 1928 he helped to found the Liturgical Arts Society. His only official position in the society was chaplain, which post he held until his death.

The Liturgical Arts Society was generally dedicated to the improvement of church art, for both aesthetic and religiously inspirational reasons. Too much of that art, the founding members felt, was tawdry and

poor in workmanship. To get this message across, the society began publishing a quarterly magazine in 1931, called simply *Liturgical Arts*. Due
to shortage of funding (because of the Great Depression, 1931 was a bad
time to launch a new publication), the magazine barely managed to survive its first few years. LaFarge recalled its slow start when he wrote
about it in 1956.

> The early years of the magazine's existence were handicapped by
> a lack of suitable material, so that it leaned heavily upon material
> which now seems to have been of archeological value but to bear
> little relation to present-day needs.[26]

Three of LaFarge's relatives were involved in founding the society
and publishing the magazine. Henry Binsse, his cousin, was the first editor of *Liturgical Arts*. Both his brother Bancel and his nephew Bancel,
an architect, were on the editorial board. Cardinal Francis Spellman,
archbishop of New York, was the society's patron. Except for LaFarge,
all the early members of the society were lay people, although later on
clerics, members of the American hierarchy, nuns, and even some foreign prelates were involved. In *The Manner Is Ordinary*, LaFarge disclaimed any significant role for himself in the society. "Neither the ini-
tiation of the Society," he wrote, "nor the magazine itself were my
doings: they were started by the group that I mentioned. But I was glad
to be identified with them as a not very active or useful chaplain, but one
deeply convinced of the value and importance of the work itself."[27]

As usual, LaFarge was being modest. His role in the society was not
nearly so passive as he claimed. Mary LaFarge, who knew him very well,
told the author that he was the "guiding spirit" of the society.[28]

In a 1973 interview Maurice Lavanoux, a major authority in liturgical
art who succeeded Binsse as editor of the magazine, stressed the part
played by LaFarge.

> During the growing pains of these early years, Fr. LaFarge was a
> tower of strength. When his advice was sought, he would listen in-
> tently. His suggestions were always effective and understood by
> the rest of us. The gyrations, apathy, indifference in high places
> during those early years (and later, too!) were made bearable by Fr.
> LaFarge's understanding and continued encouragement.[29]

Writing in *Liturgical Arts* in 1961, the publication's thirtieth year, La-
Farge recounted its history. He broke it down into three periods, each

about a decade long. During the 1930s, while short of funds, the society
and the magazine were long on promises.

> The Society's early days, in the 1930's, were the forerunners of an
> important decline. This was the demise of the pseudo-archaeolog-
> ical revival that had dominated the scene for much too long a pe-
> riod. These early days marked the beginning of the time when ar-
> chitects and artists would look for inspiration not in the mere
> imitation of the past, but would seek guidance, as I have just said,
> in a positive approach.[30]

The second ten years, the 1940s, were still years of struggle for funds.
Churches had taken a financial battering during the depression and the
war that followed, and were only just recovering by the end of the
decade. Purveyors of church art had to be persuaded that cheaply produced art meant inferior art. "The client needed to be convinced of the
fact that limited budgets made it all the more important that the talents
of the best architects and artists should be brought into play, even though
the initial expense of fees was higher than before."[31]

The 1950s, however, witnessed a change of fortune for the society. A
generous trust fund was established, enabling the society's "secretary to
travel in many lands and gather valuable material for publication." He
examined and assessed church art in Europe, Latin America, Japan, In-
dia, Asia and Africa, as well as some remote corners of the United States.
Some whole issues of *Liturgical Arts* were devoted to a single country
or region. The magazine became something of a work of art itself, containing beautiful illustrations of liturgical art from all over the world.

The society wanted art, and the church buildings themselves, to reflect
the times, not simply copy the past. Gothic cathedrals were beautiful ed-
ifices, but they should not be built in the twentieth century. "Only in a
few isolated instances today," LaFarge wrote, "would anyone risk building a pseudo-style church."[32]

LaFarge himself saw the mission of the society as one of encouraging
the creation of church art that would both conform to the liturgy in
changing times, while simultaneously inspiring greater feelings of devotion in the worshipper. "At the same time," he wrote, "the release of
this rich field of artistic creation would redound to the deepening of religious life itself. If *worship* were clothed in its rightful dignity and mag-
nificence, then men would be drawn to do worship in an age of indifference and mediocrity."[33]

The building and decorating of a church is not a simple matter. He concluded:

> A church is not a set of parts to be assembled and erected like a child's toy. Study and skill alike must work together. Our Society does not claim to furnish all the answers. But our Society and our quarterly will have done their work if they arouse our readers to the attraction, the complexity, and the promise of this great task; not in some abstract dreamland, but in our changing American civilization.[34]

This paragraph contained the last words that LaFarge wrote for *Liturgical Arts*. He was not a regular contributor to the publication. While intensely interested in the subject, he realized he lacked the artistic competence to write about church art as an authority. His rare contributions included occasional obituaries of society members, or articles that summarized work done by the society, as on its twenty-fifth and thirtieth anniversaries. *Liturgical Arts* continued publication until 1972. Why it ceased in that year is uncertain, although there is some evidence that it was having financial problems.

While admitting to an occasional lapse or mistake while on the altar, he was very interested in the liturgy of the mass. In *The Manner Is Ordinary,* he wrote that if the celebrant found he was doing the wrong thing, he should "do it with grace and dignity." He recalled once having sung a High Mass as chaplain of the society in the presence of Cardinal Spellman. "I succeeded," he wrote, "in omitting the solemn *Dominus Vobiscum* after the *Credo*. But calm deportment usually helps to compensate for defect of rubrical exactitude."[35]

What increasingly disturbed him about the Catholic mass was, in effect if not by design, its limiting participation to the celebrant and the few members of the congregation who really knew what was going on. He wanted the liturgy to be understood by everyone attending, not just a select few. As early as 1933 he wrote that the "plain fact is that people, in the English-speaking Catholic congregations of the US of A, *do not* sing at Mass." He deplored the turning-off of parishioners who wanted to join in, but were discouraged because there was so little for them to do, and much they did not comprehend.

> Most of our intelligent Catholics, young and old, feel the need of participation outwardly as well as inwardly in the services of the Church, particularly the most sacred and vital of them all, the Holy Mass. Rather they feel that they will participate better inwardly,

with more devotion and fewer distractions, if they can also take part outwardly.[36]

In a 1942 article, "Explaining Liturgy," he returned to the theme of understanding what was being said and done during the Mass. He emphasized the importance of explaining the liturgy to Catholic laymen so they would have a better appreciation of what was occurring on the altar. He had recently attended a mass in Peoria, Illinois, where an attempt had been made to do this.

> When the altars were consecrated in the Cathedral of Peoria, one of the Catholic clergy read from the pulpit at intervals a simple and interesting explanation of the ceremonies and a translation of some of the high points of the prayers.[37]

It is tempting to read a forecast of Vatican II in these words. LaFarge, however, was not rash enough at this point to predict, or even urge, use of the vernacular instead of Latin in the Mass. When English did replace Latin in some rituals in the late 1950s and early 1960s, he was very pleased. And while he died in the second year of the council in 1963, he was delighted with the direction it was taking.[38]

In December 1948 and January 1949, he published a series of three articles in *America* that summed up his thinking on the liturgy. In the first article he began by noting that *America* had been criticized by some of its readers for not paying more attention to the liturgical movement in its pages, despite the large number of books and articles appearing on the subject. His articles, he hoped, would satisfy these critics.

"The liturgical movement," he wrote, "is not just a movement for promoting greater faithfulness to the ceremonial rubrics of the Church. Nor is it a mystery cult for a few adepts. It is a normal project planned to effect two main results."

One of these was to arouse a practical knowledge of the Church's liturgy as a means of doctrinal instruction and devotional inspiration. Laymen left on their own without guidance, frequently misunderstood the meanings in the service. "The words, the ceremonies, the sacred objects, the symbolism of the liturgy are in truth a vast encyclopedia of supernatural wisdom, ranging from the preaching of the most sublime truths to the simplest of moral homilies."[39]

Learning the meaning of the liturgy was essential to more meaningful participation by the laity in the rituals of the Church. In this article he quoted extensively from Pope Pius XII's recent encyclical *Mediator Dei,* in which the pope argued a similar line. While Pius wrote nothing specific about reciting the liturgy in the vernacular, it is generally agreed, that by stressing the goal of greater lay participation in the mass, he was pointing in that direction. The 1967 edition of the *Catholic Encyclopedia* called *Mediator Dei* "the crowning of the modern liturgical movement that began in the early years of the 20th century." The document "laid down principles but did not work out all their conclusions. In many ways it was a point of departure rather than a final goal."[40]

LaFarge quoted the following critical paragraph from the encyclical.

> Therefore they are to be praised who with the idea of getting the Christian people to take part more easily and more fruitfully in the Mass strive to make them familiar with the "Roman Missal," so that the faithful, united with the priest, may pray together in the very words and sentiments of the Church. They are also to be commended who strive to make the liturgy even in an external way a sacred act in which all who are present share. This can be done in more than one way. When, for instance, the whole congregation in accordance with the rules of the liturgy, either answers the priest in an orderly or fitting manner, or sing hymns suitable to the different parts of the Mass, or do both, or finally in High Masses when they answer the prayers of the minister of Jesus Christ and also sing the liturgical chant.[41]

In his second article on the liturgy, one week later, he dealt with liturgical art. Art, he wrote, is intimately associated with worship. Much statuary is mass-produced and displeasing to the eye. We must improve the quality of the art in our churches. The artists do not necessarily have to be practicing Catholics, but they must understand what the Church is looking for in its art.

In his youth he remembered hearing "that one of the most intensively devoted woodcarvers that the Austrian Tyrol ever produced had the reputation of being personally not very devout. But the scandal, if any, is mitigated by the thought that Bachlechner's crucifixes and Stations of the Cross expressed the faith of the profoundly Catholic milieu in which he grew up and lived."[42]

In his last article on the liturgy, in mid-January 1949, "The Mass for the Masses," he again referred to *Mediator Dei,* where Pius stressed that only the Church can make changes in the liturgy. There are two elements to the liturgy, one divine, the other human. The divine comes from God, and cannot therefore be changed in any way by man. But the human el-

ements can be variously modified, "as the needs of the age, circumstances and the good of souls may require, and the ecclesiastical hierarchy, under guidance of the Holy Spirit, may have authorized."[43]

That the Church reserves the authority to make changes does not mean
they will not be made. "It only means that they shall be done in the proper
way, and not by unauthorized persons." There was extraordinary need to
popularize the Mass for the masses, and to bring them into "the Sacrifi-
cial Action, as participants. They must be drawn in from the highways
and byways into God's House of Prayer, into an intimate participation
both inwardly and outwardly in the Living Sacrifice, until God's House
is filled."[44]

While not openly calling for the use of the vernacular in the Mass, La-
Farge clearly wanted that to someday happen. In February 1952, for example, he wrote of this to Edwin V. O'Hara, bishop of Kansas City.

> My years of priesthood and of parochial life over and over again
> impressed on me the dire need of being able to use the English lan-
> guage. Each additional year of the priesthood, each additional ex-
> perience of the various functions makes the use of the Latin always
> more difficult, sometimes really intolerable. I had the experience a
> couple of years ago of being able to conduct a sort of improvised
> service. It was the case of a body which was in the city merely tem-
> porarily resting where the funeral service was to be conducted in
> another city and I was asked to perform some sort of a private cer-
> emony just out of devotion. There were a number of non-Catholics
> there; in fact, most of the family, the immediate family, were non-
> Catholics. I simply took the Requiem Mass and read it in English,
> plus some of the words from the funeral Office. I was deeply moved
> myself to see how touched and really moved were the bystanders.
> One felt then the force of the use of the English language and the
> freedom one felt in not having the veil or wall of Latin between
> oneself and the hearers.[45]

The slowly increasing use of the vernacular in various Catholic services in the late fifties and early sixties, was pure gold to LaFarge. He
was thrilled with the changes being made, hoping for even greater
changes in the near future. Latin, mysterious and arcane for the great majority of Catholics, was giving way to English translations. "One of the
most significant developments in recent years," he wrote in *America* in
August 1960, "is the constantly increasing use of the vernacular in the
liturgy of the Church." Somebody just arrived from the 1930s would be

amazed at the changes. "Yet such is the scene he would witness today, and the spectacle but mirrors the extensive use of the vernacular which the Church has sanctioned to quicken and deepen the spiritual life of her children." The Church is a living thing. It grows and adapts. LaFarge and his co-author, John A. O'Brien of Notre Dame, exulted at the changes. They would dramatically alter the role of the congregation.

> The basic cause of the apathy enveloping the vast majority of the Sunday congregation is undoubtedly the exclusive use of Latin, even in those parts of the Mass which call for the active participation of the faithful. There is a barrier between sanctuary and the nave: a palpable lack of any vital link. With the exception of the few who try with a missal to keep pace with the celebrant, the congregation sits in bored silence with little sense of union with what is being done by the celebrant. He is reading, in silence for the most part, an unknown language, with his back turned toward them. A greater lack of rapport could scarcely be contrived.[46]

While he would not live to see the vernacular replace the Latin in the Mass, LaFarge was confident that it was imminent. For the most part his prediction of greater involvement of the congregation has followed the change. Few Catholics in the United States miss the old way. LaFarge would not be surprised.

Chapter 15

Father John LaFarge, S.J. (1880–1963)

To be human is to be complicated, but some humans are more complicated than others. Father John LaFarge belonged in the latter category.
But with persistence, documents, and a lot of help from relatives, friends,
and other people who knew him, it has been possible to fathom some
parts of this remarkable man's life. To begin with, his belief in the
Catholic Church and its teachings was nearly total. The Faith was his
beacon, the Church his touchstone.

He was willing, however, to see his Church change over time, as long
as it brought people closer to God and one another, as in changing the
liturgy of the Mass from Latin to the vernacular. He deplored Communism from its beginnings to where it stood at the end of his life; but he
preached communalism, if it promoted religious solidarity. He wanted
religion to permeate not only his own life, but every one else's life as
well. While he appeared to be an early and consistent supporter of ecumenism, deep down he would have been happy to convert the whole
world to Roman Catholicism.

When family members strayed from the faith, he either kept his silence, or admonished them mildly and indirectly. He wanted to keep the
door open for their return, praying that before their deaths they would repent and be saved.

His niece, Phyllis LaFarge Johnson, recently speculated on LaFarge's
own deep commitment to the Church, and his concern for the faith of his
family. These are simply her thoughts, but they do offer a few insights
about LaFarge from someone who knew him well. They should not be
taken as anything more than that.

> As I said to you on the phone, I think the position of youngest child
> in a failed marriage is a very special one. Possibly it is true, too,
> that a child growing up in such a situation—especially an innately
> spiritual child—would grow up to feel that it was very important

for people he cared about to marry within a church that stressed the permanence of the institution of marriage by viewing it as a sacrament. A kind of institutional guarantee against the possibility of loss or abandonment.[1]

He bitterly opposed birth control. How he would have felt about that issue were he alive today is no mystery. The pope's continued condemnation of its practice would have been enough for him. As for abortion, that was something so heinous it hardly merited discussion. *Roe v. Wade,* constitutionally sanctioning abortion through the second trimester, would have shocked and saddened him beyond description.

The amount, quality, and variety of his writings was prodigious. Until his last hours on earth he was still correcting proofs of material to be published in *America*. His last book, which had evolved from one of his previous articles in *America* in 1961, came out just a few months before his death. He facetiously dedicated the book, *Reflections on Growing Old,* to "Jim Lawrence, Joe O'Gorman, Bill Reid, And Other Survivors of H.C. '01, The First Class Of The Century."

In this brief volume he neither sentimentalized nor deplored old age. He called it "a natural phase of our human life that stands in its own right, just as does every other human life-phase: infancy, childhood, youth, adulthood. It enjoys its own dignity, its own privileges and character."[2] Old age in itself is not a calamity, although it can become one for those whose frenzied attempts to remain, or try to remain young make them look foolish.

Old age is a time to reflect on things you were too busy to think about earlier in your life. It is also a time to start loving one's neighbor. "Old age has at its disposal the exercises of the *greatest social power* in the world, that of genuine love for one's fellow human beings. This love is inspired by the Creator's own love for us and His willingness to become one of us and share our joys, our experiences, and our suffering."[3]

Some say it is too depressing to talk about aging and dying. Is it not "better to discuss them frequently, to clarify our thoughts, to rid ourselves of false fears, to settle upon those points that are essential?"[4] If we do this then we are prepared when the time comes to leave.

> If by chance death comes suddenly and unannounced—and who can be sure that it won't—it will not then find us unprepared. If its approach is gradual, if we have learned to "die a little" as well as "live a little," it will come as a friend. Our own terminal Amen will ring true as the response to the Creator's primal Amen which sent

us into this world. In all penitence and contrition for our failings, we will say, like St. Patrick's *Grazagham,* "thanks be to God," for the gift of the golden bowl of life.[5]

Almost prophetically, his own death came suddenly and unannounced. By far his most popular and successful book (based on the number of copies sold) was *The Manner Is Ordinary,* a book he almost did not write. The Book of the Month Club offered the autobiography as an alternate selection. Jacques Barzun, historian and critic, reviewed it on page one of the *New York Times Book Review Section* on February 14, 1954.

> The admirable simplicity, one might say transparency, with which Father LaFarge lets us share in this way the whole of his conscious life, the humble detail he gives so effortlessly even about remote events, the kaleidoscope he puts before us of men and principalities, of priests and secular thinkers, of ideas and common emotions close to sensations—all these define the image of a saintly character so wholly at ease in two worlds that for him everything finds somewhere its place if not its justification—the happy state of mind, one would say, of a lovable pilgrim from "The Canterbury Tales" whose accent was nonetheless pure American.[6]

Other reviews, equally praiseworthy, included one by George N. Shuster, president of Hunter College in New York, in the *New York Herald Tribune,* also on February 14, 1954.[7]

LaFarge confided to a fellow Jesuit shortly after these reviews appeared that he had been very reluctant to write the book. He "had always felt that a Jesuit should not write his autobiography." When he mentioned this feeling to his father provincial, however, he was told to go ahead anyway, and that if LaFarge did not write it, he would get someone else to do it for him. He then agreed to write the book, but still with reservations.

> I take little pleasure in going over things that happened long ago. I have no feeling of nostalgia for my youth, not that it was an unhappy youth but I just felt that I had outgrown it. However, when told to do the job I felt certain compensations, because through the medium of an autobiography one can get across to the world certain ideas which they will not take in a less personal form. I was able to set a number of things right about my parents, who after all are more or less historical figures and about whom undoubtedly more will be written in the future, at least with regard to my father,

and I wanted to get my mother properly in the picture too. Again, I wanted to make clear the nature of a Jesuit vocation as exemplified in an individual, and I was anxious particularly to show the growth of the interracial work, how it came from real experience and was not simply the result of an enthusiasm or purely theoretical approach to the problem. Finally, I was anxious to nail down certain points about the conduct of AMERICA and its editorial policy, and so on. If the book brings a certain amount of prominence or popularity it gives one a chance to speak one's mind more plainly on certain topics and to be heard over a wide area which, if you have something to say, is all to the good as long as you keep your head.[8]

Keeping his head was a LaFarge specialty. Contemporaries consistently described him as soft-spoken, thoughtful, and extremely modest about his achievements. This is not to say that he was indifferent to praise from others. It certainly pleased him to get a good book review, or an honor from some university or organization. But he seldom claimed to be more than an ordinary Jesuit priest, working for God and man to the best of his ability.

Once in a while, however, he did preen himself somewhat on making an impression. One such occasion came in March 1947 during a luncheon at the Century Club in New York, in honor of Lord Inverchapel, the British ambassador to the United States. LaFarge sat on one side of the ambassador, with Father Gannon, president of Fordham University, on the other. Lord Inverchapel raised a number of subjects for discussion, including hummingbirds. Neither LaFarge nor Gannon knew much about hummingbirds, so they quickly dropped that topic.

A subject then came up which LaFarge did know something about. The conversation, somehow, steered around to John Constable, the English painter, and especially his painting of Salisbury Cathedral. "I think I amazed him," LaFarge wrote to his sister Margaret, "by the fact that I showed remarkable familiarity with Constable, particularly with the painting of Salisbury Cathedral. I was also able to tell him about the price for which Constable's paintings recently sold."

After bragging about his knowledge of Constable, however, LaFarge quickly brought himself down to earth. "By the tone of this," he wrote, "you can see the slight note of vanity on the part of myself, and of course that is quite reprehensible. . . ."[9]

LaFarge had many and varied contacts both inside and outside the United States. After his death, the priest who discovered his body wrote that his address book, "which we used to notify friends, read like a

'Who's Who,' not only of the ecumenical and interracial leaders, but of the art world as well."[10]

He numbered among his personal friends Jacques Maritain, the famous French Thomist philosopher, and a convert to Catholicism. Maritain had left France in 1940, settling down first at Princeton as a visiting professor, then at Columbia in New York. Aside from royalties from his writings, miniscule after the fall of France in June 1940, Maritain had only a two thousand dollars per annum grant from the Rockefeller Foundation. Columbia was glad to have him as a professor, but could not pay him anything, concerned that this would stimulate a flood of applications from other refugee professors. LaFarge asked his sister-in-law Mabel to help raise funds for Maritain from private donors. How successful she was is not known.[11]

Another friend of LaFarge was Dr. Alexis Carrel, an expert on nutrition and author of *Man the Unknown*. Both Carrel and Maritain expressed a desire to LaFarge to meet the other, since each was curious about how the other's mind worked. LaFarge obligingly invited them to dinner at the Century Club, where they talked for hours.

> After the meeting Dr. Carrel remarked to me: "Monsieur Maritain is a perfectly wonderful man, a delightful character and I am charmed to have met him. I feel like loving him, but I still don't understand how his mind operates." If my memory does not fail me, Mr. Maritain made somewhat the same remark about Dr. Carrel.[12]

Maritain returned to France after the war, but he did not forget LaFarge. On the occasion of LaFarge's eightieth birthday, Maritain described him in the *Interracial Review* "Under 'a manner' that 'is ordinary,' he conceals an extraordinary grandeur of the mind and heart."[13]

LaFarge also tried to help another French intellectual, the physicist Lecomte du Noüy, author of the very popular book *Human Destiny*. In September 1947 du Noüy was in New York's Roosevelt Hospital dying of cancer. At the request of du Noüy's wife, LaFarge visited the critically ill man in the hospital. Among other things, *Human Destiny* contained a vigorous defense of God's existence, although the author had drifted away from the Catholic Church years before.

"I went down and talked to him," LaFarge wrote a Jesuit friend in Paris, "and found him in a most admirable state of mind, marvelously resigned, wonderfully spiritual and most anxious to do everything in every way and to obey the Church in every detail. He professed his faith most beautifully and in the most childlike fashion; so I had the privilege of giving him all the Sacraments, even including that of Extreme Unction on account of his condition."[14] Du Noüy died shortly afterward.

As already mentioned, Julian Green, from whose balcony in Paris he peered down on Molotov in 1947, was another of LaFarge's intellectual friends. Green wrote him at the end of 1957, congratulating him on *The Manner Is Ordinary,* which he had read and enjoyed. Praise from some-one like Green, for whom he had the greatest respect as a writer, was surely welcome to LaFarge.

In replying to Green's letter, LaFarge took the opportunity to express some of his own thoughts on the current state of American religion. He also explained to Green, how despite his own total commitment to Roman Catholicism, he was able to get along well with people of other faiths.

> There is a sort of external religiosity current and fashionable in the U.S., which is variously interpreted by various peoples, but is of only limited importance. But at the same time, I think there is a real spiritual revival in a large number of minds despite so much superficiality. I have had for several years the interesting experience of dialog with scientists (physical and social), with Jewish theologians, with all sorts of belief and unbelief, and find so much good can be accomplished merely by *being oneself,* most simply—as a believer, as a priest, even as a Jesuit, as long as you honor others' sincerity. Then one can affirm one's beliefs honestly, without arousing suspicion.[15]

Many demands for speeches, writings, and other activities came his way. At times he tried to resist at least some of them, and probably succeeded. He once complained to a niece, "Publishers make me write, because that is the kind of people they are; and they work it by getting you out to lunch, or having some third party say how nice it would be, etc., or ask you how you are getting along. But they usually lick you in the end, and you find yourself signing what is called the dotted line . . . Ahwah!"[16]

On February 25, 1952, LaFarge was honored at a testimonial dinner to celebrate his twenty-five years as an editor at *America.* Held at the Waldorf-Astoria Hotel in New York, some eight hundred people attended, including a table of his relatives. While Catholic prelates and lay people predominated, representatives of other faiths came out in force. These included Rabbi Louis Finkelstein, chancellor of the Jewish Theological Seminary; A. Philip Randolph, president of the Brotherhood of Sleeping Car Porters; and Dr. Anson Phelps, dean of the Episcopal National Cathedral in Washington, D.C. Francis Cardinal Spellman served as honorary chairman, although due to illness did not attend.

As happens at this sort of affair, speaker after speaker extolled the virtues and achievements of the guest of honor. Msgr. Cornelius A. Drew, representing the New York archdiocese, and pastor of St. Charles Borromeo Church in predominantly black Harlem, said that he had admired and reverenced Father LaFarge for years from afar. He found his path at St. Charles's made smoother because of LaFarge's work in interracial affairs. "He is so far ahead of us," he said, "that we have difficulty in keeping within hailing distance of him."

Before making his response, LaFarge was presented with a gold chalice, which he promised to use for the first time at a mass of thanksgiving he was to celebrate on March 2, at St. Peter's Church on Barclay Street in New York. After this tribute he expressed his gratitude for the evening. According to the *Catholic News,* however, he characteristically gave credit to others for what he had accomplished. What was said about him, he insisted, really belonged to the friends, colleagues, and religious superiors who had been his "constant collaborators."

In his address he acknowledged that men differ greatly on God's message and its meaning. While we follow different creeds, we are still drawn to persons who come to different conclusions, as long as those conclusions are based on sincere convictions. He took strong exception with those who charge that religious differences are a divisive force in society.

> To let such a notion gain a foothold in American life would, as I see it, destroy the very unity and peace we seek and cherish in our communities. Mere subjective religious emotionalism might well divide us into quarreling factions. But a religious faith that prizes the full dignity of human reason as a path toward discovering the holy will of God is the surest and only guarantee of peace and unity in our city, our country, and our world.

> If religious divisions are to be healed by outlawing religion itself and creating a nation of doubters, every man will be divided from his brother and the path laid open for the master mind of the ideologist to take charge. On the other hand, I know no surer pledge of a unified community than the company of men and women who apply the teachings of religion to the problems of daily life as consistently, as intelligently, yes, as scientifically as they can.

> I see in this gathering another proof that all persons of good will in our communities can unite to preserve our American heritage of reason and reverence and respect for religious faith.[17]

His well-deserved reputation for fostering ecumenism was apparent in these remarks. No matter what he believed about the higher truth of the Catholic faith, the infallibility of the pope, and the need for Catholic leadership of the world, he had constantly to be aware that he lived and worked in New York City, where diversity of race, religion, and ethnicity were facts of life. Anyone who sought to accomplish what he sought to accomplish, basically peace and the brotherhood of man, had to begin from that starting point. It is greatly to his credit that he recognized and acted upon this reality.

Three and a half years later, in November 1955, he celebrated a double jubilee—fifty years as a priest and his seventy-fifth birthday. Earlier, in a *New York Times* interview, the reporter asked him to make an informal, desk-side assessment of race relations in the United States. He replied briefly and optimistically, "there has been 'extraordinary improvement' within the last ten or fifteen years and the pace is accelerating." When asked to comment on recent violent acts of racism in the South, he said they would "blow themselves out in a few years as a sense of Christian responsibility mounts."[18]

This was the year after the *Brown* decision, which gave hope that integration would now come more rapidly. As the decade wore on, however, and the next one began, LaFarge gradually lost his optimism about the future of American race relations. He became increasingly uneasy, in fact, about the whole of American society and where it was heading.

On the eve of his eightieth birthday, a reporter from the *New York World-Telegram* asked him two questions. The first was "What was good about America?" The second was, "What was bad about America?" "Very provocative questions," he murmured. After closing his eyes for a few moments, he responded to the first question. America, he said, has a remarkable talent for "developing voluntary organizations." Americans were becoming more culture conscious. More people, for example, visited the Metropolitan Museum of Art in 1957 than ever before. Americans, he continued, are generous, resourceful, hospitable, and heroic. They were also moving forward on new ways to combat religious and racial tensions.

On the second question, what was wrong with America, he declared himself neither an optimist nor a pessimist. Rather, he considered himself a realist. His realism, however, led him to see some worrisome things about his country that, despite his disclaimer of being a pessimist, sounded very pessimistic indeed.

I am seriously concerned about the moral fiber of America. I'm more afraid of internal decay than I am of external danger—although the hypothesis of our being destroyed by nuclear weapons is a very real one.

I see in this country a moral erosion which is the result of our very great affluence, our comfortable living, our preoccupation with personal security, and our lavish expenditure on luxuries, stimulated by the ever-increasing pressure of advertising.

We have altogether too much Momism [sic], if you will, too much preoccupation with social conformity and a very marked lack of information and interest regarding those world issues that intimately concern us.

The Van Doren case was very alarming because it was a symptom of our moral problem and a symptom of an educational vacuum. I'm not so concerned that Van Doren behaved as he did, but by the fact that he was enthusiastically defended by so many people.

It seems to me that we've drifted into the notion that what is good or bad should be judged only by the question: What can you get away with?[19]

On the day of his eightieth birthday, a reception and luncheon in his honor was held at the Waldorf-Astoria. Greetings were given by Lester B. Granger of the National Urban League; Benjamin R. Epstein, director of the Anti-Defamation League of the B'nai B'rith; Roy Wilkins, secretary of the NAACP; and Dr. John Slawson of the American Jewish Committee.

Both gratitude and humor displayed themselves in LaFarge's response—gratitude to his friends and co-workers, and all who had helped him in his labors in the interracial movement; humor in his comment that so many people, now that he had reached the milestone of eighty years of living asked him so often to comment on his past life. "All sorts of questions are popped at you—and no payola—about your past, but that's easy, since the autobiography takes care of anything that needs to be known as to the personal record. Mr. Delaney will let you have it for $1.95 in paper-back form."

In the serious part of his response, he noted outbreaks of anti-Semitism in several parts of the country. People have asked what he thought was their cause. He could not be sure if these were merely a "passing skin eruption of youthful vandalism, or whether they indicate a deeper infection." He was sure, however, that they could escalate into greater danger for everyone. "The disrespect and violence that attack one set of your fellow-citizens today, may be turned against you tomorrow; the Jew and the Negro bombed today, the Catholic later," he told the audience.

He acknowledged that differences among groups will always exist. The question is, how do we deal with them? "Out of the problem of racial division and differences and annoyances they create we can build a positive program. Differences that naturally lead to discord and even open conflict if merely left to take their course, can be the building stone of a strong and lasting unity, in our cities and in the nation, in our church parishes, and finally in the world at large. Provided, that is to say, we do not degenerate into a hopelessly smug and comfort-loving people. Provided: that the leaders really lead."

While his address at the Waldorf was more positive than his interview with the *World-Telegram* reporter the day before, it was still a worried assessment of the world and its future. As for himself, he personally prayed for courage. Life, for him, became more precious as he grew older. "When the time allotted you on earth is drawing to an end," he said, "the hours still remaining mean a great deal."[20]

A little more than three and a half years of that life remained to him after this birthday celebration. Although he stayed mentally alert until the very end, old age eventually started taking its toll on his body.

While he lived to be eighty-three, LaFarge nonetheless had some serious illnesses during his lifetime. As an infant he was so puny and listless he was expected to die. As a teen he suffered an acute attack of appendicitis that kept him out of school for more than a year. The appendix eventually had to be removed. As a priest in Maryland he had occasional bouts of severe and protracted headaches, possibly migraines brought on by overwork and tension. He had been sent from Woodstock in Baltimore to the county missions in the first place, because his rector realized he was pushing himself too hard and bordered on the verge of physical and mental collapse.

During his four years as editor in chief of *America*, from 1944 to 1948, he had three operations, all unspecified as to cause. His nephew's wife Mary thought one might have been for a prostate condition, but no one really seems to know. It is not that he was secretive about his ailments; he just did not give details. "A completely disproportionate amount of time," he wrote in *The Manner Is Ordinary*, "had been spent those four years . . . in the hospital or in convalescence."[21]

After laying down the reins as editor in chief in 1948, however, and recovering from the three operations, he seems to have enjoyed reasonably good health for the remainder of his life. Father Walter Abbott, on the staff of *America* at the time of LaFarge's death, remembers that for the last year or so of his life he had trouble with one leg, and dragged his foot when he walked.[22]

On one of the last trips before his death, to participate in a meeting of a committee on religion and race, one of the workmen at *America* saw him pushing his bag with his foot, trying to get out to hail a taxi to take him to the airport. He was clearly in pain. A hernia on his left side could explain the trouble he was having with his left leg.

LaFarge had a complete physical examination by Dr. W. S. Morton on October 28, 1960. Morton sent him the results a few days later, and they were not bad for an eighty year old man.

> At your examination on October 28, I found your blood pressure normal. There were some evidences of mild hardening of the arteries which is consistent with your age. The left hernia does not need attention at this time.
>
> Laboratory tests including urinalysis, blood hemoglobin and cell count and chemistry test for sugar protein and cholesterol were all within normal limits.
>
> I see no reason for you to take any particular medicine at this time in fact, provided your ankles do not swell up; there is no reason to restrict salt in your diet. If you have any questions please write or phone.[23]

Two months before his death he wrote to his cousin, Father Schuyler Brown, "I am obliged to go slow, and restrict my movements, for various reasons. After all, the mechanism runs down after a while. Wonderful it has worked as long as it has."[24]

The mechanism stopped working on Sunday afternoon, November 24, 1963 — two days after the assassination of President John F. Kennedy. The president's death devastated LaFarge, who could barely speak about it. Father C.J. McNaspy, S.J., who had been working at *America* since 1960, and who discovered and anointed the body, told the writer what happened that day.

In the morning, LaFarge asked McNaspy to escort the ambassador to the United Nations from Upper Volta in Africa around the city. He had been scheduled to do this himself, but worn out from the hours and hours of television about the assassination, he decided to take a nap after lunch.

When McNaspy returned he had with him a young priest from New Orleans, who had once been his student, Father Charles Coyle, S.J. As a treat and an honor he offered to introduce Coyle to LaFarge. Around noon they went up to his bedroom. When they arrived they found the door slightly open. Peering in, McNaspy saw LaFarge lying quietly on his bed. Later he realized he might have already been dead. The two Jesuits decided to go downstairs and have lunch, agreeing to return to LaFarge's room later in the day.

When they went back, however, he was still quietly stretched out on his bed. Now thoroughly alarmed, McNaspy hastened downstairs and called LaFarge on the phone. When there was no answer, he hurried back to his room, went in and found him dead. To this day he vividly recalls rushing from the room, shouting "Uncle John is dead! Uncle John is dead!"[25]

In an editorial in *America* on December 14, 1963, Editor in Chief Thurston N. Davis wrote of the deaths of Kennedy and LaFarge, expressing poignantly the tragedy of the first and the great sadness of the second.

> That long last week of November left us with an immemorial ache. Indeed, the whole earth ached, as the messages and reflections we publish in this issue prove. Many were eager to express their baffled grief. They sent poems and prose tributes. Wives mailed up copies of letters their husbands had written that black night of November 22, to be read one day by children now too young to understand the awful meaning of what had happened.
>
> At AMERICA's editorial residence, grief over the President was merged with the sense of loss we felt at the death of Fr. John La-Farge. He died just two days after the President, and I can't escape the feeling that the Dallas tragedy had something to do with it. On Sunday, fully clothed, Fr. LaFarge lay down on top of his bed to read the paper, first carefully spreading the financial section under his feet. He apparently read for a while, then put the paper aside, took off his glasses, and dozed off. Death came some little time later. When we found him at four o'clock that afternoon, one of the Fathers anointed him and called the police to get a doctor. When the police examined his person for "valuables" — a routine procedure — they found two worn rosaries.
>
> Cardinal Cushing had flown from Washington to Boston after the President's funeral Mass on Monday. Yet when we asked him that

night if he would celebrate the Mass for Fr. LaFarge, he immediately agreed. So it was that Fr. Walter Abbott and I met him early Wednesday morning at LaGuardia Airport and brought him into Manhattan in Cardinal Spellman's car. After the Mass, the Cardinal preached a stirring eulogy on Fr. LaFarge and on his long years of work for the poor. As we accompanied the body to the rear of St. Ignatius Loyola Church, the Cardinal leaned over and shook hands with La-Farge's old friend, Roy Wilkins, the head of the NAACP. He was one of the hundreds who were there to pay their last respects.[26]

The writer wondered why *America's* editors asked Cardinal Cushing of Boston, rather than Cardinal Spellman of New York, to say the mass and deliver the homily. Father Abbot explained that Cushing was a well-known, long-time admirer of LaFarge, whom he first met in Boston forty years before. It was LaFarge who urged the cardinal to work harder for blacks.

A year or so before LaFarge's death, *America* decided to move its headquarters and residence from One hundred eighth Street down to Fifty-sixth Street in Manhattan. About one and a half million dollars would be needed to buy and renovate the building they were interested in, most of which would have to be raised by donations. Father Davis asked Father Abbott to see Cardinal Cushing in Boston, and ask him for five hundred thousand dollars. Abbott doubted that Cushing would donate such a large sum, figuring that he would contribute twenty-five thousand dollars at most, but agreed to try anyway. After speaking to the cardinal for a few minutes, making his best pitch, Cushing silenced him with a raise of his hand. He asked Abbott how much he wanted, then stunned the priest by immediately agreeing to the half million. In agreeing, however, he made it clear that it was because of Father LaFarge's long association with *America*. His admiration for him went beyond praise; it went all the way to his pocketbook.[27]

And so Father John LaFarge, who had said so many funeral masses for so many friends and relatives over his fifty-eight years as a priest, was now to have one said for himself. At ten o'clock on the morning of November 27, 1963, mourners filled the Church of St. Ignatius Loyola, come to pay their last respects. Cardinal Cushing said the mass and preached the sermon. Father McNaspy, who had discovered the body and anointed it, was one of the two Jesuit servers assisting the cardinal. Father Schuyler Brown, LaFarge's young Jesuit cousin, was the other.

While Cushing denied that he was delivering a eulogy, for one of the "sacred rules" of the Jesuits was "no eulogy" for any of its members, he did in fact say a eulogy for LaFarge, disguising it as a "personal appreciation." He told of first meeting him four decades before, when he asked him to come to Boston to inspect a new information and recreation center for blacks, established by Mother Drexel's Sisters of the Blessed Sacrament.

He stressed LaFarge's early involvement in civil rights for blacks. At that time, Cushing conceded, the "Church was dragging its heels" on the issue. It seemed content to let things find their own way. Not so LaFarge, who would not wait for the problem to solve itself.

He especially singled out his starting the Catholic interracial councils, his work in rural areas, and his ecumenism, long before that word was current. He called him an "instrument of God, the true tool of Christ." Yet in the midst of endless activity, he always remained calm, "never disturbed, never upset, always reaching the root and core of every discussion and calmly, intelligently coming forth with a common denominator acceptable to all."

Cushing's final words called for a continuation of LaFarge's work in the interracial movement.

> Now all is calm, all is peaceful. Please God, he is now in the mansions of Heaven. Let us cherish the memory of this great crusader for the truth. And we can do it best not only by our prayers, but by perpetuating more and more the wonderful spirit of Catholic interracial work.[28]

Lengthy obituaries appeared in the *New York Times* and the *New York Herald Tribune,* as well as countless other newspapers and magazines around the country. The *Times* placed him in the company of other religious trailblazers of the New World. "What he stood for really was the tradition of service in European and American history, which took a Marquette and a Joliet to trading posts on the Mississippi, a Rene Guptil to Huron villages, and himself to the water courses and swamps of Maryland mission stations."[29]

The *Herald Tribune* was even more effusive. Far from leaving the world when he became a priest, the obituary read, "Father LaFarge went on to become one of his Church's most forceful spokesmen on many controversial subjects—especially racial justice . . . and champion of many another seemingly lost cause. He reflected the best of Christianity.

> To many of his colleagues, and to the laity of all faiths as well, Father LaFarge was the embodiment of what St. Thomas Aquinas

adumbrated as the Roman Catholic ideal: the balance of faith and reason. His convictions on social problems were as deeply seated as those on religion; to him, they were inextricably woven into a passionate mosaic that spelled the salvation of man.[30]

LaFarge was not buried in the family plot in Newport, but in the Jesuit cemetery at Shrub Oak, New York, about an hour's drive north of New York City. Between 1959 and 1974, one hundred and ten Jesuits were laid to rest there. Formerly a Jesuit seminary situated in the midst of 140 sprawling acres of forest and lawns, it had to be sold for lack of use. Since 1981 it has served as a rehabilitation center for teenagers with drug problems. But the small cemetery is well preserved and cared for. The tombstones are laid out in chronological order based on date of death. LaFarge's is one of the early ones. The inscriptions, in Latin, are all in the same style. LaFarge's reads:

P. IOANNES LAFARGE S.I.
NATUS 13 FEB. 1880
INGRESSUS 12 NOV. 1905
OBIIT 24 NOV. 1963
RIP

Honored during his life, LaFarge continues to be honored after the end of that life. Thanks in part to the generous gift from Cardinal Cushing, *America* purchased and renovated the nine-story building it still occupies at 106 West Fifty-sixth Street. One large room in the building was dedicated to LaFarge in 1964, and named *The John LaFarge Institute*. In the years since, seminars, lectures, and discussions on a broad array of topics have been held in this charming room. Father Abbott was named the first director of the institute. On the first anniversary of LaFarge's death. Father Davis celebrated a mass in his honor, and delivered a short sermon on his life. It concluded with one more tribute.

> In its modest but, we hope, truly effective way, the newly founded John LaFarge Institute, to be located in the new *America* House at 106 West 56th Street, pledges its energies and its resources to this central concern of the man whose name it bears. In so doing it humbly takes alongside the venerable Catholic Interracial Council of New York — alongside all the Catholic Interracial Councils of the United States — all of them products of the foresight of Father LaFarge — hoping to be of help in our common struggle for justice. Together today at this Mass, on John LaFarge's first anniversary,

the Catholic Interracial Councils and the John LaFarge Institute
dedicate themselves with fresh purpose to the ideals of faith, hope,
love and justice that were his greatest bequest to all of us.[31]

The influences and effects on others of LaFarge's long and fruitful life
have not ended. Every year the Catholic Interracial Council of New York
holds a dinner in his honor. The main purpose of this gathering is to present the annual Father John LaFarge awards for interracial justice to men
and women who have excelled in that field. It is a happy occasion, as the
writer, who attended a recent dinner, can personally testify. LaFarge is
no longer mourned. Too much time has passed for mourning. But he is
far from forgotten. The author of the Book of Daniel could have written
these lines with him in mind.

But the wise shall shine brightly
like the splendor of the firmament,
And those who lead the many to justice
shall be like the stars forever.

Amen.

Abbreviations Used in Citations

BLC   Ben LaFarge Collection
GUL   Georgetown University Library
HGU   *Humani Generis Unitas*
MLC   Mary LaFarge Collection
MLHC   Margaret LaFarge Hamill Collection
NYHS   New York Historical Society
PA   Paulist Archives
SBC   Schuyler Brown Collection
TMIO   *The Manner Is Ordinary*
YUL   Yale University Library

Notes

Chapter 1

1. John LaFarge, *The Manner Is Ordinary* (New York: Harcourt, Brace and Company, 1954), p. 18. Hereinafter cited *TMIO*.
2. *Ibid.*, p. 19.
3. Notes of Oliver LaFarge's conversation with his mother Margaret LaFarge, January 4, 1923, Margaret LaFarge Hamill Collection. Hereinafter cited MLHC.
4. *TMIO*, p. 20.
5. John LaFarge (senior) to Margaret Perry, March 1860, MLHC.
6. Notes of Oliver LaFarge's conversation 1/4/23.
7. *TMIO*, p. 25.
8. Margaret LaFarge to Fr. Isaac Hecker, November 23, 1860, Paulist Archives, Washington, D.C. Hereinafter cited PA.
9. Margaret LaFarge to Fr. Isaac Hecker, April 22, 1861. PA.
10. *TMIO*, p. 26.
11. Henry James to Thomas Perry, April 18, 1864, Leon Edel, ed. *Henry James's Letters,* vol. I (Cambridge, Mass.: Belknap Press, Harvard University, 1974), p. 52.
12. Oliver LaFarge conversation with Margaret LaFarge, January 9, 1923, MLHC.
13. Quoted in James Yarnell, *John LaFarge: Watercolors and Drawings* (Yonkers, N.Y.: The Hudson River Museum of Westchester, 1990), p. 68.
14. Oliver H. P. LaFarge, *The Gold Rush of 1898 and Other Reminiscences* (Privately printed by his daughter Margaret LaFarge Hamill, 1990), pp. 87–88.
15. John LaFarge to Mrs. Michael Kurch, July 28, 1954, John LaFarge Papers, Georgetown University Library. Hereinafter cited GUL.
16. John LaFarge, *An American Amen: A Statement of Hope* (New York: Farrar, Straus and Cudahy, 1958), p. 25.
17. *Ibid.*, p. 27.
18. Oliver LaFarge, *The Gold Rush,* p. 113.
19. *Ibid.*, p. 115.
20. Undated, unnamed newspaper clipping, MLHC.
21. *TMIO*, p. 3.
22. *Ibid.*, p. 27.

23. Mary A. LaFarge and James Yarnell, *Margaret Mason Perry LaFarge,* (Manuscript accepted for publication by Newport Historical Society) p. 29.
24. *TMIO,* pp. 29–30.
25. John LaFarge (father) to Mary Whitney, Easter 1882, LaFarge family collection, New York Historical Society. Hereinafter cited as NYHS.
26. *Ibid.,* September 8, 1882.
27. *Ibid.,* January 1, 1910.
28. Margaret LaFarge (sister) to Henry LaFarge, March 12, 1947, Mary LaFarge Collection. Hereinafter cited MLC.
29. *TMIO,* p. 30.
30. Oliver LaFarge, *The Gold Rush,* p. 94.
31. John LaFarge, "LaFarge and the Truth," *America,* March 30, 1935, p. 586.
32. Royal Cortissoz, *John LaFarge: A Memoir and a Study* (Boston: Houghton Mifflin Co., 1911), p. 31.
33. Henry James, *Henry James: Autobiography* (New York: Criterion Books, 1956), p. 287.
34. Royal Cortissoz, *John LaFarge,* p. 183.
35. Henry Adams, *The Education of Henry Adams: An Autobiography* (Boston: Houghton Mifflin Co., 1918), p. 371.
36. John LaFarge to Susan LaFarge. March 3, 1962, Ben LaFarge Collection. Hereinafter cited BLC.
37. *TMIO,* p. 46.
38. *Ibid.,* p. 31.
39. *Ibid.,* p. 34.
40. *Ibid.*
41. *Ibid.,* p. 35.
42. James Huneker, *New Cosmopolis* (New York: Charles Scribner's Sons, 1915), p. 333.
43. *Ibid.,* p. 332.
44. *TMIO,* p. 43.
45. *Ibid.,* p. 42.
46. Laura E. Richards and Maud Howe Eliott, *Julia Ward Howe, 1819–1910,* vol. II. (Dunwoody, Georgia: Norman S. Berg, 1970), p. 74.
47. *TMIO,* p. 43.
48. *Ibid.,* p. 30.
49. John LaFarge to Harold Voorhis, May 1, 1940, NYHS.
50. Bertha L. Lyons to John LaFarge, May 6, 1940, NYHS.
51. John LaFarge to Most Rev. Russell J. McVinney, July 13, 1961, GUL.

Chapter 2

1. *TMIO,* p. 34.
2. *Ibid.,* p. 38.

3. *Ibid.*
4. John LaFarge to Margaret LaFarge, January 30, 1885, NYHS.
5. *TMIO*, pp. 54–55.
6. Interview with Mrs. Peter Morris, November 29, 1992.
7. Oliver LaFarge, *The Gold Rush,* p. 113.
8. *TMIO*, p. 37.
9. Phyllis LaFarge Johnson to the author, August 10, 1991.
10. John LaFarge to Margaret LaFarge, June 8, 1893, NYHS.
11. John LaFarge to Margaret LaFarge, December 30, 1894, NYHS.
12. John LaFarge to Margaret LaFarge, January 30, 1895, NYHS.
13. John LaFarge to Margaret LaFarge, February 5, 1895, NYHS.
14. *TMIO*, p. 47.
15. *Ibid.*, pp. 39–40.
16. *Ibid.*, p. 53.
17. *Ibid.*, p. 40.
18. *Ibid.*, p. 55.
19. John LaFarge (senior) to Henry Adams, Yale University Library. Hereinafter cited YUL.
20. *TMIO*, p. 49.
21. *Ibid.*, p. 56.
22. Ibid., *p. 57.*
23. L. R. Briggs to W. K. Brice, September 1897, GUL.
24. L. R. Briggs to John LaFarge (senior), May 9, 1899, NYHS.
25. Hugh Hawkins, *Between Harvard and America: The Educational Leadership of Charles W. Eliot* (New York: Oxford University Press, 1972), p. 108.
26. *Ibid.*, p. 109.
27. John LaFarge to Margaret LaFarge, March 23, 1898, NYHS.
28. John LaFarge to Margaret LaFarge, September 29, 1900, NYHS.
29. *TMIO*, p. 64.
30. *Ibid.*, p. 63.
31. John LaFarge, "Feature X, re. death of George Santayana at age 88," *America,* October 11, 1952, p. 42.
32. *TMIO*, p. 68.
33. John LaFarge to Rev. Philip Hughes, June 26, 1945, GUL.
34. *TMIO*, p. 67.
35. John LaFarge, undated memo, GUL.
36. *TMIO*, p. 67.
37. John LaFarge, "In Place of the Foundation," *America,* December 13, 1926, pp. 424–25.
38. *TMIO*, p. 63.
39. *Ibid.*
40. John LaFarge to Margaret LaFarge, March 23, 1898, NYHS.
41. *TMIO*, p. 7.
42. John LaFarge to Margaret LaFarge, November 27, 1899, NYHS.

43. *TMIO,* p. 61.
44. Hugh Hawkins, *Between Harvard and America,* p. 108.
45. *TMIO,* p. 62.
46. John LaFarge to Margaret LaFarge, May 19, 1900, NYHS.
47. Henry LaFarge to Rev. Edward S. Stanton, S.J., May 30, 1982, Mary La-Farge Collection.
48. *Ibid.*
49. John LaFarge, "Harvard Culture and Jesuit Humanism, *America,* November 9, 1926.
50. John LaFarge to Rev. Dr. W. L. Sperry, April 14, 1947, GUL.
51. *TMIO,* p. 74.

Chapter 3

1. John LaFarge to Margaret LaFarge, August 5, 1901, NYHS.
2. *Ibid.*
3. *TMIO,* p. 81.
4. John LaFarge to Margaret LaFarge, August 8, 1901, NYHS.
5. *Ibid.*
6. *Ibid.*
7. *TMIO,* p. 81.
8. John LaFarge to Margaret LaFarge, August 8, 1901, NYHS.
9. John LaFarge to Margaret LaFarge, August 12, 1901, NYHS.
10. *Ibid.*
11. *TMIO,* pp. 83–84.
12. *Ibid.*
13. *Ibid.,* p. 86.
14. *Ibid.,* p. 90.
15. *Ibid.,* p. 90–91.
16. *Ibid.*
17. *Ibid.,* p. 92.
18. *Ibid.,* p. 93.
19. *Ibid.,* p. 103.
20. *Ibid.,* p. 108.
21. *Ibid.,* p. 110.
22. *Ibid.,* p. 111.
23. Henry James to Margaret LaFarge, June 10, 1904, "Henry James's Letters to the LaFarges," *The New England Quarterly,* June 1949, p. 184.
24. John LaFarge to Margaret LaFarge, October 4, 1903, NYHS.
25. John LaFarge to Margaret LaFarge, October 8, 1903, NYHS.
26. Henry James to Margaret LaFarge, January 9, 1904, NYHS.
27. John LaFarge to Margaret LaFarge, November 18, 1903, NYHS.

28. John LaFarge to Margaret LaFarge, December 6, 1903, NYHS.
29. *TMIO*, pp. 99–100.
30. *Ibid.,* p. 98.
31. John LaFarge to Margaret LaFarge, January 21, 1904, NYHS.
32. John LaFarge to Margaret LaFarge, February 29, 1904, NYHS.
33. John LaFarge to Margaret LaFarge, April 20, 1904, NYHS.
34. John LaFarge to Margaret LaFarge, May 28, 1904, NYHS.
35. *TMIO*, p. 115.
36. John LaFarge (senior) to Mrs. Jones, August 2, 1904, YUL.
37. *TMIO*, p. 116.
38. *Ibid*, p. 118.
39. John LaFarge to Margaret LaFarge, October 21, 1904, NYHS.
40. *TMIO*, p. 124.
41. *Ibid.,* p. 119.
42. *Ibid.,* pp. 118–120.
43. John LaFarge to Margaret LaFarge, March 22, 1905, NYHS.
44. *TMIO*, p. 122.
45. *Ibid.,* p. 123.
46. *Ibid.,* p. 125.
47. Margaret LaFarge to Frances LaFarge, August 6, 1905, MLHC.
48. *TMIO*, p. 125.
49. John LaFarge (senior) to Mrs. C. Jones, July 25, 1905, YUL.
50. Margaret LaFarge to Frances LaFarge, August 6, 1905, MLHC.
51. John LaFarge to Mrs. A. E. Fekete, Dec. 13, 1948, GUL.
52. Margaret LaFarge to Mabel LaFarge, November 6, 1906, YUL.
53. Ben LaFarge to the author, August 1992.
54. Bancel LaFarge to John LaFarge, August 9, 1905, NYHS.
55. Margaret LaFarge to Bancel LaFarge, April 12, 1910, YUL.

Chapter 4

1. *TMIO*, p. 133.
2. *Ibid.,* p. 126.
3. *Ibid.,* p. 129.
4. John LaFarge to Margaret LaFarge, November 27, 1905, NYHS.
5. John LaFarge (senior) to John LaFarge, January 13, 1906, NYHS.
6. John LaFarge to John LaFarge (senior), December 25, 1906, NYHS.
7. *TMIO*, p. 137.
8. John LaFarge to Margaret LaFarge, April 25, 1907, NYHS.
9. John LaFarge to Margaret LaFarge, August 6, 1907, NYHS.
10. John LaFarge to Margaret LaFarge, August 18, 1907, NYHS.
11. John LaFarge to Margaret LaFarge, October 20, 1907, NYHS.

12. *TMIO,* p. 141.

13. John LaFarge to Margaret LaFarge, May 24, 1907, NYHS.

14. *TMIO,* pp. 142–143.

15. John LaFarge to Margaret LaFarge (sister), August 8, 1908, NYHS.

16. John LaFarge to Margaret LaFarge, November 10, 1908, NYHS.

17. John LaFarge to Margaret LaFarge, December 29, 1908, NYHS.

18. John LaFarge (senior) to John LaFarge, January 29, 1907, NYHS.

19. John LaFarge to John LaFarge (senior), June 21, 1908, NYHS.

20. John LaFarge to Margaret LaFarge, September 28, 1908, NYHS.

21. John LaFarge to John LaFarge (senior), June 3, 1909, NYHS.

22. John LaFarge to Margaret LaFarge, February 16, 1910, NYHS.

23. John LaFarge to Margaret LaFarge, October 2, 1910, NYHS.

24. John LaFarge to Margaret LaFarge, January 17, 1912, NYHS.

25. John LaFarge, "John LaFarge," *America,* May 27, 1911, p. 152.

26. *TMIO,* p. 145.

27. Margaret LaFarge to Bancel LaFarge, September 30, 1910, YUL.

28. John LaFarge to Margaret LaFarge, May 16, 1910, NYHS.

29. *TMIO,* p. 147.

30. John LaFarge to Margaret LaFarge, October 19, 1910, NYHS.

31. John LaFarge to Thomas Sergeant Perry, October 19, 1910, Perry Family Papers, Colby College Library, Special Collections, Waterville, Maine.

32. Margaret LaFarge to Bancel LaFarge, December 5, 1910, YUL.

33. Margaret LaFarge to Mabel LaFarge, January 12, 1911, YUL.

34. John LaFarge to Margaret LaFarge (sister), July 1, 1909, NYHS.

35. *TMIO,* p. 147.

36. *Ibid.,* p. 148.

37. *Ibid.,* p. 149.

38. *Ibid.*

39. *Ibid.,* p. 151.

40. John LaFarge to Margaret LaFarge, February 26, 1911, NYHS.

41. *TMIO,* p. 152.

Chapter 5

1. *TMIO,* p. 156.

2. *Ibid.,* p. 158.

3. *Ibid.,* p. 384.

4. John LaFarge to Margaret LaFarge, January 1, 1912, NYHS.

5. John LaFarge to Margaret LaFarge, May 7, 1899, NYHS.

6. *TMIO,* p. 191.

7. *Ibid.,* p. 192.

8. John LaFarge to the Very Rev. David Nugent, S.J., July 11, 1947, GUL.

9. John LaFarge to Margaret LaFarge, December 3, 1911, NYHS.

10. John LaFarge to Margaret LaFarge, January 1, 1912, NYHS.

11. John LaFarge to Margaret LaFarge, January 17, 1912, NYHS.

12. John LaFarge to Margaret LaFarge, April 19, 1912, NYHS.

13. John LaFarge to Margaret LaFarge, September 3, 1912, NYHS.

14. *TMIO*, p. 166.

15. John LaFarge to Margaret LaFarge, February 12, 1913, NYHS.

16. *TMIO*, p. 167.

17. *Ibid.*, p. 170.

18. *Ibid.*

19. *Ibid.*, p. 178.

20. John LaFarge to Margaret LaFarge, May 10, 1914, NYHS.

21. John LaFarge to Margaret LaFarge, November 16, 1915, NYHS.

22. John LaFarge to Margaret LaFarge, December 28, 1915, NYHS.

Chapter 6

1. John LaFarge diary entry July 31, 1916, GUL.

2. *TMIO*, p. 197.

3. *Ibid.*

4. John LaFarge to Margaret LaFarge, November 1, 1917, NYHS.

5. John LaFarge to Margaret LaFarge, December 27, 1917, NYHS.

6. John LaFarge diary entry, March 5, 1916, GUL.

7. John LaFarge to Margaret LaFarge (sister), November 18, 1917, NYHS.

8. John LaFarge to Margaret LaFarge, February 25, 1918, NYHS.

9. John LaFarge to Margaret LaFarge, April 2, 1918, NYHS.

10. *Ibid.*

11. John LaFarge to Margaret LaFarge, Easter Sunday, 1917, MLC.

12. John LaFarge to Margaret LaFarge, April 2, 1918, NYHS.

13. *TMIO*, p. 198.

14. John LaFarge to Margaret LaFarge, April 19, 1918, NYHS.

15. *TMIO*, p. 202.

16. *Ibid.*, pp. 202–203.

17. John LaFarge to "my dear children," May 9, 1918, NYHS.

18. John LaFarge to Margaret LaFarge, June 17, 1918, NYHS.

19. John LaFarge to Margaret LaFarge, July 11, 1918, NYHS.

20. John LaFarge to Margaret LaFarge (sister), September 19, 1919, NYHS.

21. *TMIO*, p. 200.

22. *Ibid.*, p. 201.

23. *Ibid.*, p. 199.

24. John LaFarge to Margaret LaFarge, June 6, 1919, NYHS.

25. John LaFarge to Margaret LaFarge, January 19, 1919, NYHS.

26. John LaFarge to Margaret LaFarge, August 28, 1919, NYHS.
27. John LaFarge to Margaret LaFarge, November 16, 1920, NYHS.
28. John LaFarge to Margaret LaFarge, December 13, 1920, NYHS.
29. John LaFarge to Margaret LaFarge, March 12, 1921, NYHS.
30. John LaFarge diary entry, March 26, 1921, GUL.
31. Interviews with Mary LaFarge and Margaret LaFarge Hamill, 1992 and 1993.
32. John LaFarge to Margaret LaFarge, December 13, 1920, NYHS.
33. John LaFarge to Margaret LaFarge, December 19, 1921, NYHS.
34. John LaFarge to Margaret LaFarge, March 13, 1918, NYHS.
35. John LaFarge diary entry, November 16, 1916, GUL.
36. *TMIO*, p. 209.
37. John LaFarge to Margaret LaFarge, January 24, 1924, NYHS.
38. John LaFarge memo, September 12, 1935, GUL.
39. *TMIO*, p. 216.
40. John LaFarge to Margaret LaFarge, July 30, 1924, NYHS.
41. *TMIO*, pp. 224–25.
42. *Ibid.*, p. 226.
43. *Ibid.*

Chapter 7

1. John LaFarge, *Interracial Justice: A Study of the Catholic Doctrine of Race Relations* (New York: America Press, 1937), p. VI.
2. *Ibid.*, p. 3.
3. *Ibid.*, p. 5.
4. *Ibid.*, p. 15.
5. *Ibid.*, p. 24.
6. *Ibid.*
7. *Ibid.*, p. 45.
8. *Ibid.*, p. 47.
9. *Ibid.*
10. *Ibid.*
11. *TMIO*, p. 184.
12. John LaFarge, *Interracial Justice*, p. 52.
13. *Ibid.*, p. 59.
14. *Ibid.*, p. 60.
15. *Ibid.*, p. 111.
16. *Ibid.*, p. 113.
17. *Ibid.*, p. 124.
18. *Ibid.*, p. 126.
19. *Ibid.*, p. 128.
20. *Ibid.*, p. 132.

21. *Ibid.,* p. 133.
22. Thurston Davis, S.J. and Joseph Small, S.J. eds., *A John LaFarge Reader* (New York: America Press, 1956), p. 162.
23. John LaFarge, *Interracial Justice,* p. 139.
24. *Ibid.,* p. 143.
25. *Ibid.,* p. 144.
26. *Ibid.*
27. *Ibid.,* p. 146.
28. *Ibid.*
29. *Ibid.,* p. 147.
30. George H. Dunne, S.J., *King's Pawn: The Memoirs of George H. Dunne, S.J.* (Chicago: Loyola University Press, 1990), p. 98.
31. Editorial, *America,* October 16, 1948, p. 36.
32. John LaFarge, *Interracial Justice,* pp. 155–56.
33. *Ibid.,* p. 158.
34. *Ibid.,* p. 164.
35. *Ibid.*
36. *Ibid.,* p. 194.
37. *TMIO,* p. 272.
38. *Ibid.,* p. 273.
39. John LaFarge to Fr. Francis Talbot, S.J., July 3, 1938, GUL.
40. *Ibid.*
41. *Ibid.*
42. *Ibid.*
43. Fr. Talbot to John LaFarge, August 13, 1938, GUL.
44. Jim Castelli, "Unpublished Encyclical Attacked Anti-Semitism," *National Catholic Reporter,* December 15, 1972, p. 1.
45. Telephone interview with Fr. George Abbott, February 24, 1994.
46. Edward S. Stanton, "John LaFarge's Understanding of the Unifying Mission of the Church" (Ph.D. dissertation, St. Paul University, Ottawa, Canada, 1972), p. 181.
47. Interview with Fr. John Donahue at *America* headquarters, September 1993.
48. Notes on galley proofs of draft encyclical *Humani Generis Unitas* sent to Georgetown Library, November 18, 1993, GUL. Hereinafter cited as HGU.
49. *Ibid.*
50. John LaFarge to Fr. Talbot, August 23, 1938, GUL.
51. Fr. John Kileen to John LaFarge, October 27, 1938, GUL.
52. Father Gundlach to John LaFarge, October 27, 1938, GUL.
53. Stanton, "Unifying Mission," p. 1.
54. Jerry Filteau, "Did Church Miss Chance to Condemn Racism?" *Boston Pilot,* January 12, 1973, p. 16.
55. Robert G. Weisbard and Wallace P. Sillonpor, *The Chief Rabbi, the Pope, and the Holocaust* (New Brunswick, N.J.: Transaction Publications, 1992), p. 35.

56. *Ibid.,* p. 37.
57. *Ibid.,* p. 39.
58. *Catholic Transcript,* December 22, 1972.
59. *Ibid.*
60. J. Derek Holmes, *The Papacy in the Modern World, 1914–1978* (New York: Crossroads, 1981), p. 116.
61. *Catholic Transcript,* December 22, 1972.
62. *HGU,* p. 5.
63. *Ibid.,* p. 9.
64. *Ibid.,* p. 16b.
65. *Ibid.,* p. 21.
66. *Ibid.,* p. 32b.
67. *Ibid.,* p. 33b.
68. *Ibid.*
69. *Ibid.,* p. 34.
70. *Ibid.*
71. *Ibid.,* p. 34b.
72. *Ibid.,* p. 35.
73. *Ibid.,* p. 36.
74. *Ibid.*

Chapter 8

1. F. Jay Taylor, *The United States and the Spanish Civil War* (New York: Bookman Associates, 1956), p. 24.
2. *Ibid.,* p. 25.
3. José Sanchez, *The Spanish Civil War as a Religious Tragedy* (South Bend, Indiana: University of Notre Dame Press, 1987), p. 8.
4. *Ibid.,* p. 52.
5. *Ibid.,* p. 123.
6. Joseph F. Thorning, "Why the Press Failed on Spain," *Catholic World,* December 1937, pp. 289–91.
7. F. Jay Taylor, *The United States and the Spanish Civil War,* p. 122.
8. *New York Times,* August 17, 1936.
9. *Time,* May 16, 1938, p. 9.
10. *Christian Century,* April 12, 1939, p. 467.
11. *New York Times,* September 3, 1937.
12. *Ibid.,* September 11, 1937.
13. *Ibid.,* October 15, 1937.
14. *Ibid.,* October 5, 1937.
15. *Ibid.,* October 14, 1937.
16. Herbert L. Matthews, *Half of Spain Died: A Reappraisal of the Spanish Civil War* (New York: Charles Scribner's Sons, 1973), p. 180.

17. John LaFarge to Fr. Talbot, May 7, 1938, GUL.
18. *Ibid.*
19. *TMIO,* p. 255.
20. John LaFarge to Fr. Talbot, May 15, 1938, GUL.
21. John LaFarge, "The Munich Agreement Demands Further Adjustments," *America,* November 5, 1938, p. 100.
22. John LaFarge to Fr. Talbot, May 15, 1938, GUL.
23. *Ibid.*
24. *Ibid.*
25. *TMIO,* p. 257.
26. *Ibid.*
27. *Ibid.,* p. 258.
28. *Ibid.,* p. 260.
29. *Ibid.,* p. 263.
30. *Ibid.*
31. *Ibid.,* p. 264.
32. *Ibid.,* p. 262.
33. *Ibid.,* p. 266.
34. John LaFarge to Fr. Talbot, June 8, 1938, GUL.
35. *Ibid.*
36. *Ibid.*
37. *TMIO,* p. 277.
38. Editorial, *America,* July 2, 1938, p. 292.
39. John LaFarge, draft of article, July 8, 1938, GUL.
40. *Ibid.*
41. *Ibid.*
42. Fr. Talbot to John LaFarge, August 13, 1938, GUL.
43. *TMIO,* p. 284.
44. *Ibid.,* p. 276.
45. *Ibid.,* p. 283.
46. *America,* October 8, 1938.
47. *TMIO,* p. 283.
48. C. F. Carsley, "Democracy in Spain Under the Hammer and Sickle," *America,* January 28, 1939, pp. 388–89.
49. Gault Macgowan, "Festering Barcelona as the Stooge of Stalin," *America,* February 11, 1939, pp. 439–40.
50. Joseph B. Code, "The New Spain Merits—Demands Recognition by the United States," *America,* April 1, 1939, pp. 604–05.
51. Daniel Sargent, "Madrid: The City That Was Drugged," *America,* May 20, 1939, pp. 124–26.
52. *TMIO,* p. 305.
53. Hugh Thomas, *The Spanish Civil War* (New York: Harper and Row, 1961) pp. 606–07.

Chapter 9

1. John LaFarge, *No Postponement: United States Moral Leadership and the Problem of Racial Minorities* (New York: Longman, Green and Co., 1950), p. 152.
2. *TMIO*, p. 212.
3. *Ibid.*, p. 216.
4. Marilyn Wenzke Nickels, "The Federated Colored Catholics: A Study of Three Variant Perspectives On Racial Justice As Represented by John La-Farge, William Markoe, and Thomas Turner (Ph.D. dissertation, the Catholic University of America, Washington, D.C., 1975), p. 7.
5. Edward Stanton, "Unifying Mission," p. 55.
6. Roy Wilkins to Edward Stanton, September 22, 1972. *Ibid.*, p. 241.
7. Bishop John Ruard, "The Advent of the Black Bishops," in *Catholics U.S.A.: Makers of a Modern Church,* ed. Linda Brandi Cateuri (New York: William Morrow Co., 1989) p. 142.
8. John LaFarge, *The Catholic Viewpoint on Race Relations* (Garden City, New York: 1956), p. 64.
9. Nickels, "The Federated Colored Catholics," pp. 18–19.
10. John LaFarge, "The Laymen's Union," *Interracial Review,* April 1934, p. 42.
11. John LaFarge to Gov. Thomas E. Dewey, May 19, 1945, GUL.
12. Nickels, "The Federated Colored Catholics," p. 282.
13. George K. Hunton, *All of Which I Saw, Part of Which I Was: the Autobiography of George K. Hunton as told to Gary MacEoin* (New York: Doubleday and Co., 1967), p. 187.
14. Walter G. Murphy, "Father John LaFarge—Friend of the Negro," *Catholic Home Messenger,* April 1964, p. 3.
15. George K. Hunton, "Father John LaFarge, Priest and Jesuit," *America,* November 2, 1955, p. 179.
16. *TMIO*, p. 339.
17. Martin Adam Zielinski, " 'Doing The Truth' ": The Catholic Interracial Council Of New York, 1945–1965," (Ph.D. dissertation, the Catholic University of America, Washington, D.C., 1988), p. 20.
18. John LaFarge to the Reverend Dr. George Moneris, November 3, 1942, GUL.
19. John LaFarge, "Interracial Justice," *Interracial Review,* October 1934, p. 121.
20. Martin Adam Zielinski, " 'Doing The Truth,' " p. 20.
21. *TMIO*, 344.
22. *Ibid.*
23. *Ibid.*
24. John LaFarge, "Communism and the Negro," *Interracial Review,* March 1936, p. 39.

25. John LaFarge to Rev. Charles E. Leahy, S.J., April 7, 1936, GUL.
26. *TMIO,* pp. 246–47.
27. John LaFarge to the Very Rev. Edward C. Philips, S.J., February 2, 1934, GUL.
28. George H. Dunne, S.J. *King's Pawn,* pp. 130–31.
29. John LaFarge review of *An American Dilemma* by Gunnar Myrdal, *America,* February 5, 1944, p. 496.
30. Telephone conversation with Fr. Frank Carnavon, S.J., November 22, 1993.
31. John LaFarge, *The Catholic Viewpoint on Race Relations,* pp. 65–67.
32. *Ibid.,* p. 67.
33. Interview with Mary LaFarge, December 8, 1993.
34. Martin Adam Zielinski, " 'Doing the Truth,' " p. 25.
35. John LaFarge, *The Catholic Viewpoint on Race Relations,* pp. 71–72.
36. John LaFarge, *Interracial Justice,* May 1936, p. 75.
37. John LaFarge, *The Catholic Viewpoint on Race Relations,* p. 73.
38. John LaFarge, "Let's Accept the Challenge," *Interracial Review,* May 1956, pp. 41–42.
39. John LaFarge, "A Call For Catholic Interracial Councils," *Interracial Review,* December 1948, p. 185.
40. John LaFarge to William J. Junkin, S.J., May 3, 1957, GUL.
41. John LaFarge, *The Catholic Viewpoint on Race Relations,* p. 139.
42. Walter G. Murphy, "Father John LaFarge—Friend of the Negro," *Catholic Home Messenger,* April 1964, p. 3.
43. John LaFarge to Most Rev. Vincent S. Waters, March 19, 1951, GUL.
44. John LaFarge to Most Rev. Patrick O'Boyle, May 27, 1954, GUL.
45. *Ibid.*
46. John LaFarge to Rev. Theodore F. Cunningham, S.J., December 16, 1960, GUL.
47. Martin Adam Zielinski, " 'Doing the Truth,' ", p. 449.
48. *The Catholic Transcript,* August 1, 1963, MLHC.
49. John LaFarge, "Four Eyes on the Washington March," *America,* September 14, 1963.
50. Sermon by Rev. Thurston Davis, S.J., St. Ignatius Church, New York, November 21, 1964.
51. John LaFarge, "Judgment on racial segregation," *America,* December 12, 1953, p. 289.
52. John LaFarge, *Saturday Review of Literature,* December 14, 1963, pp. 42–43.

Chapter 10

1. Rev. John K. Daly to John LaFarge, August 12, 1947, NYHS.
2. John LaFarge to Fr. Daly, August 22, 1947, NYHS.
3. John LaFarge to Evelyn Waugh, November 12, 1948, NYHS.

4. *Ibid.*
5. *TMIO*, p. 245.
6. *Ibid.*, p. 246.
7. *Ibid.*
8. *Ibid.*, p. 245.
9. *Five Great Encyclicals* (New York: The Paulist Press, 1939), p. 133.
10. Telephone conversation with Fr. Walter Abbott, S.J., February 24, 1994.
11. John LaFarge, "The Nation Can Cure Causes of Race Riots," *America,* July 17, 1943, p. 298.
12. *TMIO*, p. 230.
13. John LaFarge, "Catholic Light on the Rural Life Problem," *America,* July 30, 1927, p. 368.
14. John LaFarge, "The Church Harvests Her Rural Life, *America,* September 13, 1930.
15. *TMIO*, p. 231.
16. John LaFarge to the Rev. Philip Hughes, June 26, 1945, GUL.
17. *TMIO*, p. 211.
18. John LaFarge, "Lifting the Burden Off the Land," *America,* November 21, 1931, p. 152.
19. John LaFarge to Margaret LaFarge (sister), October 30, 1932, NYHS.
20. *TMIO*, p. 238.
21. *Ibid.*, p. 234.
22. *Ibid.*, p. 235.
23. *Ibid.*, p. 238.
24. *Ibid.*
25. *Ibid.*, pp. 238–39.
26. *Ibid.*, p. 239.
27. *Ibid.*
28. John LaFarge, "Machines and Rural Life Need Not Be In Conflict," *America,* March 16, 1940, p. 620.
29. John LaFarge, "The Good Nebraska Earth Grows a Plan for Rural Life," *America,* November 7, 1942, p. 122.
30. John LaFarge, "The Negro Worker and the Land," *Interracial Review,* November 19, 1942, p. 172.
31. John LaFarge, "Few Farms Mean More Rationing," *America,* March 6, 1943, pp. 598–99.

Chapter 11

1. Interview with Phyllis LaFarge Johnson, March 30, 1990.
2. Bancel LaFarge to John LaFarge, March 27, 1962, GUL.
3. John LaFarge to Hester LaFarge, April 16, 1962, BLC.

4. Hester LaFarge to John LaFarge, April 25, 1962, BLC.
5. Telephone interview with Ben LaFarge, January 5, 1994.
6. John LaFarge to W.E.R. LaFarge, July 6, 1956, GUL.
7. *TMIO*, p. 36.
8. *Ibid.*, p. 60.
9. Telephone interview with Margaret LaFarge Hamill, December 29, 1993.
10. Ben LaFarge to Ms. Joanne Rees, February 6, 1990, BLC.
11. *Ibid.*
12. Fr. Frances Talbot, S.J., to John LaFarge, August 18, 1938, GUL.
13. John LaFarge to the Rev. M. Hayes, July 21, 1944, NYHS.
14. Phyllis LaFarge Johnson to the author, January 7, 1994.
15. John LaFarge to Bancel LaFarge (nephew), October 2, 1944, NYHS.
16. *TMIO*, p. 390.
17. Grant LaFarge to John LaFarge, August 2, 1938, NYHS.
18. *TMIO*, p. 284.
19. Taylor Caldwell to John LaFarge, April 17, 1960, GUL.
20. John LaFarge to Taylor Caldwell, April 22, 1960, GUL.
21. Dr. Grant LaFarge to the author, January 6, 1994.
22. Robert A. Hecht, *Oliver LaFarge and the American Indian: A Biography* (Metuchen, N.J.: Scarecrow Press, 1991), p. 3.
23. Wanden Kane to John LaFarge, January 20, 1954, NYHS.
24. John LaFarge to Rt. Rev. Msgr. Carlos Blanchard, January 25, 1954, NYHS.
25. *Ibid.*
26. Oliver LaFarge to John LaFarge, March 4, 1954, NYHS.
27. Oliver LaFarge to Christopher LaFarge, March 7, 1954, NYHS.
28. Wanden Kane to John LaFarge, June 24, 1954, NYHS.
29. Consuelo LaFarge to John LaFarge, January 14, 1955, NYHS.
30. Oliver LaFarge to Christopher LaFarge, February 11, 1955, NYHS.
31. John LaFarge to Margaret LaFarge (sister), March 7, 1951, GUL.
32. *Ibid.*
33. Margaret LaFarge (sister) to John LaFarge, July 18, 1936, NYHS.
34. Margaret LaFarge (sister) to John LaFarge, November 26, 1942, NYHS.
35. John LaFarge to Elizabeth Storer (niece), May 31, 1956, NYHS.
36. *Ibid.*
37. *Ibid.*

Chapter 12

1. John LaFarge, "War May Be in Europe While America Is at Peace," *America,* November 4, 1939, p. 88.
2. John LaFarge, "Injustices in Peace Foster Reasons for War," *America,* February 24, 1940, p. 371.

3. John LaFarge, "In Any United Europe Religion Must Find a Place," *America,* February 24, 1940, p. 542.

4. John LaFarge, "What Think You of Peace Even Though War Rages?" *America,* November 23, 1940, p. 179.

5. John LaFarge, "No Penance Is Needed for French Catholic Action," *America,* September 14, 1940, p. 620.

6. John LaFarge, "The Church in France," *America,* December 23, 1944, p. 329.

7. John LaFarge, "What Democracy Are We Defending?" *America,* January 18, 1941, p. 403.

8. John LaFarge, "The Soviets Bring No Joy to Soothe the World in 1940," *America,* December 30, 1939, p. 313.

9. John LaFarge, "Issues that Are Involved in American War Aid to Russia," *America,* September 30, 1941, p. 650.

10. John LaFarge, "Comes Comrade Litvinov to Sell U.S. Out to Soviets," *America,* November 29, 1941, pp. 206–07.

11. *TMIO,* pp. 295–96.

12. *Ibid.,* p. 296.

13. John LaFarge, "Italy Needs Democratic Spirit More Than Forms," *America,* August 21, 1943, p. 537.

14. *Ibid.*

15. John LaFarge, "Russia Challenges the Allied Conscience," *America,* June 9, 1945, p. 191.

16. *TMIO,* p. 313.

17. Editorial, *America,* August 18, 1945, p. 394.

18. John LaFarge, "Control of Atomic Energy," *America,* November 17, 1945, p. 17.

19. *TMIO,* p. 313.

20. John LaFarge to the Very Rev. Msgr. Howard J. Carroll, January 2, 1945, GUL.

21. Statement by John LaFarge on the atomic bomb and the United Nations, undated, NYHS.

22. John LaFarge, "Perspective for World Government," *America,* May 4, 1948, p. 106.

23. John LaFarge to Norman Cousins, August 15, 1950, GUL.

24. Editorial, *America,* July 30, 1949, p. 91.

25. Editorial, *America,* October 29, 1949, p. 91.

26. Editorial, *America,* March 25, 1950, p. 715.

27. Editorial, *America,* April 22, 1950, p. 79.

28. Editorial, "Is the Red peril a distraction?" *America,* May 27, 1950, p. 325.

29. Editorial, *America,* March 17, 1951.

30. Editorial, "Loyalty of Communists," April 21, 1951, p. 63.

31. Robert C. Hartnett, S.J. "Pattern of GOP Victory," *America,* November 22, 1952, p. 209.

32. John LaFarge to Mrs. Mary P. Sinclair, April 15, 1952, GUL.
33. John LaFarge, "Forty Years of Soviet Russia," *America,* November 2, 1957, p. 131.
34. John LaFarge, "The Future of Spain," *America,* December 30, 1944, p. 246.
35. Editorial, *America,* September 22, 1945, p. 494.
36. John LaFarge, "Carlton Hayes and Friendship for Spain," *America,* December 1, 1945, p. 233.
37. Editorial, "Freedom in Spain," *America,* March 2, 1946, p. 166.
38. Editorial, *America,* June 15, 1946, p. 218.
39. Editorial, "Decision in Spain," *America,* December 28, 1946, p. 342.
40. John LaFarge, "Spain and the Americas," *America,* April 14, 1951, p. 36.
41. Editorial, "Cooperation with Spain," *America,* February 24, 1951, p. 608.
42. Editorial, "Spanish Bishops Speak," *America,* July 14, 1951, p. 374.
43. Editorial, "Cardinal Segura on the Spanish Workers," *America,* December 15, 1951.

Chapter 13

1. *TMIO,* pp. 314–15.
2. *Ibid.,* p. 319.
3. Captain Warren L. Richardson to John LaFarge, April 28, 1947, GUL.
4. *TMIO,* p. 320.
5. *Ibid.,* p. 323.
6. *Ibid.,* p. 324.
7. John LaFarge, "Was Soll Es Hedeuten?" *America,* August 2, 1947, p. 485.
8. *Ibid.,* p. 487.
9. *TMIO,* p. 327.
10. *Ibid.,* p. 329.
11. *Ibid.*
12. *Ibid.,* p. 330.
13. John LaFarge to Julian Green, December 9, 1947, GUL.
14. John LaFarge, "Backdrop for the Marshall Plan," *America,* July 26, 1947, pp. 457–58.
15. *TMIO,* p. 355.
16. John LaFarge to Dr. LeRoy E. Colby, July 7, 1950, GUL.
17. John LaFarge to Mr. Manuel Espinosa, August 23, 1950, GUL.
18. John LaFarge to Mr. Manuel Espinosa, February 21, 1951, GUL.
19. Lawrence S. Wittner, *Cold War America: From Hiroshima to Watergate* (New York: Holt, Rinehart, and Winston, 1978), p. 54.
20. *TMIO,* pp. 356–57.
21. John LaFarge, "Catholic Interracial Program—From a European Window," *Interracial Review,* July 1951, p. 107.
22. *TMIO,* p. 356.

23. John LaFarge, "Nazi Policies Survive in Austria," *America,* September 22, 1951, p. 597.
24. John LaFarge to Margaret LaFarge (sister), May 10, 1951, NYHS.
25. *TMIO,* p. 369.
26. *Ibid.,* p. 372.
27. J. Manuel Espinosa to John LaFarge, October 9, 1951, GUL.
28. John LaFarge to Bishop J.J. Dauenhauer, August 1, 1951, GUL.

Chapter 14

1. John LaFarge to Mabel LaFarge, March 16, 1918, MLC.
2. John LaFarge to Mabel LaFarge, December 12, 1918, MLC.
3. *Ibid.*
4. *TMIO,* pp. 173–74.
5. Ernest Samuels, *Henry Adams* (Cambridge: Belknap Press, Harvard University Press, 1989), p. 450.
6. *TMIO,* pp. 174–75.
7. John LaFarge, "Catholic Marriages and Mixed Marriages," *America,* April 30, 1932, p. 83.
8. John LaFarge to Margaret LaFarge (sister), March 16, 1932, NYHS.
9. John LaFarge to Phyllis LaFarge Johnson, December 13, 1950, GUL.
10. Marie LaFarge to John LaFarge, July 28, 1958, GUL.
11. Telephone conversation with Phyllis LaFarge Johnson, February 4, 1994.
12. Telephone conversation with Sheila LaFarge, February 3, 1994.
13. Telephone conversation with Anne LaFarge, February 3, 1994.
14. John LaFarge to Schuyler Brown, June 14, 1955, GUL.
15. John LaFarge to Mary Lathrop Allen, October 7, 1946, MLC.
16. *Ibid.*
17. John LaFarge to Ben LaFarge, March 21, 1950, BLC.
18. *Ibid.*
19. Telephone conversation with Ben LaFarge, February 7, 1994.
20. John LaFarge to Ben LaFarge, May 21, 1950, BLC.
21. John LaFarge to Ben LaFarge, January 25, 1955, BLC.
22. Telephone conversation with Schuyler Brown, February 6, 1994.
23. John LaFarge to Schuyler Brown, December 17, 1955, Schuyler Brown Collection, Hereinafter cited as SBC.
24. Telephone conversation with Schuyler Brown, February 6, 1994.
25. Sermon by John LaFarge, June 23, 1963, GUL.
26. John LaFarge, "A Quarter Century Retrospect L.A.S." *Liturgical Arts,* November 1956, p. 3.
27. *TMIO,* p. 291.
28. Interview with Mary LaFarge, March 8, 1990.

29. C.J. McNaspy, "The Arts and John LaFarge," *America,* November 24, 1973, p. 404.
30. John LaFarge, "Foreword," *Liturgical Arts,* November 1961, p. 14.
31. *Ibid.,* p. 15.
32. *Ibid.*
33. *Ibid.,* p. 14.
34. *Ibid.*
35. *TMIO,* p. 291.
36. John LaFarge, "Shall the People Sing at Mass," *America,* June 24, 1933, p. 270.
37. John LaFarge, "Explaining the Liturgy," *America,* November 21, 1942, p. 180.
38. Interview with Mary LaFarge, March 8, 1990.
39. John LaFarge, "Thoughts on the Liturgical Movement," *America,* December 1, 1948, p. 288.
40. *Catholic Encyclopedia,* 1967 edition, vol. 9, p. 571.
41. John LaFarge, "Thoughts on the Liturgical Movement," *America,* December 18, 1948, p. 288.
42. John LaFarge, "New view of an old problem," *America,* December 25, 1948, pp. 317–18.
43. John LaFarge, "The Mass for the Masses," *America,* January 15, 1949, p. 401.
44. *Ibid.*
45. John LaFarge to the Most Rev. Edwin V. O'Hare, February 2, 1952, GUL.
46. John LaFarge and John A. O'Brien, "The Language of the Liturgy," *America,* August 20, 1960, p. 557.

Chapter 15

1. Phyllis LaFarge Johnson to the author, February 5, 1994.
2. John LaFarge, *Reflections on Growing Old* (New York: Doubleday and Co., 1962), p. 22.
3. *Ibid.,* p. 51.
4. *Ibid.,* p. 137.
5. *Ibid.*
6. *New York Times Book Review,* February 14, 1954.
7. *New York Herald Tribune Book Review,* February 14, 1954.
8. John LaFarge to Br. Peter S. Brown, N.S.J., February 23, 1954, GUL.
9. John LaFarge to Margaret LaFarge (sister), March 14, 1947, NYHS.
10. C.J. McNaspy, "The Arts and John LaFarge," *America,* November 24, 1973, p. 404.
11. John LaFarge to Mabel LaFarge, July 18, 1942, NYHS.

12. *TMIO*, p. 331.

13. Jacques Maritain, "Father John LaFarge," *Interracial Review,* February 1960, p. 31.

14. John LaFarge to Rev. René d'Ouince, S.J., September 11, 1947, GUL.

15. John LaFarge to Julian Green, December 8, 1957, GUL.

16. John LaFarge to Elizabeth LaFarge, December 8, 1957, Anne LaFarge Collection.

17. *The Catholic News,* March 1, 1952, p. 2.

18. *New York Times,* November 8, 1955.

19. Edward Ellis, "Father LaFarge Sees America Land of Greatness, Fears Decay," *New York World Telegram,* February 12, 1960.

20. Address by John LaFarge on the occasion of his eightieth birthday celebration, February 13, 1960, GUL.

21. *TMIO*, p. 334.

22. Telephone conversation with Fr. Walter Abbott, S.J., May 4, 1994.

23. Dr. W. S. Morton to John LaFarge, November 3, 1960, GUL.

24. John LaFarge to Fr. Schuyler Brown, S.J., September 28, 1963, SBC.

25. Telephone conversation with Fr. C. J. McNaspy, S.J., May 9, 1994.

26. Editorial, *America,* December 14, 1963, pp. 42–43.

27. Telephone conversation with Fr. Abbott, May 10, 1994.

28. Sermon delivered by Cardinal Cushing at funeral mass of Fr. John LaFarge, November 1963, MLHC.

29. *New York Times,* November 25, 1963, p. 19.

30. *New York Herald Tribune,* Obituary, November 26, 1963, p. 26.

31. Sermon by Fr. Thurston Davis, S.J., on the first anniversary of Fr. John LaFarge, November 21, 1964, MLHC.

Bibliographical Essay on
Documents and Interviews

The two most important documentary collections for this work were the LaFarge Family Papers at the New York Historical Society in New York City (NYHS), and the John LaFarge Papers at the Georgetown University Library in Washington, D.C. Those in New York are especially useful for the first half of LaFarge's life. Most of the letters in the collection are from him to his mother, many of which she kept. The letters she wrote to him, while probably just as numerous, if not more so, were not kept. After 1925, the year his mother died, the collection thins out considerably.

Fortunately, however, the Georgetown collection picks up the slack at about this point. As LaFarge became increasingly prominent, his correspondence with non-relatives also increased. Most of these that have been preserved are in Georgetown. The only restriction on their use by scholars is that letters to LaFarge cannot be photocopied. Those from him to others can.

I also located a small number of letters in the LaFarge Collection at the Yale University Library (YUL). These are mainly between him and his mother and his brother Bancel's family.

A number of friends and relatives were interviewed, some of them several times, in person, on the telephone, or both. I spoke more often to Mary LaFarge (wife of his nephew Henry), Phyllis LaFarge Johnson (wife of his nephew Tom), and Ben LaFarge (son of his nephew Bancel), than others. Mary loaned me a number of photographs of LaFarge and his family which are used in this volume. All three had me to their homes (usually accompanied by my wife), and patiently guided me through the maze called the LaFarge family. I am very grateful to them all.

Other relatives interviewed were Anne LaFarge (wife of his nephew Edward), Sheila LaFarge (another daughter of his nephew Tom), Margaret LaFarge Hamill (daughter of his brother Oliver), W.E.R. and C. Grant LaFarge (sons of his nephew Oliver), and Fr. Schuyler Brown (a cousin on his mother's side). As is typical of LaFarge family members, they were eager to help. Several of them loaned me their private correspondence with Father LaFarge. These are appropriately cited in the notes.

It also helped that I had previously published a biography of his nephew Oliver LaFarge (son of his brother Grant), since it gave me a headstart on understanding the family and its importance in American history. Part of the chapter on Fr. LaFarge's family has been drawn from this book.

The Jesuit priests who knew him while he worked at *America*—Fr. John Donahue, Fr. Walter Abbott, Fr. Frank Carnavon, Fr. Culhane, and Fr. C.J. McNaspy—all contributed memories of LaFarge. Father Donahue is still active at *America*. The others are retired and living in various parts of the country. I was able, however, to track them down in their various lairs by telephone. Fr. Donahue supplied me with their numbers. He was more patient with me than I probably deserved, and it was he who discovered the "lost encyclical," *Humani Generis Unitas,* and had it photocopied for me at America House. I thank them all.

My sincerest thanks also to James Yarnell of Newport, Rhode Island, who is organizing a catalogue of LaFarge's father's works, and is planning to write a biography of the artist. He supplied me with a number of LaFarge family papers, which I would not have found on my own.

Then of course, there were LaFarge's own writings—his books and hundreds of articles, mostly in *America*, but some from other publications as well. Articles that are cited in the text are listed in the bibliography.

The Manner Is Ordinary, LaFarge's autobiography, was invaluable. Wherever possible I tried to follow his career mainly through letters, other documents, and interviews. Occasionally, however, there were gaps in the primary sources which forced me to turn to his own story.

A SELECTED BIBLIOGRAPHY

Books by John LaFarge

An American Amen: A Statement of Hope. New York: Farrar, Straus and Cudahy, 1958.

The Catholic Viewpoint on Race Relations. Garden City, N.Y.: Hanover House, 1956.

Interracial Justice: A Study of the Catholic Doctrine of Race Relations. New York: America Press, 1937.

The Jesuits in Modern Times. New York: America Press, 1927.

The Manner Is Ordinary. New York: Harcourt Brace, 1954.

No Postponement: U.S. Moral Leadership and the Problem of Racial Minorities. New York: Longmans, Green and Co., 1950.

The Race Question and the Negro: A Study of the Catholic Doctrine on Interracial Justice. New York: Longmans, Green and Co., 1943.

Reflections on Growing Old. Garden City, N.Y.: Doubleday, 1963.

A Report on the American Jesuits. (Photographs by Margaret Bourke-White). New York: Farrar, Straus and Cudahy, 1956.

Articles by John LaFarge

"Backdrop for the Marshall Plan." *America,* July 26, 1947.

"A Call for Catholic Interracial Councils." *Interracial Review,* December, 1948.

"Carlton Hayes and Friendship for Spain." *America,* December 1, 1945.

"Catholic Interracial Program—From a European Window." *Interracial Review,* July 1951.

"Catholic Light on the Rural Life Problem." *America*, July 30, 1927.

"Catholic Marriages and Mixed Marriages." *America,* April 30, 1932.

"The Church in France." *America,* December 23, 1944.

"The Church Harvests Her Rural Life." *America,* September 13, 1930.

"Comes Comrade Litvinov to Sell U.S. Out to Soviets." *America,* November 29, 1941.

"Communism and the Negro." *Interracial Review,* March 1936.

"Control of Atomic Energy." *America,* November 17, 1945.

"Explaining the Liturgy." *America,* November 21, 1942.

"Feature X, re. death of George Santayana at age 88." *America,* October 11, 1952.

"Few Farms Mean More Rationing." *America,* March 6, 1943.

"Forty Years of Soviet Russia." *America,* November 2, 1957.

"The Good Nebraska Earth Grows a Plan for Rural Life." *America,* November 7, 1942.

"Harvard Culture and Jesuit Humanism." *America,* November 9, 1926.

"In Any United Europe Religion Must Find a Place." *America,* February 24, 1940.

"Injustices in Peace Foster Reasons for War." *America,* February 24, 1940.

"Interracial Justice." *Interracial Review,* October 1934.

"Issues that are Involved in American War Aid to Russia." *America,* September 20, 1941.

"Italy Needs Democratic Spirit More Than Forms." *America,* August 21, 1943.

"John LaFarge." *America,* May 27, 1911.

"LaFarge and the Truth." *America,* March 30, 1935.

"The Language of the Liturgy." (with John A. O'Brien) *America,* August 20, 1960.

"The Layman's Union." *Interracial Review,* April 1934.

"Let's Accept the Challenge," *Interracial Review,* May 1956.

"Lifting the Burden Off the Land." *America,* November 21, 1931.

"Machines and Rural Life Need Not Be In Conflict." *America,* March 16, 1940.

"The Mass for the Masses." *America,* January 15, 1949.

"The Munich Agreement Demands Further Adjustments." *America,* November 5, 1938.

"The Nation Can Cure Causes of Race Riots." *America,* July 17, 1943.

"Nazi Policies Survive in Austria." *America,* September 22, 1951.

"New view of an old problem." *America,* December 25, 1948.

"No Penance is Needed for French Catholic Action." *America,* September 14, 1940.

"Perspective for World Government." *America,* May 4, 1948.

"A Quarter Century Retrospect L.A.S." *Liturgical Arts,* November 1956.

"Russia Challenges the Allied Conscience." *America,* June 9, 1945.

"Shall the People Sing at Mass?" *America,* June 24, 1933.

"The Soviets Bring No Joy to Soothe the World in 1940." *America,* December 30, 1939.

"Spain and the Americas," *America.* April 14, 1951.

"Thoughts on the Liturgical Movement." *America,* December 1, 1948.

"War May Be in Europe While America Is at Peace." *America,* November 4, 1939.

"Was Soll Es Hedeuten." *America,* August 2, 1947.

"What Democracy Are We Defending?" *America,* January 18, 1941.

"What Think You of Peace Even Though War Rages?" *America,* November 23, 1940.

Books by Other Authors

Adams, Henry. *The Education of Henry Adams: An Autobiography*. Boston: Houghton Mifflin Co., 1918.

Cateura, Linda Brandi. *Catholics USA: Makers of a Modern Church*. New York: William Morrow and Company, Inc., 1989.

Cortissoz, Royal. *John LaFarge: A Memoir and a Study*. Boston: Houghton Mifflin Co., 1911.

Davis, S.J., Thurston, and Joseph Small, S.J. (eds.). *A John LaFarge Reader*. New York: America Press, 1956.

Dunne, George H. *King's Pawn: The Memoirs of George H. Dunne, S.J.* Chicago: Loyola University Press, 1990.

Hawkins, Hugh. *Between Harvard and America: The Educational Leadership of Charles W. Eliot*. New York: Oxford University Press, 1972.

Hecht, Robert A. *Oliver LaFarge and the American Indian: A Biography*. Metuchen, N.J.: Scarecrow Press, 1991.

Hills, George. *Franco: The Man And His Nation*. New York: The Macmillan Co., 1967.

Holmes, J. Derek. *The Papacy in the Modern World, 1914–1978*. New York: Crossroad, 1981.

Huneker, James. *New Cosmopolis*. New York: Charles Scribner's Sons, 1915.

Hunton, George K. *All of Which I Saw, Part of Which I Was: the Autobiography of George K. Hunton as told to Gary MacEoin*. New York: Doubleday and Co., 1967.

James, Henry. *Henry James: Autobiography*. New York: Criterion Books, 1956.

LaFarge, Oliver H.P. *The Gold Rush of 1898 and Other Reminiscences*. Privately printed by his daughter Margaret LaFarge Hamill, 1990.

Matthews, Herbert. *Half of Spain Died: A Reappraisal of the Spanish Civil War*. New York: Charles Scribner's Sons, 1973.

Mitchell, David. *The Jesuits: A History*. New York: Franklin Watts, 1981.

Morison, Samuel Eliot. *Three Centuries of Harvard: 1636–1936*. Cambridge: The Belknap Press of Harvard University Press, 1963.

Richards, Laura E., and Maud Howe Elliott. *Julia Ward Howe, 1819–1910*. Dunwoody, Georgia: Norman S. Berg, 1970.

Samuels, Ernest. *Henry Adams*. Cambridge: The Belknap Press of Harvard University Press, 1989.

Sanchez, José. *The Spanish Civil War as a Religious Tragedy*. South Bend, Indiana: University of Notre Dame Press, 1987.

Taylor, F. Jay. *The United States and the Spanish Civil War*. New York: Bookman Associates, 1956.

Thomas, Hugh. *The Spanish Civil War*. New York: Harper and Row, Publishers, 1961.

Treacy, Gerald C. *Five Great Encyclicals*. New York: The Paulist Press, 1939.

Weisbard, Robert G., and Wallace P. Sillonpor. *The Chief Rabbi, the Pope, and the Holocaust*. New Brunswick, N.J.: Transaction Publications, 1992.

Wittner, Lawrence S. *Cold War America: From Hiroshima to Watergate*. New York: Holt, Rinehart, and Winston, 1978.

Yarnell, James. *John LaFarge: Watercolors and Drawings*. Yonkers, N.Y.: The Hudson River Museum of Westchester, 1990.

Articles by Other Authors

Castelli, Jim. "Unpublished Encyclical Attacked Anti-Semitism." *National Catholic Reporter*, December 15, 1972.

Code, Joseph B. "The New Spain Merits—Demands Recognition by the United States." *America*, April 1, 1939.

Ellis, Edward. "Father LaFarge Sees America Land of Greatness, Fears Decay." *New York World Telegram*, February 12, 1960.

Carsley, C.F. "Democracy in Spain Under the Hammer and Sickle." *America*, January 28, 1939.

Hartnett, S.J., Robert C. "Pattern of GOP Victory." *America*, November 22, 1952.

Hunton, George K. "Father John LaFarge, Priest and Jesuit." *America*, November 2, 1955.

Macgowan, Gault. "Festering Barcelona as the Stooge of Stalin." *America*, February 11, 1939.

McNaspy, C.J. "The Arts and John LaFarge." *America*, November 24, 1973.

Maritain, Jacques. "Father John LaFarge." *Interracial Review*, February 1960.

Murphy, Walter G. "Father John LaFarge—Friend of the Negro." *Catholic Home Messenger*, April 1964.

Sargent, Daniel. "Madrid: The City That Was Drugged." *America*, May 20, 1939.

Thorning, Joseph F. "Why the Press Failed on Spain." *Catholic World*, December 1937.

Index

About the Author

ROBERT A. HECHT (A.B. Queens College; Ph.D. City University of New York) is a professor of history at Kingsborough Community College, Brooklyn, New York. He has published extensively on a variety of historical and contemporary subjects in recent years, emphasizing the American Indian. His *Oliver LaFarge and the American Indian: A Biography* was published by Scarecrow Press in 1991. He has also been published in *Pacific Historical Review, Journal of Arizona History, American Indian Culture and Research Journal, Centerpoint, America, Commonweal, Archaeology,* and *Fidelity*. His interest in Father LaFarge stemmed from his research on Oliver, Father LaFarge's nephew, who won a Pulitzer Prize for literature in 1929, and was a major twentieth-century Indian reformer.